"Although commissioned to honor the Upjohn Institute's 75th anniversary, *A Future of Good Jobs* could hardly be better timed with respect to current trends in the American economy. While most of these trends—widening wage inequality, underemployment of the less educated, increased global competition, and cutbacks in health insurance and retirement coverage—are far from new, it is only recently that policymakers and mainstream economists have come to acknowledge that they are not necessarily self-correcting. The practical, concrete remedies offered in this book are especially welcome in that they are sensitive both to the realities of the U.S. labor force and to the needs and resources of U.S. employers."

―Jodie Allen, Senior Editor, Pew Research Center

"This book provides a readable and highly interesting discussion of some of the key problems facing American workers. The chapters are well-written and the facts are clearly presented. The policy discussions are on-target. I particularly liked the discussion of policies to improve job quality in low-wage jobs; others will be interested in the chapters on immigration, older workers, employer-provided health insurance, or employment and training programs. Any reader who wants to know more about work, jobs, and the economy will find this book useful reading."

―Rebecca Blank, Henry Carter Adams Collegiate Professor of Public Policy and former Dean of Gerald R. Ford School of Public Policy, University of Michigan

"Since 1980 American workers with average and below-average skills have received anemic pay gains. Many have seen erosion in crucial employment benefits, including health insurance. The surge in productivity after the mid-1990s gave a temporary boost to wages, but the relief proved short-lived. Workers who are not in the top ranks of the pay distribution have seen meager wage gains in recent years, even when the economy is growing robustly. Timothy Bartik and Susan Houseman have assembled a first-rate team of economists to assess the problems of struggling workers. They offer cogent analyses of America's workplace problems. More importantly, they provide a timely set of prescriptions to address those problems. Many writers wring their hands at the challenges facing workers who are at the bottom of the pay ladder. The authors of this volume focus on the more difficult task of crafting humane but tough-minded solutions to the problem of shrinking wages. For readers who are interested in clear-eyed analysis as well as shrewd policy advocacy, this book offers an excellent starting place for thinking about solutions to the problem of lousy jobs and lousy pay."

―Gary Burtless, Senior Fellow, Economic Studies, The Brookings Institution

---

$\infty \cdot \infty \cdot \infty$

"Leading policy analysts not only frame the major challenges facing U.S. labor policy in this book, but they provide possible solutions. Growing inequality, declining coverage and generosity of employer-sponsored benefits, soaring health insurance costs, less job security, and a sharp decline in the employment of less-educated men are serious problems. The presidential candidates, economic policy analysts, and concerned citizens would do well to study the ideas in this book to prepare for the challenges ahead."

–*Richard A. Hobbie, Executive Director, National Association of State Workforce Agencies*

"The middle class is anxious and for good reasons. Recent productivity increases have done little to raise the wages of most workers, health and retirement benefits along with jobs are less secure, and education and training policies have not kept pace with new global challenges. The authors of this volume provide both good diagnosis and some interesting ideas for how the nation should respond."

–*Isabel Sawhill, Senior Fellow, Economic Studies, The Brookings Institution*

$\infty \cdot \infty \cdot \infty$

A Future of Good Jobs?

A Future of Good Jobs?

America's Challenge in the Global Economy

Timothy J. Bartik
Susan N. Houseman
Editors

2008

W.E. Upjohn Institute for Employment Research
Kalamazoo, Michigan

Library of Congress Cataloging-in-Publication Data

A future of good jobs? America's challenge in the global economy / Timothy J. Bartik,
Susan N. Houseman, editors.
  p. cm.
  The outgrowth of a conference sponsored by the Upjohn Institute in Washington,
D.C., in June 2007. Includes bibliographical references and index.
  ISBN-13: 978-0-88099-331-9 (pbk. : alk. paper)
  ISBN-10: 0-88099-331-6 (pbk. : alk. paper)
  ISBN-13: 978-0-88099-332-6 (hardcover : alk. paper)
  ISBN-10: 0-88099-332-4 (hardcover : alk. paper)
  1. Labor market—United States—Congresses. 2. Labor supply—United
States—Congresses. 3. Manpower policy—United States—Congresses. 4. Industrial
management—United States—Congresses. 5. Occupational training—United
States—Congresses. I. Bartik, Timothy J. II. Houseman, Susan N., 1956- III. W.E.
Upjohn Institute for Employment Research.
  HD5724.F88 2008
  331.10973—dc22
                2008003946

The facts presented in this study and the observations and viewpoints expressed are
the sole responsibility of the authors. They do not necessarily represent positions of
the W.E. Upjohn Institute for Employment Research.

Cover design by Alcorn Publication Design.
Index prepared by Diane Worden.
Printed in the United States of America.
Printed on recycled paper.

Contents

Acknowledgments

First and foremost, we appreciate the strong support that the Board of Directors of the Upjohn Institute and Randy Eberts, the Institute's executive director, gave to this project, which was commissioned in honor of the seventy-fifth anniversary of the W.E. Upjohn Institute Trustee Corporation.

Many individuals made important contributions at various stages of the project, which culminated in a conference in June 2007 in Washington, DC, and the publication of this book. Kevin Hollenbeck of the Institute's research staff played an especially important role in developing the project's concept. Katharine Abraham, Rebecca Blank, Phyllis Eisen, Robert Haveman, Len Nichols, and Paul Osterman, who attended planning meetings, provided helpful advice in selecting and refining the topics covered in this book. We thank Claire Black for ably overseeing conference logistics; Sarah Klerk and Leslie Lance for their assistance with conference administration; Linda Richer and Babette Schmitt for their help with the preconference publicity; Wei-Jang Huang and Lillian Vesic-Petrovic for research assistance; Benjamin Jones, Richard Wyrwa, and Allison Colosky for their excellent job of editing and producing the book under a tight deadline; and Erika Jackson for typesetting the book. We also thank Jodie Allen, Beth Buehlmann, Dalmer Hoskins, Wendell Primus, Ray Uhalde, and Stacey Wagner for moderating sessions and facilitating lively discussion at the conference.

Finally, we greatly appreciate the contribution each of the authors made to this project. They did an exemplary job of analyzing challenging labor market issues and making policy recommendations that, if implemented, will substantially improve conditions for U.S. workers and the competitiveness of the American economy.

1
Introduction and Overview

Timothy J. Bartik
Susan N. Houseman
W.E. Upjohn Institute for Employment Research

Can the U.S. economy generate healthy growth of "good" jobs—jobs that will ensure a steady improvement in the standard of living for the middle class and that will offer a way out of poverty for low-income Americans? This is the fundamental economic policy challenge facing our country in an age of intense global competition. By some measures, the U.S. economy appears poised to perform well in the long-term, whatever its short-term difficulties. With Gross Domestic Product (GDP) and productivity growth high and unemployment relatively low in recent years, key economic indicators suggest a fundamentally strong U.S. economy that can withstand downward cyclical pressures.

Beneath these aggregate statistics, however, are signs that those at the bottom and a growing number in the middle are being left behind. Rapid globalization and technological progress have brought substantial benefits to American consumers in the form of better and cheaper goods and services. But globalization and technological improvements have also been associated with substantial dislocation, stagnant or declining real wages and benefits, and reduced job security for many workers. The gains from economic growth in recent years have accrued primarily to those at the very top of the income distribution, as evidenced by the growth of inequality in this country.

In this book, which was the outgrowth of a conference sponsored by the Upjohn Institute in Washington, D.C., in June 2007, leading policy analysts frame the major challenges facing U.S. labor policy:

- Improving the skills of American workers so that they can better compete in a global economy;
- Addressing the crisis in our system of employer-sponsored health insurance;

- Minimizing the effects of dislocation due to immigration and trade;
- Removing barriers to employment for older workers;
- Improving the quality of jobs for low-wage workers without harming the competitiveness of American companies;
- Addressing the serious employment barriers of the disadvantaged.

Each chapter in this volume tackles one of these policy challenges, identifying the key problems, evaluating the effectiveness of current policy approaches, and offering innovative, forward-thinking, but pragmatic alternative policies. Collectively, the chapters in this volume offer a clear road map for future labor market policy.

SIGNS OF TROUBLE FOR U.S. WORKERS

The difficulty that the United States will have in generating good jobs and improving living standards for *all* Americans is readily apparent in problems already facing middle-class and low-wage workers.

Growing Inequality

Wage inequality has widened substantially in recent years. From 2000 to 2006, average real hourly wages dropped by 0.5 percent for those in the fifth to the fifteenth percentiles of the wage distribution, increased by 3.4 percent for those in the forty-fifth to fifty-fifth percentiles, and rose by 5.9 percent for those in the eighty-fifth to ninety-fifth percentiles.[1] Indeed, this recent increase in inequality is a continuation of a general trend evident since the 1980s, during which time wages for the middle and lower classes have risen far less than the rate of productivity growth, and most of the increased wealth generated by productivity gains has gone to the highest income households. From 1979 to 2006, hourly wages for the median worker grew only 16 percent in real terms, or about 0.5 percent per year.[2] In contrast, the U.S. economy's total output per hour over that same period grew 58 percent, or about 1.7 percent per year.[3] Figure 1.1, which shows the growth in real hourly wages at various percentiles of the overall U.S. wage distribution between 1979 and 2006, depicts the increase in inequality.[4] Wages at the bottom 10 percent of the distribution have actually declined in real terms since 1979. Real wage growth has been low for workers between the tenth percentile and the eightieth percentile—increasing by less than 20 percent over this 27-year period—compared to the much more rapid wage growth for those at the ninetieth percentile and above.

Real hourly wage growth of approximately 1.1 percent per year from 1979 to 2006 would have been needed for the growth in total compensation to match labor productivity growth over the period.[5] Only earnings at the ninetieth percentile and above matched or exceeded this rate. To understand the extent to which inequality in this country has grown, consider the fact that if wages below the ninetieth percentile had grown at a rate consistent with productivity growth from 1979 to 2006, earnings for these workers would have been $734 billion higher in 2006.[6] This amount represents about 12 percent of all wage and salary income and about 7 percent of GDP in 2006.

Figure 1.1 Growth in Wage Inequality in the United States, 1979–2006

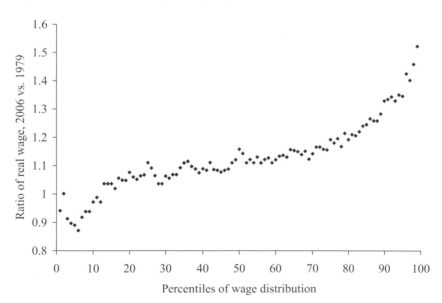

NOTE: These data are based on our calculations from the CPS-ORG for 1979 and 2006. See Note 4 for details.

Declining Coverage and Generosity of Benefits

Employer-sponsored health insurance has been the foundation of the U.S. health insurance system for over 50 years. Yet the fraction of the nonelderly population with employer-sponsored health insurance has dropped sharply in recent years, accompanying the steep increase in health insurance costs. In 2005, health insurance was as costly to employers as paid leave, historically the most expensive benefit (GAO 2006). From 2000 to 2006, the percentage of firms offering health insurance benefits declined by 8 percentage points, and the percentage of the nonelderly adults with employer-sponsored health insurance coverage declined by 5 percentage points. By 2006, only 62 percent of the nonelderly population was covered by employer-sponsored health insurance.

The fraction of the working population with retiree health insurance benefits similarly has dropped. The largest drop occurred among private-sector workers following an accounting rule change in 1993 that required companies to show future retiree health-benefit costs as liabilities on their financial statements. The fraction of private-sector workers working in companies that offer some type of retiree health-insurance benefits has continued to fall since then, however, dropping from an estimated 32 percent in 1997 to 25 percent in 2003 (Buchmueller, Johnson, and Lo Sasso 2006). Analysts believe that recent changes in government accounting rules will lead to a sharp drop in the incidence of retiree health-insurance coverage offered to public-sector workers as well (Johnson 2006).

Besides health insurance and paid leave, the primary workplace benefit is a retirement plan. Although the fraction of workers who are covered by some retirement plan has not declined in recent years, companies' shift from traditional defined-benefit to defined-contribution retirement plans shifts investment risks to workers. In addition, although defined benefit plans are not intrinsically more generous than defined contribution plans, companies' shift to defined contribution plans typically has been associated with reduced benefits (Ghilarducci and Sun 2006).

Less Job Security

Long-term employment with a single company is becoming less common. Mean and median job tenure have declined among men over the last 50 years, and the fraction of men in a long-term job (whether it be for 10 years or 20) has declined for all age groups, with the decline most notable for older men (Farber 2007). Related to this phenomenon, there is evidence of a persistent trend towards increased job loss in recent years, especially among more educated and older workers (Farber 2005). Thus, American workers appear more likely than in the recent past to experience dislocation and are more likely to have to make a late-in-life job change.

Sharp Drop in Employment among Low-Educated Men

The employment rates of men of all ages with a high school education or less have declined precipitously since the 1980s. Among prime-age (25–54) white, non-Hispanic men, the employment rate (the percentage ratio of employment to population) has dropped by 13 percentage points since 1979 among high school dropouts and by 5 percentage points among those with only a high school degree.[7] Among prime-age black men, the employment rate has dropped by 21 percentage points for high school dropouts and by 10 percentage points for those with only a high school degree.[8] The employment rate of prime-age black men who had dropped out of high school stood at only 54 percent in 2006. The sharply declining employment rates among low-educated men contrast with the employment rate trend for college-educated men, which has changed little over this period.

Offsetting these large declines in the employment rates of low-educated men would require significant expansion of employment in the U.S. economy. For example, in 1979 the employment rate among prime-age, white non-Hispanic men without a high school degree was 84.6 percent.[9] If all prime-age men without a high school degree had been employed at that rate in 2006, more than 600,000 additional jobs would have been required. Similarly, if all prime-age men with only a high school degree in 2006 had been employed at the same rate as that experienced by white prime-age men with only a high school degree in 1979 (93.5 percent), an additional 2.2 million men would have been employed. Taken together, such an expansion of employment among prime-age, less-educated men would require an additional 2.9 million jobs, or about a 2 percent expansion of employment in the U.S. economy, if all else remained the same.

Less-educated men in their 50s, which are traditionally the immediate preretirement years, have also experienced sharp declines in employment. From 1979 to 2006, employment rates among men in their 50s declined by 12 percentage points for high school dropouts and by 11 percentage points for high school graduates.

Although one might argue that declining employment rates among low-educated men reflect increased employment among women, this explanation is insufficient. Employment rates for college-educated men have not fallen, in spite of the sharp increase in employment among college-educated women. Moreover, employment rates among prime-age, high-school-dropout women have been relatively constant and thus would appear to explain none of the sharp drop in employment rates among their male counterparts.[10] Instead, the fact that employment rates have remained quite low among prime-age women without a high school degree—in spite of the overall high growth in employment among other prime-age women and in spite of declining marriage rates and welfare reform, which has decreased public support for many of these women—suggests insufficient employment opportunities for low-educated women as well.

FORCES SHAPING THE AMERICAN WORKPLACE

These problems of growing inequality, declining generosity and coverage of benefits, reduced job security, and declining employment rates among low-educated men are attributable to a range of economic and social forces. Widespread involvement of large institutional investors in the stock market beginning in the 1980s led to greater focus on lowering costs to boost short-term earnings and stock prices, which in turn contributed to downward pressure on compensation and reduced job security.

Rapid technological advances have also played an important role. Developments in health technology have reduced mortality and improved the quality of life for many Americans. But these advances have greatly increased the cost of health care and placed severe strains on our employer-financed system of health insurance.

Economists generally believe that computer technology introduced into the workplace in the 1980s and 1990s has favored more-skilled workers and helps explain growing inequality. However, by opening up the possibility of offshoring many service jobs, the development of the Internet and other communications technologies potentially will have far-reaching implications for American workers at all skill levels in the future.

Globalization reinforces pressures from financial markets and new technology. Recent political and economic reform in China, Eastern Europe, and elsewhere has enabled tremendous expansion of trade to occur in large sections of the world. Bilateral and multilateral trade agreements have further paved the way for the expansion of trade. These factors—coupled with lower transportation and communications costs and financial market pressures on U.S. companies to lower costs through offshore outsourcing—have greatly increased the importance of trade in the U.S. economy. Figure 1.2 displays the manifestation of this trend through U.S. exports and imports as a percentage of GDP. From 1980 to 2006, the combination of exports and imports rose as a proportion of GDP in the United States from 20 to 28 percent. Almost all of that increase was attributable to the growth of imports, reflecting the steep increase in the U.S. trade deficit, particularly in the last several years (Figure 1.3). While Americans broadly benefit from lower-priced imports, the growth of the global economy has led to substantial worker dislocation and placed further downward pressure on many workers' wages.

At the same time that these economic forces are placing strains on middle-class and low-wage workers, institutions that historically have helped to mitigate income inequality have significantly weakened. Most notable are the decline in the value of the minimum wage and the decline in union representation. Before its increase in July 2007, the minimum wage had fallen to 77 percent of its real value in 1996, the year the minimum wage was last increased.[11] Unionization rates have continued to fall from their peak in the 1950s. In 2006 just 12 percent of all U.S. workers and just 7.4 percent of the private-sector workforce belonged to a union.

Figure 1.2 The Growing Importance of Trade in the U.S. Economy: Imports and Exports as a Percent of Gross Domestic Product

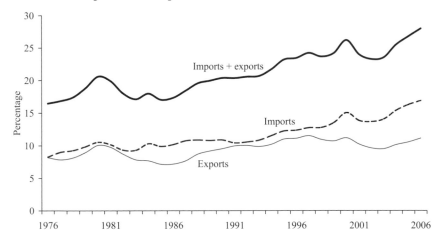

SOURCE: Authors' calculations based on data from the Bureau of Economic Analysis.

Figure 1.3 Balance of Trade for Goods and Services

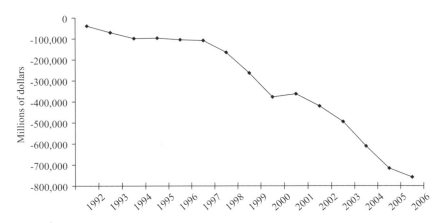

SOURCE: U.S. Census Bureau (2005, 2007).

POLICY ACTION PLAN

To address the problems of inequality and pressures from globalization, the contributors to this volume recommend several key reforms of labor market policy:

Reform the Delivery of Education and Training

Virtually all agree that improving the skills of our current and future workforce is critical to competing in a global economy. Yet, Robert Lerman points out, current federal and state policies are overly narrow and often counterproductive. According to Lerman, a key problem is that the United States lacks comprehensive measures of skills. The common focus on school completion and academic test scores leads to policies that devote too few resources to productivity-enhancing noncognitive skills and occupational skills. The results are poor preparation of many workers and an insufficient supply of workers for many jobs that are in demand and pay good wages.

Lerman urges the development of education curricula that are more closely tied to workplace needs, that meet the diverse learning styles of students, and that expand support for vocational training in high schools. High school students should be able to achieve occupational qualifications by combining school instruction with well-structured work-based learning. The K-12 system should be rewarded for raising noncognitive skills and occupational skills, even if some students do not complete all of the requirements for admission to a four-year college. The minimal federal budget allocation for apprenticeship programs should be increased. Finally, Lerman recommends changes in financial accounting rules so that firms count their workforces' human capital as assets and thereby are encouraged to invest more in worker training.

Reform Health Insurance

Can employers continue to afford health insurance coverage for employees and remain competitive in the global economy? The answer for a growing number of small and large companies is no. Katherine Swartz explains why the current system of employer-sponsored health insurance is inefficient and is leading to a downward spiral of coverage in our country. Swartz warns that the rapid drop in employer-sponsored health insurance coverage adds a new urgency to reform in the financing of health insurance, and she offers a road map for universal coverage based on three principles: 1) everyone should enroll in a health plan and pay a minimum amount, 2) additional premiums should be collected from individuals in proportion to family income, and 3) companies should contribute to financing the insurance. The Netherlands, Germany, and Switzerland have health insurance systems that meet these three principles and so offer potential models for a reformed U.S. system. The system proposed by Swartz would preserve a central role for private health insurance.

Swartz emphasizes that changing the financing of health insurance would change the way health insurance costs are shared but should not increase—and possibly would lower—the total amount spent on health care. A reformed system could avoid inefficiencies that result from lack of insurance coverage, increase productivity by allowing individuals to switch jobs without losing coverage, increase competitiveness of U.S. companies in the global market, and reduce perverse incentives employers have to contract out work or avoid hiring older workers.

Expand and Revamp Return-to-Work Programs

Federal funding of employment and training programs in 2007 is about 40 percent lower in real terms than it was a decade ago (Abraham and Houseman 2008), while the need for such programs has grown because of declining job security and a growing population. Failure to implement effective return-to-work programs is expensive for society, leading to lower employment and greater dependence on public assistance.

In their respective chapters, first Lori Kletzer and then Katharine Abraham and Susan Houseman present proposals for expanded employment and training programs, wage insurance programs, and better targeting of government programs to the needs of dislocated and older workers. Kletzer recommends expanding the Trade Adjustment Assistance program, currently limited to manufacturing workers, to include displaced service-sector workers and also to include additional monies for training. The wage-loss insurance program, started in 2002, provides trade-displaced workers over age 50 with up to half the difference between their old and new wages. Kletzer calls for evaluating this program—as Congress stipulated that it should be—and possibly extending the program to workers in their 40s. Echoing the call for program evaluation, Abraham and Houseman emphasize the need to evaluate promising older-worker initiatives being taken at the state level—including placing older-worker specialists in employment centers, instituting outreach for seniors, and providing older workers with basic computer skills—to determine their effectiveness and suitability for expansion at the national level.

Implement Special Policies for Low-Skilled Workers

The growth in inequality has hit low-skilled workers hardest. Paul Osterman calls for a two-pronged approach to improving the quality of jobs at the low end. The first is improvement in labor standards: continued increases in the minimum wage, protection for unions and other forms of worker organization, and tax incentives that promote the development of good jobs. The second strategy involves programmatic assistance to employers to encourage job upgrading. Osterman proposes that the U.S. Department of Labor establish a "Low Wage Challenge Fund" to assist employers in improving the skills of their workforce and thereby the quality of jobs. The Low Wage Challenge Fund would also provide matching funds to states for customized training programs oriented toward the low-skill workforce and would provide funding to community colleges to increase their involvement with employers and the low-skill workforce.

To boost earnings of the least skilled workers, Steven Raphael proposes expansion of the successful Earned Income Tax Credit. Specifically, Raphael proposes an expanded EITC for childless adults, with liberalization of benefits for the poorest married couples.

The rapid rise in incarceration rates and the precipitous drop in employment rates of low-skilled men require special policies to bring this growing underclass out of the cycle of crime and poverty and into productive employment. In addition to an expanded EITC program, Raphael advocates four specific policies to reduce barriers to employment for those with criminal records: 1) removing summary disqualifications of former inmates from financial assistance for education or other public assistance, 2) basing publicly mandated employment bans of former felons from certain jobs on specific offenses rather than having blanket bans, 3) expunging selected criminal records after a period of time, and 4) funding training intermediaries to prepare ex-inmates for employment.

CONCLUSION

Taken together, the policies proposed here balance the need to increase workers' wages and benefits with the need to preserve employers' competitiveness. For instance, the health insurance proposals in this book would guarantee health insurance coverage for all while lowering many employers' health insurance costs. Expanding the Earned Income Tax Credit increases workers' take-home wages without increasing employers' costs. And although the book includes proposals for increases in the minimum wage and more protection for unions' organizing rights, the book also includes proposals for greater availability of customized training grants to firms, which would increase worker productivity and, in turn, support higher pay.

In an era of tight government budgets, can the United States afford to implement the set of policies proposed in this book? We argue that any additional government expenditures required by these policies represent investments that are necessary to improve the efficiency and equity of the American economy. An education system that addresses the diversity of needs of students and prepares them for a range of jobs in the workplace is central to increasing American workers' wages and to improving the future competitiveness of our country. The United States has the highest per-capita spending on health care in the world, yet among developed countries it has the lowest rate of health insurance coverage and relatively poor health outcomes (Anderson et al. 2000; Anderson and Poullier 1999; Swartz 2008). Although reform of the employer-sponsored system of health insurance will require increased government expenditures on health care, such reform is essential to improve the efficiency of health care delivery and lower health care expenditures overall. In some cases, government expenditures to improve the effectiveness of certain programs may significantly reduce government expenditures in other program areas. For example, our failure to fund and implement effective employment and training programs and policies for dislocated workers, older workers, and the poor results in high public costs in the form of expensive and extensive dependence on public support programs, including Social Security, lower levels of employment and tax revenues, and higher crime and health problems.

Although healthy growth of the aggregate U.S. economy has accompanied rapid globalization in recent years, the benefits of economic expansion have accrued disproportionately to those at the very top of the income distribution. Many lower and middle income Americans have instead experienced less security and lower employment rates, stagnant or falling real wages, and lower benefit levels. The policies advocated in this book would go a long way toward guaranteeing a future of good jobs for all Americans.

Notes

1. These statistics are based on our analysis of data from the Current Population Survey—Outgoing Rotation Group (CPS-ORG). We averaged over multiple percentiles to minimize the statistical noise for individual percentiles.

2. It is sometimes asserted that much of the gap between wage and productivity growth can be explained by the growth of the cost of benefits such as health insurance (see, for example, Council of Economic Advisers 2007, p. 51). This is largely true if we focus on the gap between productivity growth and mean wage growth using consistent price deflators. But the growth of nonwage compensation only explains a small portion of the gap between U.S. economic output and measured real wage growth for the median worker, or for most workers. For example, in the National Income and Product Accounts of the United States, average real wages per hour grew 1.27 percent per year from 1979 to 2005, whereas average real compensation (including benefits) per hour grew 1.42 percent per year from 1979 to 2005, a difference of 0.15 percent per year.

3. Productivity for the nonfarm business sector grew 2.0 percent per year, according to figures published by the Bureau of Labor Statistics. The estimated 1.7 percent annual growth rate of productivity for the overall economy adjusts for the lower productivity growth in the farm sector, as reported in Dew-Becker and Gordon (2005).

4. We exclude all observations with imputed earnings, hours, or wages. For workers paid by the hour, we use hourly wages. For other workers, we use usual weekly earnings divided by usual weekly hours, where available. For workers whose usual weekly hours vary, we use actual weekly hours the previous week. For workers whose usual weekly earnings are top-coded, we multiply the top code by 1.4. Wage observations are treated as outliers and dropped if the real wage is less

than $2 per hour or more than $200 per hour in 2004 dollars, deflated using the Consumer Price Index research series produced by the Bureau of Labor Statistics. The percentiles are then calculated over all remaining workers in the CPS-ORG sample for each year. The CPS earnings weights are used in calculating the percentiles. The reported statistics in the figure equal the ratio of the 2006 wage to the 1979 wage at each percentile.

5. Wage growth consistent with productivity growth would be less than 1.7 percent, for a couple of reasons. First, total compensation includes benefits, such as health insurance and retirement plans, whose value grew at a rate greater than 1.7 percent. Second, the GDP deflator used to deflate real output in the productivity statistics grew more slowly than the Consumer Price Index (CPI) deflator used to calculate the real wage trends. The first factor might explain an annual growth difference of 0.2 percent (see Note 1). The second factor suggests that real wage growth using the CPI will be lowered by 0.4 percent per year relative to real productivity statistics using the GDP deflator. These figures come from Bureau of Labor Statistics data on the CPI research series (BLS 2007) and Bureau of Economic Analysis data on the GDP price deflator, taken from Table 1.1.4 of the National Income and Product Accounts (BEA 2007).

6. These estimates are based on data on earnings or hourly wages and weekly hours of work from the outgoing rotation groups in the Current Population Survey in 1979 and 2006. First, we computed real hourly wages in 2006 consistent with a 1.1 percent annual growth in real hourly wages from 1979 to 2006 for the first to the eighty-ninth percentile. We subtracted from these figures the actual wage rates in 2006 at each percentile to get the hourly wage increment required for wage growth to match productivity growth. The annual earnings increment at each percentile was computed as the product of this hourly wage increment, the number of workers in each CPS percentile in 2006, the average weekly hours of those in each percentile, and 52 (for the number of weeks per year). In computing these figures, we dropped all observations with imputations for earnings, hours, or wages, and excluded wage outliers. Thus, we adjusted these numbers upwards to reflect the ratio between total CPS employment, as measured by the BLS in 2006, and the smaller estimated number of weighted CPS workers in our sample. The estimate of $734 billion is the sum of this annual earnings increment across the first 89 percentiles.

7. All employment-rate statistics come from our analysis of CPS-ORG data.

8. Employment rates among low-educated Hispanic men, in contrast, have been fairly stable.

9. The employment rate among prime-age Hispanic men was slightly higher, 85.8 percent, and among black prime-age men significantly lower, 75.0 percent, in 1979.

10. This may be surprising to some because of the presumed effects of welfare reform on labor-force participation among low-educated women. Although the employment rate among high-school-dropout women aged 25–54 did increase from 45 percent to 51 percent between 1979 and 2000, it fell back to 47 percent by 2006.

11. The new minimum wage law will incrementally increase the federal minimum wage from $5.15 to $8.25 by 2009. Assuming a rate of inflation of about 3 percent

per year, the minimum wage would approximately return to its real 1996 value in 2009. However, without future policy initiatives to increase the nominal minimum wage, the real value of the minimum wage would start declining again in 2009.

References

Abraham, Katharine G., and Susan Houseman. 2008. "Removing Barriers to Work for Older Americans." In *A Future of Good Jobs? America's Challenge in the Global Economy*, Timothy J. Bartik and Susan N. Houseman, eds. Kalamazoo, MI: W.E. Upjohn Institute for Employment Research, pp. 161–202.

Anderson, Gerard F., Jeremy Hurst, Peter Sotir Hussey, and Melissa Jee-Hughes. 2000. "Health Spending and Outcomes: Trends in OECD Countries, 1960–1998." *Health Affairs* 19(3): 150–157.

Anderson, Gerard F., and Jean-Pierre Poullier. 1999. "Health Spending, Access, and Outcomes: Trends in Industrialized Countries." *Health Affairs* 18(3): 178–192.

Buchmueller, Thomas, Richard W. Johnson, and Anthony T. Lo Sasso. 2006. "Trends in Retiree Health Insurance, 1997–2003." *Health Affairs* 25(6): 1507–1516.

Bureau of Economic Analysis (BEA). 2007. *National Economic Accounts.* Washington, DC: BEA. http://www.bea.gov/National/nipaweb/index.asp (accessed November 9, 2007).

Bureau of Labor Statistics (BLS). 2007. *Updated CPI-U-RS, All Items and All items less food and energy, 1978–2006.* Washington, DC: BLS. http://www.bls.gov/cpi/cpiurs1978_2006.pdf (accessed November 9, 2007).

Council of Economic Advisers. 2007. *Economic Report of the President.* Washington, DC: U.S. Government Printing Office.

Dew-Becker, Ian, and Robert J. Gordon. 2005. "Where Did the Productivity Growth Go? Inflation Dynamics and the Distribution of Income." *Brookings Papers on Economic Activity* 2005(2): 66–127.

Farber, Henry S. 2005. "What Do We Know about Job Loss in the United States? Evidence from the Displaced Worker Survey, 1984–2004." Working Paper No. 498. Princeton, NJ: Industrial Relations Section, Princeton University.

———. 2007. "Is the Company Man an Anachronism? Trends in Long Term Employment in the U.S., 1973–2005." In *The Price of Independence: The Economics of Early Adulthood*, Sheldon H. Danziger and Cecilia E. Rouse, eds. New York: Russell Sage Foundation, pp. 56–83.

Ghilarducci, Teresa, and Wei Sun. 2006. "How Defined Contribution Plans and

401(k)s Affect Employer Pension Costs." *Journal of Pension Economics and Finance* 5(2): 175–196.

Government Accountability Office (GAO). 2006. "Employee Compensation: Employer Spending on Benefits Has Grown Faster Than Wages, Due Largely to Rising Costs for Health Insurance and Retirement Benefits." Report to Congressional Requesters. GAO-06-285. Washington, DC: GAO.

Johnson, Richard W. 2006. "Health Insurance Coverage and Costs at Older Ages: Evidence from the Health and Retirement Survey." AARP Public Policy Institute Research Report 2006-20. Washington, DC: AARP.

Swartz, Katherine. 2008. "Revising Employers' Role in Sponsoring and Financing Health Insurance and Medical Care." In *A Future of Good Jobs? America's Challenge in the Global Economy*, Timothy J. Bartik and Susan N. Houseman, eds. Kalamazoo, MI: W.E. Upjohn Institute for Employment Research, pp. 81–118.

U.S. Census Bureau. 2005. *U.S. International Trade in Goods and Services— Annual Revision for 2005*. Exhibits 1, 18. Washington, DC: U.S. Census Bureau. http://www.census.gov/foreign-trade/Press-Release/2005pr/final_ revisions (accessed December 19, 2007).

———. 2007. *FT900: U.S. International Trade in Goods and Services*. Exhibit 1. Washington, DC: U.S. Census Bureau. http://www.census.gov/ foreign-trade/Press-Release/2007pr/08/ (accessed December 19, 2007).

2
Are Skills the Problem?

Reforming the Education and Training System in the United States

Robert I. Lerman
American University, Urban Institute, and IZA

Skill formation is a life cycle process. It begins in the womb and continues on in the workplace. Education policy is only one aspect of a successful skill formation policy, and not necessarily the most important one.

—James Heckman and Dimitriy Masterov (2005)

As the larger return to education and skill is likely the single greatest source of the long-term increase in inequality, policies that boost our national investment in education and training can help reduce inequality while expanding economic opportunity. . . . The economically relevant concept of education is much broader than the traditional course of schooling from kindergarten through high school and into college. Indeed, substantial economic benefits may result from any form of training that helps individuals acquire economically and socially useful skills, including not only K-12 education, college, and graduate work but also on-the-job training, course work at community colleges and vocational schools, extension courses, on-line education, and training in financial literacy.

—Ben Bernanke, Chairman of the Board of Governors of the Federal Reserve (2007)

STATING THE ARGUMENT

The stellar economic growth of the United States since the early 1990s surprised scholars and policy analysts who had decried the mediocre skills of the American workforce and the inadequate preparation of students for careers. Unlike other countries, which have comprehensive school and career development systems, the United States lacked a well-structured approach to education and training, especially for the "forgotten half" of young people not pursuing a college education.[1] The skill development models of Germany, Japan, and other developed countries were especially compelling examples to emulate.

Certainly, the argument seemed convincing. American students and workers were underperforming compared to their counterparts in other developed countries on tests of international reading, math, and writing skills. Young people not going on to college experienced difficult transitions from high school to career-oriented jobs. Productivity growth had slowed over the 1970s and 1980s. The wage gap between high school–educated and college-educated workers had widened sharply, and compensation had actually declined for high school dropouts. Economic analyses indicated that the rising wage inequality partly resulted from the increasingly important role of the skills required to complement rapid technological changes, such as those embodied in computers. Another reason for the rising demand for skill was that changes in the organization of work were giving nonsupervisory workers more responsibility for decisions and for achieving high quality (Murnane and Levy 1996).

From today's perspective the skills problem looks overstated, since during the past 15 years the U.S. economy has far exceeded expectations. Between 1991 and 2005, national income rose in the United States by 45 percent, triple the 15 percent growth achieved in Japan and more than twice the 19 percent growth in Germany. U.S. gains in productivity also outpaced productivity growth in Japan, Germany, and most other advanced economies. The strong U.S. labor productivity performance is especially impressive in the context of a rapidly expanding job market that lowered unemployment rates and absorbed millions of poorly educated immigrants from less-developed countries, along with more than one million single parents who were former or potential welfare recipients. Since 2000, unemployment rates have averaged 4.9 percent, down from 5.8 percent in the 1990s and from 7.3 percent in the 1980s. The decline in unemployment rates has extended to workers without a high school degree; their rates of joblessness fell from about 10.5 percent in the 1992–1994 period to under 7 percent in the late 1990s and in 2006–2007.[2]

Notwithstanding these indicators of the health of the U.S. economy, not all is going well for workers. Less-educated workers have seen their wages stagnate or decline, causing them to fall further behind college-educated workers. The share of workers covered by pensions and health insurance has declined in recent years. The intensification of global competition is posing a threat to workers at all levels. Concerns are growing about immigration, outsourcing, and the expanding labor force in India, China, and other less-developed countries whose workers are now a part of a world labor market (Freeman 2007). Trade and the dynamics of companies generate worker displacement, resulting in frequent earnings losses when workers move to other jobs. The share of U.S. workers with a high school diploma and the share with a college degree are no longer the highest in the developed world. According to the New Commission on the Skills of the American Workforce (NCSAW 2007), even well-paying jobs for college graduates are threatened by outsourcing to low-paid but well-educated workers in poor countries. Given automation, outsourcing, and the need for creative workers, the commission finds that "people who prefer conventional work environments are likely to see their jobs disappear." At the same time, employers report difficulty in recruiting workers with adequate skills: over half of manufacturing firms have reported that the shortage of available skills is affecting their ability to serve customers, and 84 percent say the K-12 school system is not doing a good job of preparing students for the workplace (Deloitte Consulting 2005).

Perhaps the central concerns are shortfalls in skills and declining wages among a segment of American workers. Wages of men with less than a high school diploma have fallen. Men who graduated from high school but did not attend college have seen their wages stagnate. The worsening job market for African American men with no more than a high school degree has weakened their ability to start and maintain families. In contrast, well-educated workers, including African Americans with college degrees, enjoy low unemployment rates and earn good salaries. Apparently the demand for skill is rising faster than the supply. In 1979, the median hourly wage of college-educated workers was 34 percent higher than that of high school–educated workers. By 2005, the advantage to the college-educated reached 56 percent.[3] Thus, while expanding the skills of the current and future U.S. workforce may not be sufficient, most experts see raising educational attainment as necessary for a future of good jobs.

Translating a skills strategy into policy is, however, not straight-forward. The first problem is with the definition of skills. No one index can capture the multiplicity of skills required in a wide variety of work and occupational contexts. Reading, math, and writing capabilities are in high demand (Barton 2000) and are relevant to most jobs, including jobs held by workers with no college education (Holzer 1997). But so too are a range of other general skills (such as communication, responsibility, teamwork, allocating resources, problem-solving, and finding information) and occupation-specific skills.[4] Yet the nearly exclusive emphasis in public policy and in public funding is on academic skills. Today's goals, as espoused by leaders from politics, education, and the corporate sector, are twofold: 1) to raise educational attainment for K-12 students as high as possible, encouraging them to obtain at least a bachelor's degree, and 2) to insure that elementary and secondary students achieve at least basic academic competencies in a limited number of subjects. One measure of success is the share of students who pass academic tests of reading, math, and writing skills. A second is the share of students completing a bachelor's (or at least an associate's) degree. Implicitly, the United States has embarked on what James Rosenbaum (2001) has called a "college for all" policy.

To achieve these goals, governments have been doing four things: 1) increasing spending on elementary, secondary, and postsecondary schools; 2) mandating test-based performance measures that hold schools accountable for student performance; 3) expanding competition and school choice; and 4) offering subsidies to help students attend college. An increasing number of experts favor a skills strategy that begins at birth and uses high-quality, developmental child care before elementary school (Heckman and Masterov 2007). Although subsidized training through the public sector and through employers is a part of the nation's skill-building activities, spending on secondary and postsecondary education dwarfs the modest dollars spent training adults or youth who have dropped out of the mainstream educational system. Some secondary and postsecondary institutions, such as vocational high schools, community colleges, and proprietary private vocational schools, offer school-based programs that involve occupational training. But the traditional ways workers learned an occupational skill—through informal on-the-job training and formal apprenticeships—have attracted very little attention.

The emphasis on schooling and academic test scores as skill enhancement strategies results partly from a failure to conceptualize and measure a broader array of skills that are critical to success in the workplace. Without institutions that specify and document a range of well-accepted generic and occupational skills, public statistical agencies regularly quantify only schooling and occasionally measure verbal and math skills based on test scores. These indicators are meaningful but incomplete and sometimes inaccurate or contested.[5] As a result, we lack comprehensive measures of the job skills of the nation's workforce. We know little about the share of workers who have attained, for example, communication skills or the ability to allocate resources and to work effectively in a team environment. We have only limited information on occupational skills.

Unfortunately, the weakness in the data is not merely an academic issue; it can lead to a distorted set of education and training policies. When the public, policymakers, and educators lack information on critical generic and occupational skills, they find it difficult to diagnose trends, to identify skill gaps, to learn about the skill limitations of different subgroups, to understand the skills that are most in demand, and to determine the best mechanisms for teaching skills. The incomplete measures are a problem for the private as well as the public sector. Business firms rarely measure the skills of their employees, perhaps in part because their accounting methods disregard the asset value of the skills of their employees.

The simplified, academic-based measures of skill cause policymakers to use schooling as virtually the sole method by which students learn skills. The result is a standardized set of school-based requirements, often accompanied by a uniform approach to teaching. Such methods may be appropriate for elementary school and perhaps through early high school, but the approach has two great flaws, especially beyond this level of schooling. One is the assumption that people learn the same way—primarily through didactic teaching in a school setting. There is considerable evidence that learning styles differ markedly across students and that many learn best in a contextualized setting (Gardner 1999; Resnick 1987). The second flaw is the failure to appreciate the skill heterogeneity in the job market. Educational systems are usually large operations and typically require rules and conventions to make outcomes meaningful across students, school districts, states, and countries. Their emphasis on a few subjects, which are only marginally linked to student career interests, limits student incentives. Moreover, by their nature, school systems teach a homogeneous set of subjects and use a highly standardized approach to teaching. By comparison, the job market is strikingly heterogeneous, with hundreds of broad occupations and within each of those occupations different levels of work. The gap between the simple school-based definition of skill and the complex and varied skills required in the workplace is barely recognized in the United States. In contrast, many other countries recognize the heterogeneous and contextual nature of skills in three broad ways: 1) by using formal systems that qualify workers for most occupations, 2) by certifying workers for a variety of qualifications, and 3) by measuring the qualifications workers attain and the number of workers lacking valued qualifications.

Still, the U.S. system of skill-building has a critical asset: flexibility. The lack of formal pathways leaves space for workers to move in and out of schooling and training, which are often supplied by opportunistic community colleges, private occupational schools, on-line colleges, adult extension courses, apprenticeships, and often employers themselves. In distinguishing between the U.S. school system and the American *learning system*, Samuelson (2006) argues that these institutions offer workers a second chance, ways of combining school and work, and a close link between education and careers. Their flexibility and relevance, he says, overcome some but not all weaknesses of the mainstream system of high schools and colleges. Unfortunately, some students only use a community college to take a remedial course offering material that they should have learned in high school (Rosenbaum 2001). Others never attend, whether because their bad high school experiences make them unable or unwilling to return to school, because they get into trouble with crime or drugs, or because early parenthood creates barriers to long-term skill development.

What will it take for the training system to contribute in a greater way to helping American workers become more productive and have more rewarding careers? The central argument of this paper is that doing better requires that public policymakers and education and training practitioners recognize and address the multidimensional nature of skills, the variety of learning approaches (including the value of contextualized learning), and the desirability of close links with employers and the workplace. The next section considers conceptual and measurement issues related to the heterogeneous nature of skills demanded in the current and future U.S. economy. Section three examines the changing demand and supply of skills based on existing measures. In section four, I consider the strengths and weaknesses of the current system of U.S. skill development. Section five presents recommendations for improving and expanding skill development efforts in the United States.

DEFINING AND MEASURING SKILLS

The modern economic approach to analyzing skills begins with human capital theory (Becker 1964). The analogy with capital arises because to increase workers' skills requires an investment of real resources in the present that yields a flow of returns in the form of enhanced productivity in the future. The enhanced skills may be specific (in that they raise a worker's productivity only within one firm), general (in that the worker's added capabilities can increase productivity to a range of firms), or some of both (learning one firm's computer system can help in another firm). This specific versus general distinction affects whom we expect to finance education and training and who benefits from these investments. The added productivity potential from general skills raises the willingness of all firms to pay high salaries to workers who enhance their general skills. Since workers gain the benefits from investments in general skills, firms are unlikely to fund the education and training that generates the skills. In contrast, some of the returns to firm-specific skills will be captured by the employer. Since other firms would not benefit from specific skills, they do not bid up wages, causing workers to remain with their existing firms at a higher level of productivity and lowering the costs of turnover and recruitment. In this case, firms may finance and reap some of the benefits from training.

The language of human capital has entered the lexicon of policy-makers and professionals throughout the world. Studies of the rates of return to education have been undertaken in scores of countries (Blöndal, Field, and Girouard 2002; Psacharopoulos and Patrinos 2004). The evidence from this vast literature documents positive returns to education and finds that the highest rates of return to primary school occur in less-developed countries. The average private and social returns to education remain around 10 percent even in wealthy countries and even at high levels of education. Although these returns are healthy, they represent the average return across all workers achieving the additional education, not the individuals at the margin of either obtaining the education or not. Moreover, besides ignoring the risk and uncertainty of the returns, they often ignore the costs paid on behalf of those who do not complete the added education.

One common misperception is that education conveys general skills useful in a range of fields while training provides only specialized skills that help in very specific contexts. A second is that employers will never pay for skills that might be used outside the firm. As Acemoglu and Pischke (1999) point out, employers often have an incentive to finance general training because of transaction costs in the labor market that, in reality, make it difficult for workers to quit and costly for employers to replace them. Also, firms providing the training know more than other firms about the content and value of training and how well individual workers have absorbed the knowledge. Firms realize that specific and general skills are often complementary—the ability to achieve high productivity gains from specific training increases as the worker's general skills rise. Still another issue is that the distinction between general and specific downplays the critical role of occupational skills, which are general in the sense of having value to more than one firm but which are specific to a set of firms. Task-specific skills in one occupation are often transferable to jobs in another occupation using similar skills.

Though useful and effective in predicting a range of outcomes, the human capital perspective ignores some motivational factors that affect the accumulation and effective use of skills. Not all learning is for instrumental purposes. People often learn in order to satisfy their curiosity or to gain a sense of accomplishment. The ability to learn a skill conveys a sense of pride, and the effective use of skills in an occupation often brings workers a sense of identity. Skills rarely raise productivity in isolation; increases in productivity typically result when workers use their skills to complement the work of others in an appropriate setting within the organization (Brown 2001).

The framework provided by human capital offers little guidance as to which general, specific, or occupational skills are valuable in any given labor market. One approach is to estimate the gains in earnings associated with specific skills. While economists have developed such estimates showing that measures of math and verbal skills are correlated with earnings (Murnane, Willett, and Levy 1995), the fact that test scores do not account for much of the variation in earnings among workers suggests that other attributes or skills are relevant to job performance (Holzer 1997). To find out what these attributes might be, the U.S. Department of Labor (USDOL) created the Secretary's Commission on Achieving Necessary Skills (SCANS) in the early 1990s to study what skills effective workers require to succeed in specific settings. The commission's report highlights what have come to be called SCANS skills and characterizes them as incorporating many capabilities not directly taught in school. Some examples of SCANS skills are the abilities to allocate time and resources, to acquire and evaluate information, to participate effectively as a member of a team, to teach others, to negotiate differences, to listen and communicate with customers and supervisors, to understand the functioning of organizational systems, to select technology, and to apply technology to relevant tasks. The recent classification known as 21st Century Skills incorporates academic skills and knowledge but also emphasizes such other skills as interactive communication, teamwork, adaptability, planning, self-direction, and responsibility.[6] For all types of skills, there are many levels of competence. Context matters greatly. Responsibility and attention to detail may be necessary for both mowing lawns well and for nursing, but the required levels differ dramatically between the two occupations.

Employer hiring decisions are sensitive to an array of skills that go well beyond academic skills. In a survey of 3,200 employers in four large metropolitan areas, employers reported that such personal qualities as responsibility, integrity, and self-management are as important as or more important than basic skills (Holzer 1997). Further documentation on the importance of these job criteria comes from the National Employer Survey, which obtained responses from more than 3,300 businesses. These employers ranked attitude, communication skills, previous work experience, employer recommendations, and industry-based credentials above years of schooling, grades, and test scores administered as part of the interview (Zemsky 1997). Evidence for the relevance of occupation-specific and industry-specific skills comes from a paper by Sullivan (2006). He finds that some workers gain high wage returns to occupation-specific work experience while others gain high wage returns to industry-specific work experience.

The sociocultural approach to examining skills emphasizes the contextual nature of skills and the importance of nonacademic skills, which are often obtained in a work environment through joining experienced workers in "a community of practice" (Stasz 2001). Nelsen (1997) points out that workplaces not only require formal knowledge—facts, principles, theories, math, and writing skills—but also informal knowledge as embodied in heuristics, work styles, and contextualized understanding of tools and techniques. In a highly revealing case study of auto repair workers, she describes the importance of social skills for learning the informal knowledge, as captured in stories, advice, and guided practice. Nelsen further argues that the social skills learned at school are not necessarily useful at work and may even be counterproductive. (For example, in school, helping out one's peers on exams and on some homework is considered cheating, whereas at work the exchange of information and knowledge is essential.) By implication, years of schooling are probably not a good proxy for informal knowledge or for the attributes helpful in attaining such knowledge.

Further evidence showing the importance of noncognitive skills comes from a complex analysis by Heckman, Stixrud, and Urzua (2006) of the schooling and job market experience of a national sample of young workers as they age from 14 through 30. Although the authors use a limited set of measures to capture cognitive and noncognitive skills, their results are striking. They find that, except for college graduates, noncognitive skills (as measured by indices of locus of control and self-esteem) exert at least as high and probably a higher impact on job market outcomes than do cognitive skills (word knowledge, paragraph comprehension, arithmetic reasoning, mathematical knowledge, and coding speed as measured by the Armed Forces Vocational Aptitude

Battery). Using another major data set, the National Education Longitudinal Study (NELS), Deke and Haimson (2006) develop evidence reinforcing the importance of nonacademic competencies, such as work habits, leadership skills, teamwork and other sports-related skills, and attitudes toward whether luck or effort determines success in life. They find that for two-thirds of all high school students, a nonacademic skill is most predictive of earnings. Operators of job training programs emphasize the need for disadvantaged men to gain self-esteem, communicate effectively, envision long-term goals, and demonstrate personal responsibility as well as to avoid inflexibility, dishonesty, defensiveness, and impatience (Carmona 2007).

The importance of noncognitive skills for performance on jobs should not be taken to mean that verbal, math, and writing skills are irrelevant or unnecessary for the vast majority of positions. When employers emphasize personal qualities, many may be assuming workers have at least some basic academic skills and that, once some threshold level is reached, noncognitive skills become a priority. On the other hand, few workers use many of the academic skills that educators view as vital to success. In a survey of a representative sample of workers, only 9 percent reported using the capabilities learned in Algebra I, and fewer than 13 percent of workers below the upper white-collar level ever write anything five pages or longer (Handel 2007).

Wage rates and wage differentials offer one way to assess the skills valued in the market, since they generally reflect productivity levels and differences across workers. Wage rates indirectly capture the return to the skills of the marginal worker. Since the employer is voluntarily paying to obtain the productive services of the worker, the wage may be indirectly capturing the full complement of skills. Still, understanding which skills are most important in determining wages would require data on the multidimensional pattern of skills. Moreover, wage differences might reflect factors other than skill, such as the danger of the job and the level of unionization.

The connection between wages and productivity, along with the variability of wage rates within groups that have ostensibly similar skills, offers further evidence for the multidimensional nature of skills. Although education is highly and positively correlated with wages, educational attainment explains only a small part of the variability in earnings. Indeed, the inequality of wage rates within major educational categories is almost as high as wage inequality across the entire work-force. Work experience apparently raises wages, but the precise con-nections between actual skills and wages are rarely explicit. Higher test scores, especially on math tests, are associated with higher earnings, but they explain only a modest amount of wage variability.

The evidence provides some indicators for how best to measure skills, but, in practice, indicators of the skills of U.S. workers usually boil down to educational attainment and, in some cases, test scores and years of work experience. For example, in the 2006 *Economic Report of the President*, the chapter on "Skills for the U.S. Workforce" relies en-tirely on three considerations: 1) years of schooling and highest degree attained; 2) math and science test scores of 9-, 13-, and 17-year-olds relative to scores in other countries; and 3) the declining share of engi-neering and science degrees held by U.S. workers relative to immigrant workers (Council of Economic Advisers 2006). The concerns of the NCSAW about low skills also relate to how well the United States is do-ing relative to other countries. The commission focuses not only on the math and science test scores of current students and the literacy skills of the adult workforce, but also on an apparent shortfall in the training of U.S. engineers and scientists, especially when compared to the num-bers being turned out by China and India. The commission highlights the importance of firms using creativity to retain high-wage jobs in the future but provides no measure of this elusive concept.

Educational attainment and test scores are commonly used as prox-ies for skills, but how well do they capture the level and trend of skills in the U.S. workforce? It turns out that accurate measures of even these basic indicators of skill are more elusive than is commonly recognized. More importantly, the education-based data provide no measure of ad-ditional dimensions of skill, an omission that can lead to faulty conclu-sions and policies.

Turning to data on the capabilities of U.S. workers, we start with the figures on educational attainment and ask about broad trends and about variations in school completion across subgroups by race, sex, Hispanic status, and metropolitan area. The standard data show steady progress toward the completion of high school and college and declining and modest racial gaps in the completion of high school. Table 2.1 shows the rise in high school completion and in college completion by race, sex, and Hispanic origin. The proportion of the over-25 population with high school degrees jumped from 64 percent in 1976 to 86 percent in 2006. The share with a bachelor's degree nearly doubled, to 28 percent. In addition, the black-white gap in high-school completion narrowed from 20–24 percentage points in 1976 to less than 6 in 2006. The gains were much larger for the adult population than for successive cohorts of 25-to-29-year-olds. Still, as of 2006, 86 percent of all 25-to-29-year-olds had graduated from high school, including 83 percent of black men and 88 percent of black women. The rates of high school completion were much lower among Hispanic men and women. Growth in college graduates was especially high for all groups of women, but not nearly as strong for men.

Changes in the educational composition of the labor force are especially striking from the perspective of net additional workers. Between 1992 and early 2007, the adult labor force (ages 25 and over) expanded by about 24 million workers. Over the same period, workers with a bachelor's degree increased by 15.5 million and workers with at least some college rose by 7.9 million. Additional workers with no college amounted to only about 400,000, or 2 percent of the overall net changes. This number looks implausible given that over 40 percent of a recent cohort left school without any college.[7] Two phenomena explain the seemingly divergent pattern. First, the inflow of less-educated young people and immigrants into the labor force was offset by an outflow of less-educated older workers. Second, labor force participation rates are lower among less-educated than among more-educated workers. The demographic component will differ in the future because the segment of today's workforce nearing retirement is much more highly educated than past retirees. As a result, we are very likely to be adding many more less-educated workers than we lose to retirement.

The information for these conclusions comes from the Current Population Survey (CPS), the household survey used to measure the nation's unemployment rate since the late 1940s. These household surveys obtain information on the education, employment, and income of each member of the household from a responsible adult in the household.

Unfortunately, the CPS data do not tell the entire story and may be quite inaccurate, especially with respect to high school graduation. Data drawn from school reports (Common Core Data, or CCD) suggest much lower high school graduation rates, especially among black youth. Since schools report all ninth-graders registered and all high

Table 2.1 High School and College Completion of Noninstitutional Population by Race, Hispanic Status, and Sex: Ages 25 and Over and 25–29 at Five-Year Intervals from 1976 to 2006 (%)

Age and year	All		White		Black		Hispanic	
	Male	Female	Male	Female	Male	Female	Male	Female
Completed high school, 25 and over								
2006	85.0	85.9	85.5	86.7	80.1	81.2	58.5	60.1
2001	84.1	84.2	84.4	85.1	79.2	78.5	55.5	58.0
1996	81.9	81.6	82.7	82.8	74.3	74.2	53.0	53.3
1991	78.5	78.3	79.8	79.9	66.7	66.7	51.4	51.2
1986	75.1	74.4	76.5	75.9	61.5	63.0	49.2	47.8
1981	70.3	69.1	72.1	71.2	53.2	52.6	45.5	43.6
1976	64.7	63.5	66.7	65.5	42.3	45.0	41.4	37.3
Completed college, 25 and over								
2006	29.2	26.9	29.7	27.1	17.2	19.4	11.9	12.9
2001	28.2	24.3	28.7	24.6	15.3	16.1	10.8	11.4
1996	26.0	21.4	26.9	21.8	12.4	14.6	10.3	8.3
1991	24.3	18.8	25.4	19.3	11.4	11.6	10.0	9.4
1986	23.2	16.1	24.1	16.4	11.2	10.7	9.5	7.4
1981	21.1	13.4	22.2	13.8	8.2	8.2	9.7	5.9
1976	18.6	11.3	19.6	11.6	6.3	6.8	8.6	4.0

Completed high school, 25–29

Year								
2006	84.4	88.5	84.1	88.3	83.1	87.8	60.6	66.7
2001	85.3	88.3	84.6	88.3	85.4	87.0	58.3	67.3
1996	86.5	88.1	86.3	88.8	87.2	84.2	59.7	62.9
1991	84.9	85.8	85.1	86.6	83.5	80.1	56.4	57.1
1986	85.9	86.4	85.6	87.4	86.5	80.6	58.2	60.0
1981	86.5	86.1	87.6	87.6	78.4	76.4	59.1	60.4
1976	86.0	83.5	87.3	84.6	72.5	74.9	57.6	58.4

Completed college, 25–29

Year								
2006	25.3	31.6	25.0	31.7	14.9	21.6	6.9	12.8
2001	25.5	31.3	25.1	32.1	15.6	17.9	8.2	13.3
1996	26.1	28.2	27.2	29.1	12.4	16.4	10.2	9.8
1991	23.0	23.4	24.1	25.0	11.5	10.6	8.1	10.4
1986	22.9	21.9	24.1	22.9	10.1	13.3	8.9	9.1
1981	23.1	19.6	24.3	20.5	12.1	11.1	8.6	6.5
1976	27.5	20.1	28.7	20.6	12.0	13.6	10.3	4.8

NOTE: The four categories represent 1) the percentage of the noninstitutional population aged 25 and over that has completed four years of high school or more, 2) aged 25 and over that has completed four years of college or more, 3) aged 25–29 that has completed four years of high school or more, and 4) aged 25–29 that has completed four years of college or more.
SOURCE: U.S. Census Bureau (2007).

school diplomas awarded each year, some researchers have derived high school graduation rates by dividing the diplomas awarded by the ninth-grade enrollments four years earlier, while adjusting for the fact that ninth-grade enrollments can be swelled by high retention rates and also adjusting for internal and international migration. Unlike the case with conventional CPS-based measures, analysts using the CCD measures do not include private school students or count individuals earning GEDs as having graduated from high school.[8] Moreover, they do not capture the extent to which dropouts return to school. Still, the results are striking and troubling. Instead of only 8 percent of non-Hispanic whites in public schools not graduating from high school, the figure looks as high as 19 percent. Among African Americans, the share not completing high school jumps from 14 percent to 38 percent (Warren and Halpern-Manners 2007). The Hispanic graduation rate looks at least as high in the administrative data as in the household-based data. One broad and revealing measure is the number of public and private diplomas awarded divided by the number of 17-year-olds. It shows a decline from 77 percent in 1969 to 70 percent in 2000 (Chaplin 2002), but a recent increase back to 75 percent in 2004–2005. Overall, the trends in high school graduation look far less optimistic when using CCD-based measures than when relying on CPS-based data.

The low graduation rates based on administrative data raise serious questions about analyses of skills in the United States, as well as about public policies. Consider, for example, one of the stylized facts of labor economics, namely the rising earnings gap between high school graduates and college graduates. If many classified as high school graduates did not in fact complete high school and the misreporting is worsening, then current college–high school graduate comparisons and estimates of past trends may be highly inaccurate. Similarly, policy decisions could be influenced by this revised picture of high school completion. The nature of reforms to the nation's school system depends on whether the share of students not completing high school is small and declining or high and not declining at all, especially among African American students. If nearly everyone is graduating, administering high-stakes tests that require students to learn more in school may have a higher priority than reducing dropout rates.

From the perspective of measuring the nation's skills, one would like to know whether measurement problems extend to college completion as well. So far administrative tracking has not been undertaken to capture the accuracy of self-reported CPS data on the completion of an associate's, bachelor's, or professional degree. Although the college completion data may be entirely accurate, it is difficult to know for sure.

Test scores offer an independent indicator of skills that are rewarded in the workforce. There are a plethora of national tests, including the National Assessment of Educational Progress (NAEP), which measures reading, math, science, and writing skills over time and across states. International comparative data provide estimates of the adult literacy of U.S. workers and the academic skills of American students compared to their counterparts in other countries. Although U.S.-based policy researchers and political leaders often decry the poor performance of U.S. students in academic tests of comparative competencies, the data as a whole reveal a mixed picture (Boe and Shin 2005). In comparison to students in other industrial countries, U.S. students perform about average. U.S. students do considerably better than average in reading and civics, about the same in science, but worse than average in mathematics. Restricting the sample to the largest Western economies (the G7), Boe and Shin find that the U.S. disadvantage occurs only in math and only relative to Japan. They attribute some of the shortfall in U.S. test scores to the more heterogeneous U.S. population. When we restrict the sample to non-Hispanic white students, U.S. scores far exceed the scores of other G7 countries, except for Japan in math and science.

These data offer information only on the competency measures of current students. To learn about the literacy and basic math skills of the U.S. adult population, we turn to the 2003 National Assessment of Adult Literacy (NAAL). The NAAL tests cover prose literacy (skills in comprehending and using information from continuous text, such as news stories and instructional materials), document literacy (skills in using information from other texts, such as job applications, tables, and drug and food labels), and quantitative literacy (skills in identifying and performing computations of numbers embedded in a text, such as by filling out an order form, calculating interest on a loan, or figuring out a tip). The report (Kutner et al. 2007) defines levels of competency in terms of four categories: 1) below basic, 2) basic, 3) intermediate, and 4) proficient. "Below basic" does not necessarily mean illiterate; many in this category can, for example, find information in a short, simple prose passage and identify on an instruction sheet what is permissible to drink before a medical test. Within the below basic range of quantitative literacy, individuals can add two numbers from a deposit slip and calculate change from a $20 bill. But this group cannot calculate the weekly salary for a job based on hourly wages or locate two numbers on a bar graph and calculate the difference between them. At the high end, those individuals classified as "proficient" in terms of prose literacy can compare viewpoints in two editorials with contrasting interpretations of scientific and economic evidence. "Proficient" in quantitative literacy means individuals can calculate the yearly cost of a specified amount of life insurance using a table that gives monthly costs for each $1,000 of coverage.

The tabulations provide considerable detail on levels of literacy by demographic, education, and occupational group, as well as information on changes between 1992 and 2003, the two years NAAL was conducted. For the entire population, about 14 percent scored in the lowest category (below basic) on prose literacy, 12 percent on document literacy, and 22 percent on quantitative literacy. About 13 percent of the population was "proficient" in all literacy measures. These figures understate the skills of the workforce because the age group least likely to participate in the workforce (ages 65 and over) performed worst in terms of literacy. Only about 11 to 12 percent of the 19–64 age group fell into the below basic category in prose and document literacy; 20 percent were below basic in quantitative literacy.

Apart from the over-65 population, the two groups with low literacy levels are Hispanic adults—especially those who spoke another language, at least before starting school—and African American adults. Depending on the measure, 36 to 50 percent of all Hispanic adults scored in the below basic literacy levels; fully 61 percent of adults who grew up speaking only Spanish tested below basic in prose literacy. African Americans also showed low rates of adult literacy, as 24 to 47 percent were classified as below basic for the three categories. In contrast, only 7 to 13 percent of whites were in this low literacy category. Some improvement took place over the 1992–2003 period for African Americans, but the trend worsened among Hispanics, perhaps because of the inflow of immigrants.

The NAAL confirms a close (but far from complete) connection between literacy scores and educational attainment. Consider, for example, the prose literacy scores. While fully one-half of all adults without a high school degree or GED score in the below basic range, the proportion in this lowest category falls to 10 percent for those with GEDs. About 5 percent or fewer of those with at least some college fall into this bottom category. On the other end of the scale, the proportions reaching "proficient" rise from nearly zero among high school dropouts to 31 percent among those with a bachelor of arts and 41 percent among those with a graduate degree. Although college graduates achieve prose proficiency at levels well above less-educated adults, it is troubling that less than one-third meet this standard and that the proportion in the "proficient" group declined from 40 to 31 percent from 1992 to 2003. The overlap among categories is notable. In quantitative literacy, 63 percent of adults with associate's degrees score higher than 26 percent of adults with bachelor's degrees. For all three tests, the average performance of whites with an associate's degree is higher than the average score of African American and Hispanic adults with a bachelor's degree.

The combination of test score information and educational attainment provides considerable information on skills, but the precise connection with the job market is not clear. The evidence demonstrates that, while more education and higher literacy skills predict higher wage rates, much is left unexplained. A good example is the economic gains attached to a GED, which is sometimes considered an equivalent certification to a high school diploma. However, researchers have found that the GED by itself does little or nothing to raise the wages of workers without a high school diploma (Cameron and Heckman 1993), suggesting that the GED does not generate added skills. Yet the NAAL data show that those with a GED have test scores on prose, document, and quantitative literacy that are nearly identical to the test scores of adults with a high school diploma and that are far above the scores of high school dropouts. By implication, factors other than the academic skills measured in the NAAL must be important determinants of wages.[9]

More broadly, wage variability is high within education groups. Using data from the 2005 Current Population Survey (but excluding the upper half of the top 1 percent), I found that the Gini coefficient of wage rates is almost as high among male high school and college graduates (0.29 and 0.31) as among all adult male workers (0.33).

The rich nature of the NAAL data provides other indicators of the relevance of skills. One of special interest is the respondents' own assessments about whether their existing skills have limited their job opportunities. Not surprisingly, those at high literacy levels were much less likely to feel limited by their current skill levels. Of those in the "proficient" category of quantitative literacy, 89 percent said their current reading skills were not limiting their job options at all, and only 4 percent saw more than a very small limitation. Similarly, 80 percent of those in the "intermediate" category saw no job limitations. The unexpected result is that 66 percent at "basic" and even 40 percent at "below basic" levels believed their quantitative literacy did not limit their job opportunities. Some respondents are no doubt misinformed about their limited access to jobs, but others may actually qualify for the jobs of interest to them.

Educational attainment and test scores certainly offer important information about the nation's skills. The general skills that result from schooling and academic competencies are valued in the job market. But they do not tell the full story about the *qualifications* of American workers to perform well at the workplace. As documented by the SCANS report and other research, having a range of noncognitive, interpersonal, occupational, and industry-specific skills matters at levels that vary given the contexts in which they are used. The term "qualifications" is perhaps better at capturing the specificity of requirements of jobs and careers than the word "skills."

One common job qualification—often overlooked in discussions of skills and the workforce—is that applicants must be drug-free. Entry-level workers are frequently tested for marijuana and cocaine before obtaining employment. It is unclear to what extent illicit drug use influences the capabilities of American workers, but the evidence suggests that chronic drug use lowers employment (French, Roebuck, and Alexandre 2001).

Although job qualifications are diverse and go well beyond cognitive skills, we lack good measures of qualifications that incorporate noncognitive skills, occupational and industry skills, skills gained from general work experience, and work readiness. In part, the measurement problem arises because of the nation's complex and often informal mechanisms for certifying and qualifying worker skills in occupations and industries. Becoming a manager at a hotel requires a set of skills that hotel firms judge as being necessary for the position. Yet most managers do not receive a formal, recognized certification documenting this mix of skills. Instead, many jobs involve on-the-job training with little or no certification. In this context, it is not surprising that statistical agencies do little to measure and researchers do little to analyze occupational certification.

Contrast this pattern with the qualification systems of other advanced economies. As a National Research Council panel pointed out (Hansen 1994), several countries have national standards for work-related skills and certify those skills through training that qualifies workers for a particular occupation. Some of these countries make extensive use of apprenticeships that involve years of workplace and school-based training and formal testing to certify occupation and industry skills. The occupations are not limited to construction and craft positions but include computer work, technical sales, managerial positions, and service positions. Individuals earn one certification for completing an apprenticeship and another, much higher-level certification for becoming a master in the field.

One approach to national standards, emphasized by the United Kingdom and some other countries, is to develop a modular system of skill certification through the National Vocational Qualifications, or NVQs.[10] The NVQs set standards that define the competencies, knowledge, and understanding needed to perform well in a given occupation. The NVQs recognize workplace learning and competence based on evidence of performance at the workplace. The NVQ system takes account of skill gradations in each defined field and allows workers to gain documentation for each level, whether attained with one employer or many. The ultimate goal is that employers will place a value on their workers' attaining a qualification level, thus giving workers an incentive to learn on the job. Although this system has not worked as effectively as planned (Eraut 2001), the NVQ approach offers one example of how certifying the attainment of skills can provide the basis for measuring the heterogeneity of skills.[11]

Actually, skill standards embodied in state licensing laws and regulations and other standards adopted by industries or through apprenticeship programs have become common in the United States. About 20 percent of workers are required to have a state license to practice their occupation, up from less than 5 percent in the early 1950s (Kleiner

2006). Much of this increase has resulted from rapid growth in traditionally licensed occupations, such as medicine, dentistry, and law. However, the number of licensing laws has been increasing as well.

The distinction between certification of skills and licensing of occupations is important. Licensing requires everyone working in an occupation to meet a minimum qualification standard and excludes unlicensed workers from practicing the occupation. In the United States, licensing rules vary widely across states, and states regulate occupations as varied as alarm contractor, auctioneer, manicurist, and massage therapist. Economists have long stressed the anticompetitive nature of licensing, as incumbents in an occupation try to limit the supply of competitors (Kleiner 2006). Although licenses ostensibly offer some assurance to consumers that all providers will be of a consistent quality, Kleiner finds evidence that licensure plays more of a role in raising prices than in assuring quality. In contrast, certification provides information about a worker's skills but does not limit competition from those who lack certification. In the United States, certification is lacking in many fields, is too narrow and complex in other fields, and is not sufficiently portable and well recognized in still others (Wills 1992). In 1994, Congress established the National Skill Standards Board (NSSB) to develop a system of relevant, rigorous, portable, and well-recognized skill standards that would guide training and would provide reliable signals to worker and employers. Unfortunately, the NSSB was extremely slow to develop, rationalize, or recognize useful occupational standards.[12]

Given the uncoordinated and opaque approach to occupational certification in the United States, it is not surprising that policymakers rarely incorporate this dimension into deliberations about the skills of American workers. Measures of these skills are not readily available to capture changes over time, but occasionally statistical agencies collect data on occupational certificates. The Survey of Income and Program Participation (SIPP) provides some information on occupational certification, but only through schools. According to these data, almost 19 percent of workers reported earning "a diploma or certificate from a vocational, technical, trade, or business school." Included in this group are 7 percent of high school dropouts, 27 percent of high school graduates with no college, about 38 percent of those with some college but no associate's or bachelor's degree, 56 percent of those earning an associate's degree, and 10 percent of those with a bachelor's degree. This information suggests the importance of vocational certification for a sizable share of workers, especially those with a high school degree but no bachelor's degree. Unfortunately, these data are rarely reported, and they probably miss various occupational certifications not granted through schools, such as is the case with many apprenticeships. I know of no nationally representative data source regularly reporting whether an individual holds a license or certification in his or her occupation.

Workers who complete apprenticeships are often very highly skilled, highly trained in a field relevant to the job market, and well paid. Yet the limited information on apprenticeships illustrates the weakness of measures of the skills of the U.S. workforce. The size of the current apprenticeship system is unclear. For the USDOL and its Office of Apprenticeship, the count of apprentices includes only those within the "registered" system governed by state or federal apprenticeship councils. A program becomes registered by submitting the plans for meeting the hours of on-the-job training and classroom training required by the relevant council. Although not recognized officially by the USDOL, some unregistered positions that involve coordinated work-based and school-based training may nonetheless be called apprenticeships by many workers and firms. Given the different definitions, estimates of the number of current apprentices range widely, from 426,000 active and registered apprentices (as reported by USDOL in 2006) to 1.5 million. The latter figure is based on the number of individuals in the National Household Education Survey who reported having participated in "a formal program in the 12 months prior to the interview that led to journeyman status in a craft or trade."

Still another measurement weakness arises because businesses do not keep track of the impact of their own investments on the human capital of their employees. No doubt employers believe they earn a return on their investments in training and educating their workers. Like investments in physical capital, the dollars spent this year on human capital investments yield a flow of added productivity over time. The benefits of investments in physical and human capital are not used up within the year. For this reason, the full expenditures on this year's physical investments are not counted as costs against current-year revenues. This year's costs (depreciation) are only the amount of the asset used up this year, and the remaining value is recorded as a firm asset. Because human capital is not recorded in a similar fashion, firms do not keep records of human capital investment with the same care or include the asset of a highly trained workforce on their balance sheets.

So What?

Clearly, measures of the skills of the U.S. workforce have important weaknesses. But does it matter? Would policy development or the interpretation of economic trends change in response to a more thorough definition and measure of skills?

Certainly, the emphasis on reading and math skills looks justified by the clear shortfalls in the literacy and basic quantitative abilities of the U.S. workforce as measured by the NAAL. Nonetheless, reliance almost exclusively on educational attainment, student test scores, and limited adult testing pushes policymakers toward an unbalanced approach, one that tries to improve on the skill indicators we measure while ignoring the skills we rarely measure. One gap of particular importance and potential relevance to policy is the lack of any good measure of occupational skills or qualifications. Contrast this approach with the broader measurements and policies of many other countries that measure occupational skill certifications and encourage rigorous work-based learning.[13] Although efforts to improve outcomes for students going through high school make sense, the pessimistic data on dropouts raise questions about what and how best to teach students. In particular, focusing solely on academic skills and school-based solutions may not work as well as a balanced approach that widens the definition of skill and offers substantial opportunity for skill development in workplaces and other institutions.

DEMANDS FOR SKILLS

By nearly any indicator, the demand for skills has been increasing. To economists, the most convincing evidence is the increase in the wage premium paid to college-educated workers over high school–educated workers and the premium paid to more-experienced workers over less-experienced workers (Autor, Katz, and Kearney 2005). At the same time, the rising wage differences within educational and experience groups has been interpreted as reflecting an increasing demand for unobserved skills.

Discussions of rising skill demands often take place at a high level of abstraction and often ignore differences in occupational demands. To sense the importance of occupational demand factors in determining skill requirements, consider the job market for PhD physicists, people who have mastered science at the highest level. Raising the skills of the workforce by encouraging more people to learn enough to become physicists would increase the supply in a market with stagnant or declining demand. The 1990s saw substantially more doctorates granted than openings for physicists, and expectations are for continued slow growth in job openings in this field (BLS 2007). The example of physicists is not meant to dismiss the real increases in the demand for skills in the U.S. economy. Instead, it offers a cautionary note that raising skills does not always lead to improved jobs. Physicists certainly have the talent and capability to earn good wages in other professions, but their example and other evidence show that developing skills in fields not in demand can lead to frustration, job dissatisfaction, lower wages, and not necessarily to more good jobs (Allen and van der Velden 2001).

On the other hand, some occupations that require occupational skills but not significant formal education are in short supply. Even in manufacturing, an industry in which employment has declined by 3.4 million workers over the past 20 years, employers are having trouble finding welders and other technically competent workers.[14] Electrical occupations in the construction industry are fields in demand that require extensive occupation-specific skills but allow workers with no more than a high school diploma to enter training. Skill development for these fields takes place both in academic and in workplace settings. Moreover, demand for these workers is rising more rapidly than the workforce as a whole. In fact, the 2.8 million increase in construction jobs over the past two decades has gone largely unnoticed in comparison to the drop-off in manufacturing jobs.

On an aggregate level, the trends in occupations indicate an upgrading of skills, but one matched by the rise in educational attainment. Of the 23 million jobs added between 1992 and 2006, 22 percent were in management, business, or financial operations and 31 percent were in professional positions. These positions all require skill and considerable training, but many of these positions, such as lab technician or manager of a fast food restaurant, do not require a bachelor's degree. Over the same 14 years, the 14.4 million increase in workers holding bachelor's degrees amounted to almost 60 percent of the net increase in the 25-and-older employed population.

For the future, the projections by the Bureau of Labor Statistics (BLS) provide a starting point. Using three factors—1) projections for demand for output by each industry, 2) the composition of occupations within industries, and 3) the educational requirements of occupations— the BLS has projected the educational requirements that would enable the economy to fill both the jobs newly created in each occupation and the job openings to replace workers expected to leave the occupation. The BLS demand projections suggest that of the 19 million new jobs that will be created between 2004 and 2014, a bachelor's degree or higher will be required for about 36 percent, some college for 28 percent, and a high school degree or less for 37 percent. Counting replacement demand indicates somewhat lower educational requirements: including replacement workers, a bachelor's degree will be needed for 26 percent of openings and some college for an additional 28 percent.

The projections cover more than 700 detailed occupations, and uncertainty is inherent in such an exercise. One critique argues that the projections have systematically understated the growth of skilled occupations (Bishop and Carter 1991). A second important issue is the extent to which skill requirements *within* occupations are expected to change. Another critical set of uncertainties has to do with flexibility and unmeasured skills not captured by the occupational or even the educational breakdown. Some education and training generate skills that can be applied to a variety of occupations. In addition, some positions may require a considerable amount of relevant work experience, yet existing data do not allow us to determine whether past work experience is well or poorly matched to demand. We may match workers to broad educational categories yet generate mismatches between skills and specific occupations in demand. These mismatches create shortages and missed opportunities, especially when the occupations require more than short-term training for the worker to perform productively.

One way to minimize mismatches is to develop close linkages between education and training systems and employers, so as to glean at least some information about employers' current and future demands.

Such linkages take place every day at the community college level, at workforce agencies, and occasionally at the undergraduate and graduate levels of universities, but often the educational realm operates quite independently of patterns of employer demand.

U.S. SKILL DEVELOPMENT SYSTEM

People have long learned skills outside of formal education and training institutions (Resnick 1987). Although the vast expansion of accessible information has reinforced this tendency, formal institutions remain important in helping people gain the tools required to judge the quality of information and to use it effectively. Indeed, skills are likely complementary to the increased information flow of the Internet and other new technologies. People with sufficient skills become much more valuable because they can take the best advantage of today's computing and information revolution.

Although people become educated and learn skills for many reasons, this section focuses on skill development for productive careers. A useful way to begin is to classify these skill creation strategies as either initial preparation or continuing preparation for careers. It is true that some institutions—notably community colleges—provide each of these two kinds of skill development, but the distinction is nonetheless worth making.

Schools and Other Skill-Building Organizations

Initial preparation starts in the school system. At least 10 years of schooling is the common experience of nearly every American growing up in the United States. Spending on the nation's educational system at all levels is nearly $1 trillion, or about 7.5 percent of GDP. As of fall 2005, enrollment had reached more than 72 million students, of which 55 million were in elementary and secondary schools and 17 million were enrolled in postsecondary schools. Despite high and rising expenditures per student, national reports, public officials, and the general public have voiced dissatisfaction with the ability of the educational system to help students gain adequate skills. Going back at least to the

1983 report *A Nation at Risk: The Imperative for Educational Reform* and continuing through today, schools have been subject to withering critiques. The public has consistently rated public schools at about a C level, and its assessment has changed little since the mid-1980s.

Over the past couple of decades, we have witnessed a wide array of proposals designed to overcome the perceived weakness of the school system. Proposals for school vouchers, charter schools, school decentralization, school-based management, national standards, new math and reading curricula, and after-school programs are some of the ideas put forward for improving schooling outcomes. The No Child Left Behind (NCLB) Act, enacted in early 2002, is the most recent effort to insure that students acquire proficiency at reading, math, science, writing, and other skills. One focus of this law is on holding schools accountable for the performance of their students. To determine student progress, NCLB mandates an extensive system of annual tests for third- through eighth-graders. This level of testing is controversial because of various concerns: that state tests do not necessarily offer high standards; that excessive, high-stakes testing imposes constraints on the ability of teachers to broaden course content; and that schools get little credit for students who increase their scores if they are either well below the threshold for passing or well above the threshold. So far, the evidence for improvements in national reading, math, science, and writing skills in the wake of NCLB is mixed. Reading scores barely changed for fourth-, eighth-, and twelfth-graders; in fact, twelfth-graders scored worse in reading in 2005 than in 1992 (Perie, Grigg, and Dion 2005). In contrast, math scores have increased impressively for fourth- and eighth-graders (Perie, Grigg, and Donahue 2005). Other data comparing high school sophomores between 1980 and 2002 also revealed gains in math achievement but not in reading (Cahalan et al. 2006).

Making schools accountable for insuring that most if not all students attain basic reading and math skills is appropriate at early grades. However, in the higher grades, what is necessary for success in careers becomes less clear. More may not always be better, especially if the result is that many students fail, become discouraged, and have little chance to learn skills more relevant to their potential careers. What we know about workplace skills should play a significant role in setting benchmarks, but rarely are work-related skills considered worthy of teaching and testing. Murnane and Levy (1996) define the academic skills required for a middle-class job as the New Basics. They include the abilities to read and do math at the ninth-grade level or higher, to solve semistructured problems by forming a hypothesis and testing it, to work in groups with persons of diverse backgrounds, to communicate effectively, and to use a personal computer for tasks like word processing. For many individuals who reach these basic skill levels, the marginal gain in academic skills may yield no more benefit—and possibly less—than would a marginal improvement in other skills. Only a modest percentage of workers use many of the academic skills taught in late high school and college (Handel 2007). As noted above, Deke and Haimson (2006) report that, beyond a certain level, gains in earnings depend more on noncognitive than on cognitive skills for most students. Certainly, higher math and verbal SAT scores will help students enter more selective colleges. But this benefit only accrues to the small share of students competing for highly selective colleges.

For most jobs, the issue is not only the skill qualifications, but also the use of those skills. Although advanced math is a critical stepping stone for many engineering, scientific, and some social science endeavors, most other college students will probably not take a derivative anytime in their careers. But it is the continuing *use* of skills that leads to mastery. Students who learn—but make little use of—the tools of trigonometry or calculus are unlikely to retain them for long.

Indirectly and outside of formal courses, students often develop many of the problem-solving and common-sense skills emphasized in the SCANS report, as well as the physical, psychological, emotional, and social skills highlighted by Eccles and Gootman (2002) as necessary for healthy development of youth. Several of the assets said to promote youth development are closely linked to SCANS, including conflict resolution skills, the ability to plan and to allocate time, and working with others on a team. Other assets involve a sense of personal autonomy, efficacy, motivation, realism and optimism, and knowledge of vocations. Clubs, sports, internships, part-time jobs, and community service work are good places to develop these attributes. In 2002, about half of high school sophomores participated in athletics, 22 percent in a music activity, and 8 percent in an academic or vocational club. In addition, nearly 60 percent had worked for pay and 26 percent were working at the time of the survey. Sophomores from low-income families had somewhat lower activity levels. Although participation in these activities probably helps youth develop, no one measures the acquisition of added skill sets.

Despite the academic tests mandated by NCLB and a growing emphasis by states on a strictly academic curriculum, a sizable share of students still take vocational courses in high school. Students often take a vocational program alongside a strong academic program. Some students attend a regional vocational school part-time for vocational courses while continuing to take their academic courses at their home high schools (Silverberg et al. 2004). Some career and technical education (CTE) courses are not occupationally oriented but deal with family and consumer education as well as general workforce preparation skills, such as basic computer skills and learning about the job market (Levesque 2003). The occupational fields vary widely and include such diverse fields as business and marketing, health care, computers, food service and hospitality, construction, printing, and transportation. Students in vocational concentrations (three or more courses in a broad occupational field) are increasingly taking a solid set of academic courses as well.[15] But vocational concentrators have declined over time.[16]

Conventional high schools sometimes relate to the job market through work-based learning that counts for course credit under general programs or cooperative education. General work experience involves work for course credit that is not connected to a specific occupational program pursued in school. Cooperative education allows students to earn school credit for work related to an occupational program. Schools help place students in jobs that involve supervision by the teacher and employer, and employers evaluate students for their work-based learning and accomplishments. Work for class credit increased, from about 27 percent of students in 1982 to 32 percent in 1998.

While vocational education (now called career and technical education, or CTE) has declined in importance, alternative approaches, such as Career Academies and Tech Prep, have emerged to try to bridge the gap between career-focused learning and academic learning. Career Academies are high schools organized around an occupational or industry focus, such as finance (22 percent of Career Academies), information technology (14 percent), and hospitality and tourism (12 percent). The more than 1,588 academies involved in the program try to weave related occupational or industrial themes into a college preparatory curriculum. Students take two to four classes a year in the academy taught by a common team of teachers, and at least one course is career- or occupation-focused. Academies attempt to use applied learning in academic courses as well as career-focused courses. They try to form partnerships with employers and local colleges. However, work-based learning in real jobs is not emphasized, and many students do not experience long-term internships or jobs. Tech Prep programs build integrated sequential courses of study involving high school and community college programs. Agreements between institutions allow some courses taken in high school to count toward a two-year associate's degree. As of 2003, about 1,000 consortia involving high schools and community colleges were operating, mostly coordinated by community and technical colleges and involving at least articulation agreements allowing the transfer of high school credits. Tech Prep participation has increased substantially, from about 173,000 students in 1993 to more than 1.2 million in 2001 (Silverberg et al. 2004). But these figures may overstate concentrators since some students report being in Tech Prep although they have taken only one vocational course that has transferability.

Skill development in postsecondary education takes place mostly through two-year and four-year colleges and universities. Even as undergraduates, about 60 percent of students are in programs with a career orientation, such as engineering, accounting or other business fields, teaching, and health care. Most of the more than 1 million degrees earned every year at schools that provide degrees in less than two years are in some occupational specialty. For the 2003–2004 academic year, almost 25 percent of these subbaccalaureate degree earners were in the health care field. Another 13 percent obtained a degree in a business-related field, and 15 percent graduated in a computer-related, engineering-related, or security field. Not all these subbaccalaureate vocational students are young. As of 2000, 56 percent were aged 24 or older and 34 percent were aged 30 or older. Still, younger people recently transitioning from high school made up more than half of those entering associate's degree or certificate programs. Enrollments in vocational associate's degree programs have increased substantially since the 1980s but have leveled off in recent years.

Some students use for-profit proprietary vocational schools, such as the Coastal Truck Driving School in New Orleans, for their career-focused education and training. Although national data on enrollments and numbers of schools are limited, there is considerable evidence that millions of students enroll in proprietary vocational schools (Cellini 2006). The occupational and industry programs operating in proprietary schools are often similar to programs at community colleges.

Another route to obtaining skills is through job training, which is financed by several federal government agencies as well as state governments and private foundations. These training programs offer initial preparation for the workforce as well as retraining of adult workers. Usually, the goal is to help specific groups, including at-risk youth, displaced workers (especially those who have lost their jobs because of imports), workers with some kind of disability, senior citizens, migrants and farm workers, and workers who have been on welfare programs. Among the USDOL programs are dislocated worker, adult, and youth programs under the Workforce Investment Act (WIA), the Job Corps, Trade Adjustment Assistance, and veterans' programs. Other examples of job training programs with federal funding include YouthBuild, a program providing construction work experience and training to at-risk youth; and vocational rehabilitation grants to provide training to recipients of Food Stamps and of Temporary Assistance for Needy Families (TANF). The administration, oversight, and operation of these programs vary. WIA provides money to state and local entities which, in turn, set up One-Stop centers that provide employment placement services and contract for training with various providers, including community nonprofits or larger organizations, such as STRIVE and Goodwill Industries. In contrast, Jobs Corps is managed by the federal government, which awards competitive contracts to companies to operate Job Corps centers. Often, funds provided through federal job training programs pay for courses at community colleges or other established educational institutions.

Although the number of these programs is large, their scale is relatively small. According to estimates developed by Mikelson and Nightingale (2004), federal outlays for training provided by USDOL and other federal departments amounted to no more than about $5 billion in 2003. Counting state job training programs adds only about $500 million to the total. While these figures use a somewhat narrow definition of training and skill-building, the dollar allocation to training is very small—even under a more expansive concept of training—when compared to the hundreds of billions of dollars spent on education-oriented programs.

Often overlooked when surveying education and training institutions in the United States is the U.S. military. The Armed Forces is arguably the largest training organization in the United States (Hansen 1994; Laurence 1994). The military trains tens of thousands of military personnel in such fields as health care, electronics mechanic, auto repair, and trucking. Trainees learn skills that apply to their current employer (the military), but in many cases the occupational competencies learned have civilian applications too. However, some skilled workers exiting the military face certification and licensure problems in transferring their skills (Congressional Commission 1998). Although the military is an innovator in the job training field, the dissemination of military training approaches to the civilian economy remains limited. Of special interest but rarely studied are the training approaches used by the military in Project 100,000, launched in 1966, and in other initiatives to educate and train entrants allowed into the military despite their subpar qualifications (Sticht et al. 1987).

Some training takes place in prisons, but the quality and magnitude is uncertain and varies across states. Although many offenders are in great need of employment assistance, few prisoners receive employment-related training (Solomon et al. 2006). While one-quarter of prisoners released from Maryland and Virginia had taken part in vocational training, only 6 percent of New Jersey prisoners had, and only 1 percent of Georgia prisoners had. Many more participate in work-related activity, but only a modest effort goes into teaching work-related skills such as SCANS skills.

Outside the educational system, the largest amount of training takes place through employers in formal workplace programs and in informal, on-the-job training (OJT). In the late 1990s, over 70 percent of employers provided workers with some amount of formal training (Lerman, McKernan, and Riegg 2004). Although estimates vary, between 35 and 65 percent of workers received some formal training.

About 15 percent of workers participate in training for a full two weeks. Nearly all workers receive some informal training as well, including 95 percent of workers in firms with 50 or more employees. The training varies from a few days of instruction to several years of intensive apprenticeship training. In 1997, 82 percent of employers reported offering to reimburse workers for tuition for approved courses, including 69 percent who said they extended the offer to front-line workers.

Although only a minority of workers use tuition subsidies in a given year, 53 percent of adults enrolled in postsecondary degree programs received employer support from a tuition subsidy or paid leave. In 2001, employers apparently provided 30 hours of training for the average worker, mainly through for-credit courses or other courses. Outlays for employer-sponsored training are estimated to reach at least $60 billion a year. The training is rarely intensive enough to prepare workers for specific occupational careers, but it usually upgrades the skills of existing workers.

ASSESSING THE SKILL-BUILDING SYSTEM

To evaluate the system's effectiveness, one must answer three questions:

1) Does the system increase skills?
2) Do the added skills help workers increase productivity and earnings in the labor market?
3) Is the system cost-effective—does it generate high rates of return?

Even with excellent data and research, the questions are difficult to answer definitively. First, there is the counterfactual question—this system or system component compared to what set of alternatives? Second, benefits for individual workers and firms may not translate into gains for society as a whole. Third, the system may function well for some groups but not for others.

From the standpoint of overall productivity, the results of the U.S. training system look reasonable and, according to Lewis (2004), do not constrain U.S. productivity levels. Notwithstanding the conventional view of the ostensibly poor skills of the U.S. workforce, Lewis reviews comparative studies done by McKinsey Global Institute on many industries and finds that "the U.S. workforce achieved higher labor productivity than anyplace on earth" (p. 244).

Yet from the standpoint of high U.S. wage inequality and a weak job market for less-educated American workers, the U.S. system has much room for improvement. Many workers are in low-paying and low-skilled positions, while businesses have trouble hiring U.S. workers for many well-paying jobs, whether as welders or computer scientists, because there are not enough of them. Other workers learn skills for jobs not in high demand. Still others lack basic academic, noncognitive, and occupational skills to qualify for good jobs.

Earnings Outcomes and Skill Development from Schools and School-Linked Programs

So which parts of the skill-building system are sound, and which parts are in need of significant improvement? Although many in this country are dissatisfied with the academic outcomes of students in the K-12 education system, judging the effectiveness of the $500-billion-plus outlays is difficult. Some observers base their assessment on comparisons of academic competencies and costs in the United States and other countries. Others point to the high share of minority and low-income students who perform poorly on tests of academic performance in reading, math, science, and writing. As noted above, U.S. students perform at about the OECD average; still, about one in four cannot reach basic levels of proficiency in math, reading, writing, and science, as defined by the NAEP. In 2003, about 1.1 million families were sufficiently dissatisfied with the public and private school options available to them that they turned to homeschooling.[17]

Education experts have developed measures of school performance and academic achievement, but the relationship between these indicators and job market outcomes is unclear. On one hand, more education is associated with higher earnings; moreover, there is strong evidence that added schooling is the cause of the earnings gains. The rate of return on completing high school is over 13 percent and the return on completing college averages about 10 percent. These returns suggest a real payoff from schooling, indicating that schools must be doing something right. On the other hand, impacts vary widely across students. As many as one in four students leave school before completing high school. Although the size of the high school dropout problem is uncertain, nearly half of the dropouts attribute their leaving school to boredom and lack of interest in classes. Moreover, employers report great dissatisfaction with the quality of high school graduates. Manufacturing firms report that 60 percent of applicants that have a high school diploma or GED are poorly prepared for the typical entry job in the firm (Deloitte Consulting 2005). At the college level, the risks of wage volatility or of having a low return on one's education are high enough to reduce college completion. Finally, observed rates of return to completing high school and college do not reveal whether alternative approaches might improve earnings and occupational outcomes.

One argument for career and technical education (CTE) is that some students may remain engaged in school and earn more in the job market from a career-focused approach to learning. It is well known that high school CTE in the United States varies in intensity, quality, and interaction with employers. But, in an extensive review of overall effectiveness, Silverberg et al. (2004) find that a higher share of vocational courses raises earnings, at least in the short run and the medium run. Another recent study, Bishop and Mane (2004), estimates that taking four advanced CTE courses instead of two academic courses and one personal interest course led to substantial gains in employment and earnings about eight years after normal high school graduation. The gains were higher than average for vocational students among at-risk and minority students and in groups taking the New Basics academic curriculum. Work-based learning through cooperative education added to the earnings effects. Bishop and Mane (2003) find that employer involvement, such as employer-school partnerships, raises earnings, reduces unemployment, and leads to higher rates of students holding jobs. Even students with low grades do better in the labor market as a result of these partnerships. In fact, employer-school partnerships appear to raise the share of students graduating on time and of those earning a high school diploma instead of a GED.[18]

Other indications of the effectiveness of career-focused education come from a major evaluation of Career Academies (Kemple 2004). The evaluation involves a social experiment in eight cities, in which Career Academy applicants are randomly assigned either to the Career Academy or to the regular school. The impact analysis reveals that the academies generate an 18 percent earnings gain for young men (compared to those who applied to Career Academies but were not allowed into the program and were instead assigned to a regular school) but no change in earnings among young women. Moreover, the earnings gains are concentrated among students with a high or medium risk of dropping out of high school. For this group, Career Academies generate as much growth in earnings as would accrue from two to three years of added education. The improved outcomes may be due to the small and closely linked learning community or to the occupation or industry that is the focus of the education. It is still too early to determine the sustainability of the career academy model, especially as regards its ability to develop and maintain close links with businesses and other employers.[19]

Turning to community colleges, we find that a recent review (Silverberg et al. 2004) reports that, for men, a year in a vocational program raises earnings by almost 8 percent over no education beyond high school. No gains in earnings accrue to men with a year of academic college work or even an academic associate's degree. However, earnings jump by 30 percent for men who have completed a vocational associate's degree. Women who have taken postsecondary academic courses do better in earnings even when not completing a certificate or degree than women with no postsecondary vocational courses: a year of community college education raises their earnings by 16 percent (over a high school degree only) when they take an academic curriculum but has no effect when they take a vocational curriculum. On the other hand, women who complete associate's degrees do better with a vocational than with an academic concentration (a 47-percent earnings gain versus 40 percent for those earning an academic associate's degree).

Estimates of the impacts of career-focused, proprietary schools are rare in the literature. According to one evaluation (Washington State Workforce Training 2004), most proprietary school students report that they learn a lot (66 percent), and 96 percent of employers are very or mostly satisfied with the training these students receive. On the other hand, attendees of private career schools did not achieve statistically significant gains in earnings over a comparison group with similar characteristics who registered with the state employment service. And while *completers* of these career school programs raised their employment by 8 percent and their earnings by $373 a quarter, the gains were much smaller than among participants in community college programs. However, unobserved differences in the student populations might account for the weak performance of proprietary schools. Nearly 80 percent of proprietary school students receive a federal postsecondary grant or loan, which implies that low-income individuals often attend these schools. Despite substantial government spending on proprietary schools, the evaluative evidence concerning their impact is meager.

Another way in which the education system interacts with the world of work is through internships, co-op programs, and apprenticeships. Few students participate in intensive, career-focused programs with substantial amounts of work-based learning (Haimson and Bellotti 2001).[20] One study of the early experience of minority high school students finds high participation in career majors: 30 to 40 percent of students who were in or just completing twelfth grade were taking these majors as of 1998 (Rivera-Batiz 2003). The study estimates that participation in a school-to-work activity increased course work in math and science in high schools, along with hours worked, and that it reduced the likelihood of dropping out of high school.

A recent study finds that job shadowing, mentoring, cooperative education, and internships boost participation in postsecondary education for women and (except for internships) for men as well (Neumark and Rothstein 2005). However, the gains in earnings from these activities are largely limited to men. For men unlikely to attend college, cooperative education, school enterprises, and internship or apprenticeship increase employment and lower the share of youth who are idle after high school. Women unlikely to attend college also achieve earnings gains from the internship or apprenticeship components.

Youth apprenticeships go beyond school internships by providing in-depth, work-based learning combined with related course work. Though youth apprenticeships constitute the most intensive form of career-focused education and training, youth apprenticeships and other (including certified) apprenticeships have been the least-studied major intervention. Despite the widespread, long-term use of apprenticeships in some countries and their resurgence in others (Leitch Commission 2006; Steedman 2005), few studies have examined how entering and completing apprenticeships in the United States affects educational and job market outcomes. One analysis followed high school students who participated in a Wisconsin youth apprenticeship in printing and found that participant earnings levels were substantially above expected earnings for similar youth (Orr 1995).

Effects of Job Training

The most rigorous evaluations cover the least expensive parts of the skill development system—government-sponsored job training for low-income workers. Unlike education and training offered through the school system and employers, government-sponsored job training programs generally serve low-income, low-skilled workers who have limited skills and, often, other barriers to career success. Two large, highly cited studies are the evaluations of the Job Training Partnership Act (JTPA) and the Job Corps. Each used a social experiment in which applicants were randomly assigned either to have access to that particular job training program or to have no access. The administrative approach to the two programs differed markedly. JTPA was highly decentralized (as is its successor, WIA), whereas the federal government contracts directly with Job Corps providers, resulting in a more uniform program. The JTPA evaluation involved 16 independent, diverse sites drawn from hundreds of locally managed programs. JTPA participants typically obtain some classroom training in basic and occupation-specific skills, as well as on-the-job training and job search assistance. The Job Corps provides longer and more intensive educational and occupational-skills training, usually in a residential environment where participants have access to health care and other services.

The impacts of these programs are usually reported separately for youth and adults and for men and women. In the adult JTPA programs, the evidence shows that both adult men and adult women who are given access to JTPA earn more than the control group in the years after assignment to JTPA. Although the modest gains for both groups of adults (around 5 percent of earnings) were large enough to justify the program's modest costs, they were not sufficient to achieve a substantially improved job market outcome. Moreover, it is unclear how much additional skill the programs generated. The JPTA interventions did little or nothing to raise the earnings of youth participants (Carneiro and Heckman 2003, pp. 322–323; Orr et al. 1996).

Given the high cost per participant for those in Job Corps, the program must raise earnings substantially to achieve an adequate rate of return. Initially, the evaluation found sizable earnings increases which, when projected forward, indicated that the program's social benefits exceeded its costs. However, further analysis based on administrative data through 2001 (almost three years beyond the earlier follow-up) documented a rapid erosion of Job Corps earnings gains after the four-year follow-up and a likely overstatement of earlier earnings gains because of differential attrition (Schochet, McConnell, and Burghardt 2003). For the full sample, earnings gains from Job Corps had eroded completely soon after the 48-month follow-up. The sharp reduction in medium-term and long-term earnings gains meant that projected social benefits per participant were more than $10,000 (in 1995 prices) below social costs. Some groups of participants, such as young people entering their early 20s, sustained their earnings gains, but others (Hispanics and those with an arrest record containing serious offenses) did worse than their counterparts in the control group. The disappointing results are in some ways surprising, since Job Corps participants obtained sufficient education and training to increase their attainment of GEDs and vocational certificates.

Space does not permit a review of the evidence concerning many other government job training programs. Some have attained modest gains for participants, especially by increasing employment levels, but none are considered major successes. A meta-analysis of 31 evaluations of government-funded training programs for the disadvantaged found that annual earnings gains were about $1,400 (1999 dollars) for adult women, $300 for adult men, and zero or negative for youth (Greenberg, Michalopoulos, and Robins 2003).

Turning to employer-led training, we find wide variations in depth, purpose, and coverage of workers. Some training is brief and involves introducing workers to operations (such as a computer system or a telephone system), to safety aspects of the job, and to organizational goals. Other training aims at raising the basic skills of workers and their capability to implement new technologies or organizational methods. Some elaborate and intensive training takes place through apprenticeships, which combine three to four years of learning on the job with substantial course work. Nearly always, employer-led training occurs in the context of a work environment; indeed, that is one reason for its greater effectiveness in using contextualized learning (Resnick 1987)—for example, by teaching basic skills using materials that working students use on a daily basis.

Employer-led training is generally viewed as achieving high returns and skill development. Some estimates may overstate the true impacts because those who take the training are drawn from a more capable group of workers than those who do not take training.[21] On the other hand, those who need more training to do a good job could be drawn from a less capable group. Although training affects employers as well as workers, the most straightforward way to measure its effects is to examine impacts on earnings of workers. We look first at apprenticeship training, where the evidence indicates significant gains for participants (Cook 1989). Researchers from the W.E. Upjohn Institute for Employment Research found that the gains associated with apprenticeship training in Washington were substantial two to three years after participants had left the program (Washington State Workforce Training 2004): those completing apprenticeships earned nearly $4,300 more per quarter than the primary comparison group. These earnings gains are nearly three times the comparably estimated gains for those graduating with vocational degrees from community colleges, relative to the comparison group.

Broader studies indicate private-sector training yields modest gains in wage rates but very high rates of return on the typical training performed. One recent study (Frazis and Loewenstein 2005) finds that 60 hours of training increases wage rates by about 5 percent but has rates of return on an annualized basis of at least 40–50 percent. Employers finance 96 percent of formal company training, but they also fund 42 percent of training in the category involving business-school, apprenticeship, vocational or technical institute, and correspondence-course training (Loewenstein and Spletzer 1998). Firms certainly gain some of the benefit from training, but how much is not well understood.

A great deal of skill development takes place informally on the job as workers gain expertise in their occupations and industries (Sullivan 2006). For workers, the wage gains from occupation-specific experience are especially high in craft occupations, whereas for managers high returns occur for industry-specific experience. Professionals gain significantly from both types of experience. These wage gains provide confirming evidence of the importance of skill development through contextualized learning and communities of practice. Such situations offer workers in the same field the chance to share their understanding of how to be effective.

The significance of occupation-based and industry-based training and work experience is becoming increasingly recognized in foundation-supported and publicly sponsored job training for low-income workers. Under "sectoral strategies," programs target an industry (or a subset of an industry), become a strategic partner of the industry by learning about the factors shaping the industry's workforce policies, reach out to low-income job seekers, and work with other labor market groups, such as community colleges, community nonprofits, employer groups, and policymakers. Nonexperimental evidence indicates that the six sectoral programs taking part in the Sectoral Employment Development Learning Project (SEDLP) have yielded impressive results but without a control group (Blair 2002). Earnings jumped by 73 percent in two years for the 95 percent of participants employed for those two years. Although most of the gains came from higher work levels, wage rates increased by 23 percent. Moreover, two years after training, 69 percent of participants were employed in occupations related to their training. The focused nature of the training, the linkages with employers, the development of pathways for entry level workers to advance, and the expertise gained by the training organizations probably all have contributed to the apparent success of the sectoral strategy approach.

Learning from What Works Best

Although education and training yield mixed results when it comes to acquiring skills related to higher earnings, several lessons emerge from a review of the evidence. First, the education system, which spends nearly all of the money allocated to skill development, generates good but variable returns. Students typically learn basic academic skills that are critical for the vast majority of jobs and that yield high returns. At high levels of education, the system becomes more heterogeneous and the returns become more variable. The variations become pronounced throughout high school and postsecondary education. About 24 percent of all entering students and perhaps 40–50 percent of disadvantaged students (Warren and Halpern-Manners 2007) fail to complete high school despite free access to schooling. Thus, the cost of trying to educate these students is high but the returns are low. Other students gain more than the average student does from high school by completing vocationally oriented classes and by participating in school programs related to an industry or an occupation. Rates of return for college differ markedly between those not currently completing college and those who are new college graduates. Thus, expanding access to higher education involves high added spending, but it may not increase earnings for students who learn little of relevance to their careers or who do not complete high school or college.

Second, education and training programs work well in having students learn and retain skills when the instruction uses hands-on or project-based learning, often in a work context. Integrating training with employers or employer organizations is typically beneficial as well. Third, the modest outlays on public job-training programs for the disadvantaged yield varying returns but rarely achieve significant earnings gains. Fourth, employer-sponsored training generates high rates of return, but the dollar amount of increased earnings is often low because employer training is usually short-term. Fifth, among the most successful programs are those that build occupation-specific skills in collaboration with employers, unions, or other organizations and that involve considerable learning at the workplace.

Despite the apparent benefits of emphasizing contextualized learning, close employer linkages, a broad array of skills, and a career focus, outlays for this approach to skill-building are minimal in comparison with spending on traditional K-12 schools and four-year colleges. While U.S. schools, government training programs, and firms spend about $1 trillion a year on education and training, we are starving the programs that use highly effective strategies and meet the needs of most future workers.

DIRECTIONS FOR THE FUTURE

Doing better in building skills for good jobs requires improvements on many fronts. This section proposes a few steps aimed at raising the skills and qualifications of current and future workers. Notwithstanding the importance of investing more in prekindergarten learning to achieve increased skills, I do not cover this area.[22] This section makes two suggestions for upgrading the skills of the workforce, beginning with skill preparation during the high-school and the immediate post–high school periods. These periods form a critical time for skill-building: students learning skills at an early age have low foregone earnings, can afford to accept a lower training wage, can reap a long payoff, and can increase their ability to absorb future education and training. Providing students with a variety of skill-building options may reduce their likelihood of dropping out of high school and cause fewer to resort to job training programs for low-wage workers. Many of these programs have proven to have only modest success.

Reform the Way High Schools Prepare Future Workers

Concerns about the weaknesses of American high schools and calls for major reforms are increasingly widespread (Gates 2005). Although few would quibble with Bill Gates' assertion that "all students can and should graduate from high school ready for college, work, and citizenship," tensions arise when it comes to making the means to that end more concrete. To many, the statement's implicit goal is to prepare all students for college. This is clear from the effort to require that all students take academic courses that meet college requirements. And while the prerequisites for college are well known and broadly similar, there is little discussion or analysis of what is meant by "ready for work." We can assume that work readiness means more than the ability to find a low-wage job. But even subtituting the phrase "ready for a rewarding career" leaves open what should be the appropriate courses and other potential activities, such as workplace learning, undertaken by students. Education and political leaders seem to view "ready for work" as implying that students should complete a college-preparatory academic course, under the assumption that students will learn occupational and other workplace skills on the job or in community colleges (Achieve and National Governors Association 2005). Indeed, the agenda sponsored by the National Governors Association makes no distinction between the requirements for work and those for college. The report does little to document why these courses should be universal requirements for students in order for them to become ready for work. At the same time, the report ignores many skills that have been documented by SCANS and other projects as necessary for career success.

Another useful distinction is between the knowledge and skills all students should master and those that are particular to college preparation. While more learning is desirable, not every content standard in literature, math, science, and social science is necessary for students to be well prepared for work or even a productive career. Consider, for example, the California English content standards for grades 11 and 12 that require students to be able to analyze "the ways poets use imagery, personification, figures of speech, and sounds to evoke readers' emotions" and "the ways authors have used archetypes drawn from myth and tradition in literature, film, political speeches, and religious writings" (California State Board of Education 2007). Although such skills are desirable in themselves, there are tradeoffs in the use of student time. Forcing these content standards on all graduates may limit students from taking courses more helpful to their careers and, at worst, may worsen the dropout problem (Warren and Corl 2007). Nearly all careers involve some mastery of reading comprehension, writing, and math, but some state standards go far beyond actual career requirements. Whatever the standards, many students learn and retain information best through contextualized instruction and by applying the skills to school-based projects or to a work context (Resnick 1987; Packer 2006). Whereas schools emphasize individual instruction unaided by tools, cognitive social scientists point out the importance of learning in groups and of making use of tools; whereas schools stress symbol manipulation, cognitive scientists point to contextualized reasoning; and whereas schools focus on generalized learning, cognitive scientists favor situation-specific competencies.

What, then, are sensible high school reforms that can create a better-qualified workforce? Let's first recognize the diversity of student interests and abilities, of skills required in the workplace, of career aspirations, and of career outlets. One way of making more students "ready for work" is to permit students to focus on attaining occupational qualifications at recognized standards that incorporate academic, occupational, and other workplace skills. High school students would have the chance to combine school-based instruction with well-structured work-based learning in a program that leads to an occupational certification and entry into postprogram training. Students would learn discipline with regard to work and would make practical use of their reading, writing, math, and science skills in the context of achieving a demanding occupational standard. Of the 47 percent of dropouts who leave school because they find classes uninteresting, many could be highly engaged in a program that provides learning at work, pay, and an occupational certification.

This approach of utilizing workplaces as learning locations can be linked to several strands of research and analysis. It builds on evidence of the importance of occupational skills and other noncognitive skills, as described in SCANS. It is consistent with evidence on the effectiveness of sectoral approaches and of employer-based training, including on-the-job training. It offers good options for meeting such youth development goals as personal autonomy and efficacy, motivation, realism and optimism, and knowledge of vocations. It helps link the supply mix of skills to the composition of demands by employers. Evidence from other countries shows that the model helps students develop an occupational identity, a professional ethic, and self-esteem based on accomplishment (Rauner 2007).

A common argument against a career-oriented approach is that the mix of jobs changes so frequently that occupational skills easily become outmoded. In contrast, academic skills are said to apply broadly and make future workers more adaptable. In fact, many of the occupational and SCANS skills are as likely to provide flexibility as academic skills are. Skills erode at least as much from disuse as from the dying out of occupations. Well-developed, career-focused programs that emphasize project-based learning and allow students to use what they learn in the workplace will do as much or more to help students retain skills as traditional academic classes.

One initiative that combines high standards, project-based learning, and an occupational focus is Project Lead the Way (PLTW). It offers engineering and biomedical science curricula to high school students in more than 1,500 schools, often through CTE programs. The PLTW program emphasizes project-based learning and the application of math and science to subjects like electronics, civil engineering, and architecture. PLTW is also noteworthy for incorporating noncognitive skills, such as working in and leading a team; public speaking; listening; and managing time, resources and projects. While the PLTW option is broadly available to schools, those that have adopted the program have largely been CTE programs. A charter school movement, High Tech Schools, is trying to place technology and preengineering throughout the curriculum. Started in San Diego but expanding to other areas, the program incorporates work-based learning through a 100-hour internship, project-based goals, and the building of student portfolios.

Career Academy and Tech Prep programs also offer starting points for expanding occupational skills and noncognitive workplace skills. However, the occupational learning takes place almost entirely in school settings. Both programs would benefit if they included a larger work-based component that involved standards for achieving skills and close cooperation with employers and industry associations. Some students should be able to gain a recognized initial occupational qualification which they can build on as they acquire work experience in the occupation. Already, the two programs allow early entry into community college courses. Certainly, these and other programs should keep better track of their students' achievement of SCANS skills and of occupational qualifications.

These examples offer ways of expanding the learning approaches to enhance the skills of high school students. To diffuse the approaches across a wide variety of schools, state standards should incorporate SCANS skills and states should take steps to encourage instead of discourage the development of career-focused qualifications linked with real careers. One barrier to recognizing these skills is the disparate nature of occupational skill qualifications. As noted above, states typically have a plethora of standards for certification and licensing requirements, often influenced by current members of the occupation (Kleiner 2006). Although the National Skill Standards Board was unable to make these standards more coherent during its existence from 1994 to 2003, it is time for another try. The federal government should support states interested in developing models for judging outcomes based on SCANS and a streamlined set of occupational qualifications. Once sound standards are in place and schools see themselves and their students being judged on the basis of these broader competencies, they may be more receptive to approaches that build on these skills.

Expanding Valuable Skills of Adults

Public and private activities to increase job-related skills are increasingly turning to employer-led or employer-linked training initiatives. Both foundations and the USDOL have sponsored sectoral strategies that focus planning, recruitment, and operations on the skill requirements of employers in specific industry sectors (Blair 2002). The USDOL is sponsoring the industry-focused High Growth Jobs Training

Initiative for projects that involve coalitions of employers and training organizations. Both initiatives select a sector or group of sectors, create coalitions, assess the skill requirements for existing positions, project the skills required to upgrade jobs, recruit and target potential trainees, develop training modules, and obtain a mix of public and private funding. Often, the workers who receive training come from groups targeted under USDOL-sponsored training programs, such as disadvantaged youth, dislocated workers, veterans, and individuals with basic skill deficiencies. Participating firms often include some of their current (incumbent) workers. The focus on industry needs and close linkages with employers are sound principles and have led to some effective programs that train workers to improve their jobs and earnings. So far, the programs are ad hoc arrangements and not a systemic part of the landscape. The training is usually short-term in nature and only occasionally leads to a recognized qualification. While the programs should be encouraged, the long-term goal should be to develop a large-scale, more intense, sustainable skill-building system using these principles.

In fact, we already have such a system—apprenticeship, which provides demand-driven, long-term training to potential workers. This system generates high skills for participants, involves extensive work-based learning, requires little or no foregone earnings on the part of participants, and fills positions that are in demand, and have job ladders and long-term options. It can promote productivity and can better the life chances of workers (Steedman, Gospel, and Ryan 1998). Apprenticeship programs teach both academic subjects in classrooms and applications in the workplace—the latter in the context of the tasks, problem solving, and social interactions of the occupation. The learner can draw on help from experienced adults and from peers trying to succeed in the same career. The entry requirements vary, but some require only a high school diploma. Though such apprenticeship programs are not well known to many public officials and policymakers, the number of apprentices at least matches the number of participants in public job-training programs and exceeds the number receiving intensive, long-term training. Yet the federal budget for the Office of Apprenticeship (OA) is only $20 million, an amount that must cover the national office and all of the individuals in regions around the country who are monitoring such programs and helping to promote apprenticeship. The government provides no direct funds to help finance the training and conducts virtually no research and little monitoring of many aspects of the apprenticeship programs. In recent years, OA has funded industry efforts to establish apprenticeships in nontraditional sectors, including nursing, information technology, geospatial technology, advanced manufacturing, and maritime occupations.

An expansion of apprenticeship training would certainly increase the nation's stock of usable skills and substantially raise the earnings of participants. Although the pool of apprenticeships depends mostly on employers, apprenticeship activity is likely to increase in response to an investment by the USDOL. Tripling the current budget, which would cost only $40 million, could go a long way toward expanding outreach and technical assistance to stimulate more employers to offer apprenticeships, toward funding development and marketing of new apprenticable occupations, toward coordinating skill requirements across programs in the same occupations, and toward conducting research and analysis. If the expanded funding generated a 2–3 percent increase in apprentices, it would more than pay for itself. Ideally, apprenticeship programs should work closely with high schools to provide immediate outlets for graduates. These steps could well encourage more students to complete high school and to gain sufficient academic competencies to qualify for the new opportunities.

Expanding apprenticeships is likely to be a highly cost-effective method for skill-building in high-demand occupations and for raising productivity and earnings at intermediate levels of the job distribution. Apprenticeships vary widely, but their social cost is very low in comparison to college. Foregone earnings (and foregone output) are low or zero, depending on the alternative job available to the apprentice. The classroom instruction costs about as much as 1–2 years in a community college program, or a total of about $20,000. In comparison, the real costs of a four-year degree, some of which are borne by students and some by the government, are in the range of $180,000 (about $25,000 a year for tuition and expenses and $20,000 a year in foregone earnings). Although no definitive analysis has estimated the returns to apprentices (over, say, high school graduates with no other certification), the evidence from the state of Washington indicates earnings gains in the range of $15,000–17,000 a year. If this figure could be confirmed, the cost-effectiveness of adding apprentices would almost certainly exceed the social returns to adding college students, especially since two-thirds of community college participants do not complete a degree within four years and about 45 percent of entrants to four-year programs fail to obtain a degree within six years.

Apprenticeships are expanding in many European countries, where they play a major role in developing skills for a wide variety of careers (Steedman 2005). The Leitch Review of Skills (2006) in the United Kingdom recently recommended expanding the number of apprenticeships to 500,000 for that country. In the United States, achieving the same proportion of apprentices in the population would require a fourfold increase in apprenticeships, to about 2.3 million.

Alter Accounting Practices to Count Some Skill Development as Investment

Managers often proclaim that the skills and commitment of their employees are their companies' most precious assets. At the same time, they commonly admit that they can only manage what they can measure. These statements have consequences for human capital investment by private firms and, in turn, for the skills of the U.S. workforce. As noted above, productive investments in building the skills of a company's workforce count as current costs to firms and ultimately as consumption in national income accounts.[23] When companies invest in capital goods and plants, only a modest portion of the purchase counts as current-year costs in determining profits. The remaining value is counted as an asset on the company's balance sheet. In contrast, all of the spending on skill development counts as a cost in the current year, despite the reality that the company will gain benefits from these expenses over a period of years.

For tax purposes, it is advantageous to count training costs as expenses in the year they are incurred. However, this accounting treatment distorts the profitability of training investments relative to investments in capital, which firms depreciate over time. If investments in training were treated more in line with economic reality for measuring profits and assets (but not for tax purposes), the contributions of training investments might be measured more precisely and the benefits would become more apparent. Firms might then undertake considerably more training and increase the skills of their workforces. Employer training appears to yield high returns to workers as well as to firms. Thus, any measure that increases the incentive for companies to increase spending on training could raise the useful skills of the U.S. workforce substantially. If businesses increased their training outlays by only 1 percent of wages and salaries, the added investments in human capital would amount to more than $60 billion a year, or about double the entire education-related expenditures by all community colleges in the United States. Of course, the impact of accounting changes might be much smaller, but it is plausible to expect added training outlays in the billions of dollars.

One potential objection comes from the problem of how to measure the benefit to firms of two factors: 1) added worker capabilities and 2) the duration of these benefits. Another worry is that companies will overstate their training outlays relative to other labor costs. Such shifts would reduce accounting costs and overstate profits inappropriately, since only part of training outlays but all of salaries count against profits in a given year. Of course, similar judgments are required for allocating the costs of physical capital as well, especially concerning the length of the depreciation period. A major distinction between physical and human capital is that the firm has no property rights to the added human capital, as it has with added physical capital. If workers are not rewarded for the added human capital with wage increases, those workers may leave. Thus, training investments should count as assets to the company only to the extent that the company is able to benefit from the increased human capital. Certainly, the very fact that companies currently finance an extensive amount of training is indicative of their ability to capture some of the gains.

Valuation problems are real, but dealing in approximations is better than ignoring the reality that training does constitute an investment and should not be treated like goods or services that are used up in the current year. After all, the idea of counting the cost to the firm of providing financial options to employees was initially greeted with skepticism, both about the theory and about the feasibility of calculating an appropriate dollar amount. In fact, some measures of the costs of options depend on assumptions about longevity with the firm. Moreover, some firms already amortize some training expenses when workers are learning how to operate new equipment.

It will take some time to develop a consensus that accounting for the firm's human capital assets makes sense and to agree on a practical method for doing so. But the increase in the importance of human capital to the firm (not just to the worker) should stimulate action in the near term. The result will be additional training and ultimately better and more productive jobs.

SUMMARY AND CONCLUSION

Generating skills is a critical task of modern economies. Not counting the value of the time students themselves spend on learning, the United States invests nearly $1 trillion, or about 7 percent of its output, in education and training each year. A primary goal of this investment is to produce a well-qualified workforce that can find good jobs and rewarding careers. The stakes are high, not only for U.S. living standards but also for equality of opportunity and social cohesion.

So how well is the U.S. skill development system performing? With its schools, formal training programs, and on-the-job training activities, the U.S. system has helped develop a workforce skilled enough to achieve healthy productivity growth, especially over the past decade. The nation's universities attract hundreds of thousands of foreign students. At the same time, many workers have been left behind: they earn low wages that are stagnant from year to year, and they apparently are ill-equipped for well-paying jobs. Furthermore, employers are concerned about the lack of qualified workers in many occupations that require long-term education and training.

While the skills of the current and future U.S. workforce are a major topic for the public and for policymakers, we lack comprehensive measures of skills that are relevant to the distribution of jobs and to the achievement of high productivity. Information on school completion and on selected academic testing is widely used, and it properly forms part of the skills picture. However, these measures fall short because 1) they do not account for productivity-enhancing noncognitive skills of the type highlighted in SCANS, 2) they do not capture occupation-specific skills or broader skills learned through work experience, 3) the schooling and test score indicators are plagued by uncertainties, and 4) employers usually do not measure the increased capabilities attained by training their workforce.

Unfortunately, the weakness of existing measures affects public initiatives to improve skills. Policies are developed to raise schooling requirements and test scores, but they largely ignore other key indicators of productive skills. Investment decisions are directed at improving these imperfect indicators, leaving few resources and limited attention for other skills critical to workplace success. In the absence of well-accepted occupational qualifications for a broad range of careers, there are few measures of what share of workers have occupational qualifications and few policies to raise the share that have qualifications valued in the market. The result can be serious mismatches between the distribution of jobs in demand that pay good wages and the distribution of qualifications of the workforce. Some of these mismatches can be overcome with short-term training, but others require long-term training and work experience in the occupation.

How education and training providers conceive of skills affects curriculum content and teaching methods. When skill is viewed as knowledge in math, reading, writing and science, as measured by standardized tests, schools focus on theoretical concepts, emphasize individual learning instead of group learning and teamwork, use abstract tools instead of problem-solving in specific situations, and offer content that is weakly related to qualifications for careers. Nevertheless, classroom education works for many students. On average, more formal schooling yields solid financial returns through increased earnings, which presumably reflect increased productivity. But the gains from schooling vary widely, as do the ability and motivation of students to complete secondary and postsecondary degrees.

Only at the margins does the education system respond effectively to the diversity of learning styles, talents, and interests of students. The emphasis on college for all students leads to the adoption of curricula pushed by universities, which marginalizes career-oriented subjects and devalues experiential, work-based learning. The mismatches between the two types of curricula, approaches to teaching, student interests, and employer requirements contribute to high dropout rates (students often leaving out of boredom), low rates of qualification for many occupations, and poor earnings outcomes for a high share of young people.

As a result, many students leave the mainstream educational system without getting genuine qualifications for a good career. One reason for this is that the U.S. spends little on expanding skills that are well rewarded in the workplace or on initiatives that involve close connections with employers, including but not limited to formal apprenticeship. Employer-led training is common, but only a small share of resources is devoted to collaborative school-based and work-based learning.

Much can be done to strengthen productive skills, but the first step is to recognize the differences in academic and career interests, learning approaches, and qualifications for careers. Reforms at the high school level should reflect this diversity. Many school-based programs offer learning in context and link education effectively with careers, but they are swimming against a strong tide of sentiment for requiring all students to meet college requirements. Students should be able to seek to achieve occupational qualifications by combining school-based instruction with well-structured work-based learning. The education and training system should be rewarded for raising standards not only for all broad-based, useful skills (including SCANS and 21st Century skills) but also for occupational skills. Career-focused programs, such as apprenticeships, provide a good way of achieving these outcomes.

Many adults respond effectively to career opportunities by using the nation's private and public vocational schooling. Though these schools are flexible and often provide excellent career preparations, many lack close linkages with employers, causing trainees to experience frustration upon graduating, having spent time and money in a program only to fail to land a job. One highly successful system to train adults for rewarding careers is apprenticeship. While apprenticeship provides a large component of training for careers in some countries and is growing in others, only a small and declining share of adults in the United States participate. One way to shore up and expand apprenticeship in the United States would be to increase its federal budget allocation, which at present is minimal. Expanding apprenticeship is likely to prove far more effective in raising long-term earnings at modest cost than is increasing the share of students entering college.

Altering accounting procedures to recognize the asset value of human capital is another low-cost intervention that could be used to encourage employer training. The change would recognize in income statements and balance sheets that training investments generate assets that yield future benefits. Although this modification in a company's practice would not be easy to construct, the result would be to make accounts better reflect current operations and company assets. Whether managers were focusing on short-term or long-term profits, they would have more incentive to invest in training. Since employer-sponsored training yields a high return, additional employer-sponsored training is likely to prove productive and improve the skills, qualifications, and earnings of American workers.

Americans have long viewed the attainment of knowledge and skills as a primary mechanism for economic mobility. Unfortunately, in recent years the nation's laudable effort at promoting opportunity by enhancing skills has become too narrowly defined as raising educational attainment and academic test scores. In fact, limiting public initiatives to the goal of expanding and improving schools might actually increase inequality, since those who perform least effectively in academic settings will face continuing disadvantages. To fulfill our nation's goal of opportunity for all, we must do much more to measure and develop skills on the basis of a broader, more realistic perspective.

Notes

1. National commissions and policy researchers forcefully argued these points. Examples include the Commission on the Skills of the American Workforce (1990) and the William T. Grant Foundation Commission on Work, Family, and Citizenship (1988). Also see Lerman and Pouncy (1990) and Hamilton (1987).
2. For an intriguing explanation of the U.S. productivity advantage and the determinants of sector and country differences in productivity, see Lewis (2004).
3. These are differences in log wages based on tabulations in Table 3.17 of Mishel, Bernstein, and Allegretto (2007) and accessible on the Economic Policy Institute Web site at http://www.epi.org/content.cfm/datazone_dznational.
4. See, for example, the report of the Secretary's Commission on Achieving Necessary Skills (SCANS 1992) for one ambitious effort to document and classify an extensive array of skills that goes well beyond traditional verbal and math competencies. A recent approach that highlights similar skills is known as 21st Century Skills (see, for example, Metiri Group 2007).
5. See, for example, the recent controversy over the alternative estimates of the share of a recent student cohort that graduated from high school.
6. For an overview of 21st Century Skills, see Metiri Group (2007).
7. These numbers were tabulated by the author, using figures from the Bureau of Labor Statistics Web site, www.bls.gov.
8. In studying a youth cohort that went through high school in the late 1970s and early 1980s, Yates (2005) finds that about 40 percent of high school dropouts who left school for a year or more without a diploma ultimately completed at least a high school degree.

9. Heckman and Rubinstein (2001) make a similar point when they show that, holding constant for ability as measured by the Armed Forces Vocational Aptitude Battery, having a GED actually is associated with lower earnings than being a high school dropout.

10. For an overview on NVQ and other qualification systems in the United Kingdom, see material provided by the Qualifications and Curriculum Authority (2007).

11. The recent report by the Leitch Commission (2006) illustrates the use of qualification standards in assessing national skills and in developing policy initiatives to enhance skills.

12. Some industries issued standards through this process, but those standards have not come into common use by employers or by providers of education and training.

13. These broader measures and policies are embedded not only in systems that utilize apprenticeships extensively (including Germany, Switzerland, Austria, and Denmark), but also in the United Kingdom and other countries that use transparent approaches to occupational qualification.

14. See, for example, Brat (2006) and Deloitte Consulting (2005).

15. In 1990, only 19 percent of students with a vocational concentration completed the New Basics program of academic courses (four years of English and three years each of math, science, and social science). By 2000, 51 percent of vocational concentrators did so.

16. The share of students who were occupational (or vocational) concentrators dropped from nearly 34 to about 25 percent between 1982 and 1990 and remained at the lower rate through 2000. Seniors who were occupational concentrators and took at least one advanced course in the occupational field declined from 24 to 14.4 percent of all seniors from 1982 to 1998.

17. About two in three parents of homeschooled children report dissatisfaction with academic instruction in the schools, but their most important reasons for abandoning public (and private) schools are concerns about safety, drugs, and peer pressure and the desire to provide religious and moral instruction (National Center for Education Statistics 2007).

18. The Lansing Area Manufacturing Partnership (LAMP) offers a good example of an effective employer-school partnership. Cosponsored by the United Auto Workers, General Motors, and the local school districts, LAMP exposes students to careers in the auto industry and improves their educational and career outcomes (MacAllum et al. 2002).

19. This last comment is based on correspondence with a former president of a school board in an inner-city community. He found that several Career Academies began well, but that their performance eroded over time. He attributes part of the problem to the weak links they had with employers.

20. No more than 3 percent were participating in a school-linked, structured, long-term (one to two years or longer) experience demanding the learning of new skills at the workplace and leading to any type of certification (Hershey 2003).

21. Although the estimates typically control for observed differences in capability, there may be quality differences not readily observed in the data.

22. However, see the set of working papers on pre-K learning sponsored by the

Committee on Economic Development (CED), a business-sponsored public policy organization (CED 2007).
23. Counting education and training as investments would alter dramatically the current understatement of U.S. savings rates, in that properly accounting for human capital would increase measured investment and savings.

References

Acemoglu, Daron, and Jörn-Steffen Pischke. 1999. "Beyond Becker: Training in Imperfect Labor Markets." *Economic Journal* 109(453): F112–F142.

Achieve and National Governors Association. 2005. *An Action Agenda for Improving America's High Schools.* 2005 National Education Summit on High Schools. Washington, DC: National Governors Association.

Allen, Jim, and Rolf van der Velden. 2001. "Educational Mismatches versus Skill Mismatches: Effects on Wages, Job Satisfaction, and On-the-Job Search." *Oxford Economic Papers* 53(3): 434–452.

Autor, David H., Lawrence F. Katz, and Melissa S. Kearney. 2005. "Rising Wage Inequality: The Role of Composition and Prices." NBER Working Paper No. 11628. Cambridge, MA: National Bureau of Economic Research.

Barton, Paul E. 2000. *What Jobs Require: Literacy, Education, and Training, 1940–2006.* Princeton, NJ: Education Testing Service.

Becker, Gary S. 1964. *Human Capital: A Theoretical and Empirical Analysis, with Special Reference to Education.* New York: Columbia University Press.

Bernanke, Ben S. 2007. "The Level and Distribution of Economic Well-Being." Remarks before the Greater Omaha Chamber of Commerce, Omaha, Nebraska, February 6.

Bishop, John H., and Shani Carter. 1991. "How Accurate Are Recent BLS Occupational Projections?" *Monthly Labor Review* 114(10): 37–43.

Bishop, John, and Ferran Mane. 2003. "The Impacts of School-Business Partnerships on the Early Labor-Market Success of Students." In *The School-to-Work Movement: Origins and Destinations,* William J. Stull and Nicholas M. Sanders, eds. Westport, CT: Praeger, pp. 189–202.

———. 2004. "The Impacts of Career-Technical Education on High School Labor Market Success." *Economics of Education Review* 23(4): 381–402.

Blair, Amy J. 2002. "Measuring Up and Weighing In: Industry-Based Workforce Development Training Results in Strong Employment Outcomes." Sector Policy Project Series Report No. 3. Washington, DC: The Aspen Institute.

Blöndal, Sveinbjörn, Simon Field, and Nathalie Girouard. 2002. "Investment in Human Capital Through Upper-Secondary and Tertiary Education." *OECD Economic Studies* 34(1): 52–111.

Boe, Erling E., and Sujie Shin. 2005. "Is the United States Really Losing the

International Horse Race in Academic Achievement?" *Phi Delta Kappan* 86(9): 688–695.

Brat, Ilan. 2006. "Where Have All the Welders Gone, As Manufacturing and Repair Boom? *Wall Street Journal*, August 15, B:1.

Brown, Phillip. 2001. "Skill Formation in the Twenty-First Century." In *High Skills: Globalization, Competitiveness, and Skill Formation*, Philip Brown, Andy Green, and Hugh Lauder, eds. New York: Oxford University Press, pp. 1–55.

Bureau of Labor Statistics (BLS). 2007. *Occupational Outlook Handbook: Physicists and Astronomers.* http://www.bls.gov/oco/ocos052.htm (accessed January 24, 2008).

Cahalan, Margaret W., Steven J. Ingels, Laura J. Burns, Michael Planty, and Bruce Daniel. 2006. *United States High School Sophomores: A Twenty-Two Year Comparison, 1980–2002.* NCES Statistical Analysis Report 2006-327. Washington, DC: U.S. Department of Education, Institute of Education Sciences, National Center for Education Statistics.

California State Board of Education. 2007. *Grades Eleven and Twelve: English-Language Arts Content Standards.* Sacramento, CA: California Department of Education. http://www.cde.ca.gov/be/st/ss/enggrades11-12.asp (accessed October 23, 2007).

Cameron, Stephen V., and James J. Heckman. 1993. "The Nonequivalence of High School Equivalents." *Journal of Labor Economics.* 11(1, Part 1): 1–47.

Carmona, Rob. 2007. "Testimony of Rob Carmona." U.S. Congress. Joint Economic Committee. 110th Cong., 1st sess., pp. 1–12. http://jec.senate.gov/ Documents/Hearings/03.08.07%20African-American%20Male%20Unem ployment/Testimony%20-%20Carmona.pdf (accessed August 2, 2007).

Carneiro, Pedro, and James J. Heckman. 2003. "Human Capital Policy" and "Responses." In *Inequality in America: What Role for Human Capital Policies?* James J. Heckman and Alan B. Krueger, eds. Cambridge, MA: MIT Press, pp. 77–240 and pp. 293–326.

Cellini, Stephanie Riegg. 2006. "Smoothing the Transition to College? The Effect of Tech-Prep Programs on Educational Attainment." *Economics of Education Review* 25(4): 394–411.

Chaplin, Duncan. 2002. "Tassles on the Cheap." *Education Next* 2002(3): 24–29. http://www.hoover.org/publications/ednext/3365101.html (accessed August 2, 2007).

Chen, Stacey. 2003. "Risk Attitude and College Attendance." Department of Economics Discussion Paper 03-03. Albany, NY: University at Albany, State University of New York.

Commission on the Skills of the American Workforce. 1990. *America's Choice:*

High Skills or Low Wages! Washington, DC: National Center on Education and the Economy.

Committee for Economic Development (CED). 2007. *Invest in Kids Working Group and Partnership for America's Economic Success.* Washington, DC: CED. http://www.ced.org/projects/kids.php#working (accessed October 23, 2007).

Congressional Commission on Service Members and Veterans Transition Assistance (Congressional Commission). 1998. *Barriers to Veterans' Employment Presented by Civilian Licensure and Certification.* Washington, DC: U.S. Department of Education, Educational Resources Information Center.

Cook, Robert F. 1989. *Analysis of Apprenticeship Training from the National Longitudinal Study of the Class of 1972.* Rockville, MD: Westat.

Council of Economic Advisers. 2006. "Skills for the U.S. Workforce." In *Economic Report of the President, 2006.* Washington, DC: Executive Office of the President, pp. 49–64.

Deke, John, and Joshua Haimson. 2006. *Valuing Student Competencies: Which Ones Predict Postsecondary Educational Attainment and Earnings, and for Whom?* Princeton, NJ: Mathematica Policy Research. http://www.mathematica-mpr.com/publications/PDFs/valuestudent.pdf (accessed August 2, 2007).

Deloitte Consulting. 2005. *2005 Skills Gap Report—A Survey of the American Manufacturing Workforce.* Washington, DC: Manufacturing Institute.

Eccles, Jacquelynne, and Jennifer Appleton Gootman, eds. 2002. *Community Programs to Promote Youth Development.* Washington, DC: National Academies Press.

Eraut, Michael. 2001. "The Role and Use of Vocational Qualifications." *National Institute Economic Review* 178(1): 88–98.

Frazis, Harley, and Mark A. Loewenstein. 2005. "Reexamining the Returns to Training: Functional Form, Magnitude, and Interpretation." *Journal of Human Resources* 40(2): 453–476.

Freeman, Richard B. 2007. "Is a Great Labor Shortage Coming? Replacement Demand in the Global Economy." In *Reshaping the American Workforce in a Changing Economy,* Harry J. Holzer and Demetra Smith Nightingale, eds. Washington, DC. Urban Institute, pp. 3–24.

French, Michael T., M. Christopher Roebuck, and Pierre Kébreau Alexandre. 2001. "Illicit Drug Use, Employment, and Labor Force Participation." *Southern Economic Journal* 68(2): 349–368.

Gardner, Howard. 1999. *Intelligence Reframed: Multiple Intelligences for the 21st Century.* New York: Basic Books.

Gates, Bill. 2005. Speech to the National Education Summit on High Schools, held in Washington, DC, February 26. http://www.gatesfoundation

.org/MediaCenter/Speeches/Co-ChairSpeeches/BillgSpeeches/ BGSpeechNGA-050226.htm (accessed August 3, 2007).

Greenberg, David H., Charles Michalopoulos, and Philip K. Robins. 2003. "A Meta-Analysis of Government-Sponsored Training Programs." *Industrial and Labor Relations Review* 57(1): 31–53.

Haimson, Joshua, and Jeanne Bellotti. 2001. *Schooling in the Workplace: Increasing the Scale and Quality of Work-Based Learning.* Final Report. Princeton, NJ: Mathematica Policy Research.

Hamilton, Stephen F. 1987. "Apprenticeship as a Transition to Adulthood in West Germany." *American Journal of Education* 95(2): 314–345.

Handel, Michael J. 2007. "A New Survey of Workplace Skills, Technology, and Management Practices (STAMP): Background and Descriptive Statistics." Presented at the National Research Council Workshop on Future Skills, held in Washington, DC, May 23.

Hansen, Janet S., ed. 1994. *Preparing for the Workplace: Charting a Course for Federal Postsecondary Training Policy.* Washington, DC: National Academies Press.

Heckman, James J., and Dimitriy V. Masterov. 2005. "Skill Policies for Scotland." In *New Wealth for Old Nations: Scotland's Economic Prospects,* Diane Coyle, Wendy Alexander, and Brian Ashcroft, eds. Princeton, NJ: Princeton University Press, pp. 119–165.

———. 2007. "The Productivity Argument for Investing in Young Children." NBER Working Paper No. 13016. Cambridge, MA: National Bureau of Economic Research.

Heckman, James J., and Yona Rubinstein. 2001. "The Importance of Noncognitive Skills: Lessons from the GED Testing Program." *The American Economic Review* 91(2): 145–149.

Heckman, James J., Jora Stixrud, and Sergio Urzua. 2006. "The Effect of Cognitive and Non-Cognitive Abilities on Labor Market Outcomes and Social Behavior." *Journal of Labor Economics* 24(3): 411–482.

Hershey, Alan M. 2003. "Has School-to-Work Worked?" In *The School-to-Work Movement: Origins and Destinations,* William J. Stull and Nicholas M. Sanders, eds. Westport, CT: Praeger, pp. 79–100.

Holzer, Harry. 1997. "Is There a Gap Between Employer Skill Needs and the Skills of the Work Force?" In *Transitions in Work and Learning: Implications for Assessment*, Alan Lesgold, Michael J. Feuer, and Allison M. Black, eds. Washington, DC: National Academies Press, pp. 6–33.

Kemple, James J. 2004. *Career Academies: Impacts on Labor Market Outcomes and Educational Attainment.* With Judith Scott-Clayton. New York: MDRC.

Kutner, Mark, Elizabeth Greenberg, Ying Jin, Bridget Boyle, Yung-chen Hsu, and Eric Dunleavy. 2007. *Literacy in Everyday Life: Results from the 2003 National Assessment of Adult Literacy.* NCES 2007-480. Washington, DC: U.S. Department of Education, Institute of Education Sciences, National Center for Education Statistics.

Kleiner, Morris M. 2006. *Licensing Occupations: Ensuring Quality or Restricting Competition?* Kalamazoo, MI: W.E. Upjohn Institute for Employment Research.

Laurence, Janice H. 1994. "The Military: Purveyor of Fine Skills and Comportment for a Few Good Men." EQW Working Paper No. 25. Philadelphia: National Center on the Educational Quality of the Workforce.

Leitch Commission. 2006. *Leitch Review of Skills: Prosperity for All in the Global Economy—World Class Skills.* Final Report. London: Stationery Office. http://www.hm-treasury.gov.uk/media/6/4/leitch_finalreport051206.pdf (accessed August 3, 2007).

Lerman, Robert I., Signe-Mary McKernan, and Stephanie Riegg. 2004. "The Scope of Private Sector Training: Who, What, Where, and How Much?" In *Job Training Policy in the United States,* Christopher J. O'Leary, Robert A. Straits, and Stephen Wandner, eds. Kalamazoo, MI: W.E. Upjohn Institute for Employment Research, pp. 211–244.

Lerman, Robert I., and Hillard Pouncy. 1990. "The Compelling Case for Youth Apprenticeship." *Public Interest* 101(Fall): 62–77.

Levesque, Karen. 2003. *Trends in High School Vocational/Technical Coursetaking: 1982–1998.* NCES Statistical Analysis Report 2003-025. Washington, DC: U.S. Department of Education, Institute of Education Sciences, National Center for Education Statistics.

Lewis, William W. 2004. *The Power of Productivity: Wealth, Poverty, and the Threat to Global Stability.* Chicago: University of Chicago Press.

Loewenstein, Mark A., and James R. Spletzer. 1998. "Dividing the Costs and Returns to General Training." *Journal of Labor Economics* 16(1): 142–171.

MacAllum, Keith, Karla Yoder, Scott Kim, and Robert Bozick. 2002. *Moving Forward: College and Career Transitions of LAMP Graduates.* Findings from the LAMP Longitudinal Study. Washington, DC: Academy for Educational Development, National Institute for Work and Learning.

Metiri Group. 2007. *enGauge 21st Century Skills for 21st Century Learners.* Culver City, CA: Metiri Group. http://www.metiri.com/21/Metiri-NCREL21stSkills.pdf (accessed September 4, 2007).

Mikelson, Kelly S., and Demetra Smith Nightingale. 2004. *Estimating Public and Private Expenditures on Occupational Training in the United States.* Washington, DC: U.S. Department of Labor, Employment and Training Administration. http://wdr.doleta.gov/research/FullText_Documents/training

_expenditures_paper_6_30_06.pdf (accessed August 3, 2007).

Mishel, Lawrence, Jared Bernstein, and Sylvia Allegretto. 2007. *The State of Working America 2006/2007.* 10th edition. An Economic Policy Institute Book. Ithaca, NY: ILR Press.

Murnane, Richard J., and Frank Levy. 1996. *Teaching the New Basic Skills: Principles for Educating Children to Thrive in a Changing Economy.* New York: Free Press.

Murnane, Richard J., John B. Willett, and Frank Levy. 1995. "The Growing Importance of Cognitive Skills in Wage Determination." *Review of Economics and Statistics* 77(2): 251–266.

National Center for Education Statistics. 2007. *Participation in Education: Elementary/Secondary Education.* Washington, DC: National Center for Education Statistics, Institute of Education Sciences, U.S. Department of Education. http://nces.ed.gov/programs/coe/2005/section1/indicator03.asp#info (accessed January 24, 2008).

Nelsen, Bonalyn. 1997. "Should Social Skills Be in the Vocational Curriculum? Evidence from the Automotive Repair Field." In *Transitions in Work and Learning: Implications for Assessment,* Alan Lesgold, Michael J. Feuer, and Allison M. Black, eds. Washington, DC: National Academies Press, pp. 62–88.

Neumark, David, and Donna Rothstein. 2005. "Do School-to-Work Programs Help the 'Forgotten Half'?" NBER Working Paper No. 11636. Cambridge, MA: National Bureau of Economic Research.

New Commission on the Skills of the American Workforce (NCSAW). 2007. *Tough Choices or Tough Times.* Executive Summary. Washington, DC: National Center on Education and the Economy.

Orr, Larry, Howard S. Bloom, Stephen H. Bell, Fred Doolittle, and Winston Lin. 1996. *Does Training for the Disadvantaged Work? Evidence from the National JTPA Study.* Washington, DC: Urban Institute Press.

Orr, Margaret Terry. 1995. *Wisconsin Youth Apprenticeship Program in Printing: Evaluation 1993–1995.* Boston: Jobs for the Future.

Packer, Arnold. 2006. "The SCANS Philosophy." Unpublished manuscript. Institute for the Economy and the Future, Western Carolina University, Cullowhee, NC.

Pereira, Pedro Telhado, and Pedro Silva Martins. 2002. "Is There a Return-Risk Link in Education?" *Economics Letters* 75(1): 31–37.

Perie, Marianne, Wendy S. Grigg, and Gloria S. Dion. 2005. *The Nation's Report Card: Mathematics 2005.* National Assessment of Educational Progress. NCES 2006-453. Washington, DC: U.S. Department of Education, National Center for Education Statistics.

Perie, Marianne, Wendy S. Grigg, and Patricia L. Donahue. 2005. *The Nation's*

Report Card: Reading 2005. National Assessment of Educational Progress. NCES 2006-451. Washington, DC: U.S. Department of Education, National Center for Education Statistics.

Psacharopoulos, George, and Harry Anthony Patrinos. 2004. "Returns to Investment in Education: A Further Update." *Education Economics* 12(2): 111–134.

Qualifications and Curriculum Authority (QCA). 2007. *National Vocational Qualifications (NVQ): Purpose of Framework*. Belfast, Northern Ireland, UK: QCA. http://www.qca.org.uk/qca_7134.aspx (accessed October 25, 2007).

Rauner, Felix. 2007. "Vocational Education and Training—A European Perspective." In *Identities at Work*, Alan Brown, Simone Kirpal, and Felix Rauner, eds. Series: Technical and Vocational Education and Training: Issues, Concerns and Prospects, Vol. 5. Dordrecht, The Netherlands: Springer, pp. 115–144.

Resnick, Lauren B. 1987. "The 1987 Presidential Address: Learning In School and Out." *Educational Researcher* 16(9): 13–20.

Rivera-Batiz, Francisco L. 2003. "The Impact of School-to-Work Programs on Minority Youth." In *The School-to-Work Movement: Origins and Destinations,* William J. Stull and Nicholas M. Sanders, eds. Westport, CT: Praeger, pp. 169–188.

Rosenbaum, James. 2001. *Beyond College for All: Career Paths for the Forgotten Half*. New York: Russell Sage Foundation.

Samuelson, Robert J. 2006. "How We Dummies Succeed." *Washington Post*, September 6, A:15.

Schochet, Peter Z., Sheena McConnell, and John Burghardt. 2003. *National Job Corps Study: Findings Using Administrative Earnings Records Data*. Final Report. Princeton, NJ: Mathematica Policy Research.

Secretary's Commission on Achieving Necessary Skills (SCANS). 1992. *Learning a Living: A Blueprint for High Performance*. A SCANS Report for America 2000. Washington, DC: U.S. Department of Labor.

Silverberg, Marsha, Elizabeth Warner, Michael Fong, and David Goodwin. 2004. *National Assessment of Vocational Education: Final Report to Congress*. Washington, DC: U.S. Department of Education, Policy and Program Studies Service.

Solomon, Amy L., Christy Visher, Nancy G. La Vigne, and Jenny Osborne. 2006. *Understanding the Challenges of Prisoner Reentry: Research Findings from the Urban Institute's Prisoner Reentry Portfolio*. Washington, DC: Urban Institute, Justice Policy Center. http://www.urban.org/publications/411289.html (Accessed August 3, 2007).

Stasz, Cathleen. 2001. "Assessing Skills for Work: Two Perspectives." *Oxford Economic Papers* 53(3): 385–405.

Steedman, Hilary. 2005. "Apprenticeship in Europe: 'Fading' or Flourishing?" CEP Discussion Paper No. 710. London: Centre for Economic Performance, London School of Economics and Political Science.

Steedman, Hilary, Howard Gospel, and Paul Ryan. 1998. *Apprenticeship: A Strategy for Growth.* London: Centre for Economic Performance, London School of Economics and Political Science.

Sticht, Thomas G., William B. Armstrong, Daniel T. Hickey, and John S. Caylor. 1987. *Cast-off Youth: Policy and Training Methods from the Military Experience.* New York: Praeger.

Sullivan, Paul. 2006. *Empirical Evidence on Occupation and Industry Specific Human Capital.* Washington, DC: Bureau of Labor Statistics.

U.S. Census Bureau. 2007. *Table A-2. Percent of People 25 Years and Over Who Have Completed High School or College, by Race, Hispanic Origin and Sex: Selected Years 1940 to 2006.* Washington, DC: U.S. Census Bureau. http://www.census.gov/population/socdemo/education/cps2006/tabA-2 .xls (accessed August 28, 2007).

Warren, John Robert, and Amelia Corl. 2007. "State High School Exit Examinations, Retention in Grade 9, and High School Completion." Presented at the Population Association of America 2007 Annual Meeting, held in New York, March 29–31.

Warren, John Robert, and Andrew Halpern-Manners. 2007. "Measuring High School Graduation Rates at the State Level: What Difference Does Methodology Make?" Presented at the Population Association of America 2007 Annual Meeting, held in New York, March 29–31.

Washington State Workforce Training and Education Coordinating Board. 2004. *Workforce Training Results 2004.* Executive Summary. Olympia, WA: Washington State Workforce Training and Education Coordinating Board.

William T. Grant Foundation Commission on Work, Family, and Citizenship. 1988. *The Forgotten Half: Pathways to Success for America's Youth and Young Families.* Final Report. Washington, DC: William T. Grant Foundation.

Wills, Joan L. 1992. *An Overview of Skill Standards Systems in Education and Industry: Systems in the U.S. and Abroad.* Vol. 1. Washington, DC: Institute for Educational Leadership.

Yates, Julie A. 2005. "The Transition from School to Work: Education and Work Experience." *Monthly Labor Review* 128(2): 21–32.

Zemsky, Robert. 1997. "Skills and the Economy: An Employer Context for Understanding the School-to-Work Transition." In *Transitions in Work and Learning: Implications for Assessment*, Alan Lesgold, Michael J. Feuer, and Allison M. Black, eds. Washington, DC: National Academies Press, pp. 34–61.

3
Revising Employers' Role in Sponsoring and Financing Health Insurance and Medical Care

Katherine Swartz
Harvard School of Public Health

Globalization of markets is the straw that is breaking the camel's back of employer-financed health insurance in the United States. General Motors' (GM) CEO Rick Wagoner is perhaps the most visible chief executive to declare that the cost of health care must be reallocated away from employers and toward workers and the government. In 2006, Wagoner and his counterparts at Ford and DaimlerChrysler proposed that the federal government assume responsibility for the medical costs of the people in the top 1 percent of the health care expenditure distribution. Since people with medical expenses in the top 1 percent of the population account for about 30 percent of all health care spending each year, Wagoner and his colleagues argue for a significant shift in how we finance health insurance in the United States.[1]

GM's concerns about employee health care expenses are widely shared among employers. Between 2000 and 2006, the proportion of the nonelderly population (younger than 65) with employer-sponsored health insurance (ESI) went from 66.8 percent to 62 percent (Fronstin 2006). Employment-based health insurance coverage has contracted and expanded over the past two decades with changes in the economy, but the current decline is larger and faster than in previous periods. Moreover, the percentage of firms offering health benefits fell from 69 percent in 2000 to 61 percent in 2006 (Claxton, Gil et al. 2006). These trends reflect the rapid rise in health insurance premiums: between 2000 and 2005 they increased 73 percent (Gabel et al. 2005). The annual rates at which premiums grew are much higher than the annual increases in the Consumer Price Index and workers' wages, and they exceed productivity growth rates (Bureau of Labor Statistics 2007; Gabel et al. 2005). Perhaps not surprisingly, companies reacted by attempting to hold down increases in their health insurance costs.

Even before 2000, employers were engaged in efforts to hold down health insurance costs—some stopped sponsoring coverage, and others (generally new companies) opted not to begin sponsoring coverage; some shifted to hiring workers on a contractual basis or as temporary workers so they would not be eligible for the companies' health benefits; and others increased the employee share of premiums and/or other out-of-pocket costs (e.g., the annual deductible or co-payments when obtaining care). Although the Census Bureau's February Employee Benefit and Contingent Worker Supplement to the Current Population Survey (CPS) shows little increase in the use of contingent workers between 2000 and 2005, there is increasing anecdotal evidence of people being hired to work as contract or temporary workers or having to become self-employed workers (Swartz 2006).[2] Small service firms that in earlier decades might have been composed of a president and employees now frequently are organized as "virtual companies" in which there is a founder-president and all the other workers are technically self-employed associates or consultants. Such contingent work arrangements enable firms to avoid providing fringe benefits altogether. These moves shifted more health care costs onto employees and no doubt prevented premiums from rising faster than they did. Yet the concerns raised by the chief executives of the "Big Three" automotive makers visibly show that the future financing of ESI is far from certain. With growing competition from companies abroad, American workers can no longer assume that "good jobs" will provide ESI as part of the compensation package.

This chapter explores the question of what will happen to employer-sponsored health insurance in the next few decades with increased global competition. In particular, this chapter focuses on the question of how we might share the costs of health care between employers, employees, and government (that is, taxpayers). In the next section we review why and for whom health insurance has been a component of total compensation. In the third section we briefly describe the enormous growth in health care spending and health insurance costs over the last 50 years. It is the rapid rate of growth in these costs, particularly during the last decade, that has been causing employers to argue that they cannot continue to pay as much as they have for ESI.

We then examine in the fourth section the effects of both rising health insurance costs and global competition on employers and their efforts to reduce their ESI costs. The effects are widespread. In the fifth section we turn to the future and consider how the country might reorganize the financing of health insurance. We begin by examining different schemes that are being used in three European countries—the Netherlands, Germany, and Switzerland—to compare how other countries have chosen to share the costs between employers, workers, and individuals and companies as taxpayers to the government to help subsidize lower-income people. Three principles are then suggested for framing how we might share the costs of health insurance among individuals and employers. In the sixth section we develop back-of-the-envelope estimates of the amount of money spent by private health insurance and other sources for the medical care of the nonelderly in 2005. We use this as a starting point to estimate how that sum could be financed through premiums and different taxes on individuals and companies rather than the current system of employer and employee payments.

In the concluding section, we discuss the benefits of increased equity and efficiency in the economy that would result from restructuring the financing of health insurance, along with the fact that private insurance plans can still exist. Finally, we note that there is an urgency to creating a new financing structure—before the global competition and rising health insurance costs cause companies to cross a threshold where less than half of the nonelderly population have ESI.

HEALTH INSURANCE AS PART OF COMPENSATION FOR WORK: WHO PAYS?

Economic theory suggests that workers will accept fringe benefits in lieu of part of their wages if the value of the fringe benefits is at least equal to the value of the forgone wages. This implies that workers are paying for health insurance by giving up some of what they otherwise would have received as higher wages and salary. The tax code treatment of the share of health insurance premiums paid by employers slightly complicates the simple trade-off between wages and health insurance provided by an employer. Since 1954, premiums paid by employers (or in the case of self-insured firms, the premium equivalents) have been treated as nontaxable income by the U.S. tax code (Burman 1994).[3] This means that a dollar of premium paid by the employer, unlike a dollar of wages, is not subject to the employer and employee payroll taxes for Social Security and Medicare hospital insurance (currently a total tax of 15.3 percent) or the employee's federal and state income tax. Avoiding payroll taxes on health insurance premiums provides a strong incentive for employers to offer ESI rather than additional wages and for workers to want ESI rather than additional wages.[4]

Yet health insurance is a product that cannot be purchased in small incremental amounts, and employers cannot set up different combinations of wages and health benefits among different employees. Current laws require that employers who offer a fringe benefit must offer the same benefit to all employees; they cannot distinguish among classes of employees by offering different versions of a benefit to different sets of workers. Insurers in turn are unwilling to create many tiers of premium classes (the tiers that have come into use are: single person, married couple, parent and child[ren], and family headed by two adults) because as the number of tiers increases, there is less opportunity for spreading risks across all workers in a company. The result is that workers who earn quite different wages or salaries pay the same premium for health insurance.[5] Under these circumstances, it is almost impossible for either companies or workers to trade income at the margin for the price of health benefits for individual workers. Moreover, most employees are aware that what they pay out-of-pocket for their share of the premium for ESI is significantly less than what they would have to pay for insurance in the individual insurance market, particularly if they would be paying with after-tax income. Further, ESI policies generally cover more health care services and require lower out-of-pocket cost-sharing than policies in the individual market. As a result, almost all employees of large companies either take up ESI if it is offered or have ESI through a spouse's employer (Haas and Swartz 2007).

Despite the fact that economic theory suggests that employees pay for health insurance by forgoing wage and salary income, the common public perception is that it is employers that pay. The belief that employers pay for health insurance has roots in the decade after World War II, when unions were agitating for large companies to give them a percentage of payroll for union-run social welfare programs, including health insurance. As Klein (2003) has documented in detail, neither large insurance companies nor large manufacturing companies wanted the unions to run the health plans. The Taft-Hartley Act of 1947 made official what was already the standard of the day—unions could not run social welfare plans independently of employers, and employers could avoid collective bargaining over health insurance by simply announcing that they were paying for health insurance for the employees. The 1950 contract settlements between the United Auto Workers and the Big Three automakers—known as the Treaty of Detroit because the unions agreed to a five-year contract, reducing the threat of labor disruptions—and the subsequent 1955 bargaining agreements further solidified the public impression that it was employers that were paying for health benefits.

The perception that employers pay for ESI also was bolstered by the way in which firms use fringe benefits, including health insurance, to woo or retain workers with desirable skills, especially in a tight labor market. Although the large unions in manufacturing and mining obtained health insurance in the 1950s, the growth in ESI coverage in the 1950s and 1960s occurred especially among white-collar professionals. The large manufacturing companies that chose to provide health benefits to the unions naturally gave the same or better benefits to their white-collar workers. This set a pattern for nonmanufacturing businesses—to attract and keep college-educated and other highly skilled workers, fringe benefits, including health insurance, had to be part of the compensation package. White-collar workers who were not self-employed took it for granted that they would have ESI and treated it as an expected perk that the employers provided.

But this part of the history of health insurance as a fringe benefit should be seen not as evidence per se that employers pay for health insurance. Instead, it contributes to the argument that how the premiums are shared between companies, workers, and others—principally purchasers of a company's product and a company's stockholders—depends on the labor market and the market for the product. For example, workers who have skills that are in short supply are able to obtain greater compensation because of their bargaining position with employers. When the supply of workers exceeds the demand for them (as is often the case with people with general skills), the workers are in a weak position for obtaining compensation on a par with workers who have skills in short supply. Firms with a predominantly low-wage workforce are much less likely to offer ESI because they do not need to increase compensation to be able to recruit or retain workers. When "low-wage" companies do offer ESI, it is usually because they occupy a niche in which they provide highly desired customer services and that allows them to shift at least some of the benefit costs to the customers. Starbucks, for example, faces strong demand for its lattes and frappuccinos, so it can charge relatively high prices for coffee and offer ESI to its low-wage workers. In this case, it is the coffee drinkers who are paying a large share of the costs for Starbucks' employees' health benefits. Thus, it is too simplistic to argue that ESI is paid only by either workers or employers. Depending on the circumstances, workers, companies, consumers, and company stockholders all pay varying shares of the costs.

Several empirical studies have shown that the costs of fringe benefits are largely paid by workers (see, for example, Eberts and Stone [1985]; Gruber and Krueger [1991]; and Woodbury [1983]). Using differences in the timing when 23 states required health insurance policies to cover maternity benefits before the federal government followed suit in 1978 (with the Pregnancy Discrimination Act), Gruber estimated the states' mandates' effects on wages (Gruber 1994). He found that between 59 and 90 percent of the cost of the mandates was shifted back to workers via reduced wages in the states with the mandates, and that the wages of married women were particularly reduced relative to the wages of single women and married men. But, as Blumberg (1999) has pointed out, there has been little research on the wage effects of job-based general health insurance, and there is little evidence as to how workers' wages are adjusted to compensate for the costs of the health benefits. Thus, we do not have a clear picture of the extent or configuration of how the burden of paying for employer-sponsored health insurance is shared between workers, companies, consumers, and companies' stockholders.

Perhaps because it is not clear how much workers pay for ESI, employer claims that they pay for health benefits have been relatively unchallenged in public discussions of who pays. The tax code treatment of the share of health insurance premiums paid by employers reinforces the idea that employers pay for health insurance rather than the workers. The fact that what companies pay for health benefits is referred to as a cost in the same way that other inputs to the company's production process are costs of production also implies that employers pay for health benefits.

Thus, for more than 50 years, employer-sponsored group health insurance has been viewed as something that employers pay for, not employees. Given the history of how ESI started, it is somewhat ironic that we now find employers wanting to not pay for health benefits.

GROWTH IN HEALTH CARE SPENDING AND HEALTH INSURANCE COSTS

To see why employers are trying to limit what they pay for health benefits, it is important to understand how much health care has changed in the last half-century—how much more medicine can do and how much more it costs. In 1960, per capita health care spending in the United States was $944 (in 2005 dollars); by 2005 (the last year for which we have data) it was $6,697—a 600 percent increase (Levit et al. 1994). During those same 45 years, median family income increased from $31,390 to $56,194 (both in 2005 dollars)—a 79 percent increase—and productivity in the nonfarm business sector of the country increased by 160 percent (Council of Economic Advisers 2007, Table B-49, p. 288; U.S. Census Bureau n.d.a., Table F-7). A small portion of the increase in health care spending per capita is attributable to the aging of the population, but the vast majority is due to changes in how we are able to treat diseases and conditions (Newhouse 1992, 1993). At the end of World War II, it would have been next to impossible for large companies (or indeed anyone) to predict that medical care would change so dramatically between the midcentury point and 2000 as to increase health care spending per capita by so much more than incomes or productivity.

In the 1950s, the three biggest causes of death were heart disease, cancer, and stroke. People who had these conditions generally did not live long. But in the intervening five decades we have made enormous progress in combating these diseases. The sharp decline in smoking and tobacco use and the recognition that cholesterol increases the risks of heart disease and stroke have reduced the incidence of all three, even though they remained the leading causes of death in 2006. Yet it is the advances in medicine that have contributed the most to the increased survival rates for people diagnosed with these diseases. New drugs, new surgical techniques, and new diagnostic testing devices have increased life expectancy for people diagnosed with a wide variety of previously untreatable illnesses and conditions that are now considered chronic illnesses, including renal disease, Parkinson's disease, multiple sclerosis, and COPD (chronic obstructive pulmonary disease). Advances in medicine also have enabled millions of people to have higher quality of life when they have conditions ranging from torn ligaments to cataracts to HIV to knees or hips that need replacing. But these advances have come at a price—Americans now have per capita health care expenditures that are the highest in the world and 50 percent larger than the two countries with the next highest per capita spending, Norway and Switzerland (Anderson et al. 2006).

Thus, the shift in employer attitudes regarding sponsoring group health insurance for workers has to be seen in the context of how different medical care is today compared to what it was 50 or 60 years ago. Private industry employers did not anticipate that a fringe benefit that equaled about 1–2 percent of compensation in 1960 would equal 7 percent in 2006; for state and local governments the growth in the costs of health benefits was even higher—in 2006, health benefits equaled 10.7 percent of total compensation for their workers (Bureau of Labor Statistics 2007).

Employers' Efforts to Slow Health Care Spending

From the 1950s through the 1970s, the set of medical services covered by most health insurance policies expanded from simply a per diem payment for a limited number of hospital days to covering a high percentage of the costs for a high number (often unlimited) of hospital days, physician services, and more diagnostic tests. By the early 1980s, prescription drug coverage also began to be added to the package of covered services. The expansion of services covered by health insurance was encouraged by the tax treatment of employer payments for health insurance, especially as incomes were rising from the 1950s through the early 1970s as productivity increased.

But in the second half of the 1970s, productivity growth stalled, and when the country experienced the recession of 1981–1983, employers began to actively look for ways to slow the growth in their health care spending. Managed care plans were viewed by employers as a particularly promising mechanism. The hope was that managed care plans would restrict spending by reducing choice of health care providers and thereby obtaining discounts in fees from providers. In part because of the HMO Act of 1973, which required employers that offered ESI to offer an HMO alternative if one were located nearby, the fraction of employees at large employers (200 or more employees) who were in managed care plans increased from 5 percent in 1984 to 50 percent by 1993; by 1998, that fraction increased further to 86 percent (Marquis and Long 1999). Small firms that offered ESI also shifted their workers to managed care plans during this time: by 1995, only 31 percent of workers in small firms with ESI were enrolled in indemnity plans. The growth in health care spending did, in fact, slow during the early to mid-1990s, although it is now widely believed that the slowdown was not a direct result of managed care per se.

Workers, however, were not happy with managed care plans' restrictions on which medical care providers they could see. By the late 1990s, with a very tight labor market and a booming economy, employers worked with managed care plans to develop alternative plan structures that permitted greater choice of providers. Perhaps in part because of fewer restrictions on providers, but more likely because of the large number of new prescription drugs that came on the market in the late 1990s, as well as advances in arthroscopic surgical techniques and radiological scanning, health care spending resumed its higher growth rates after 2000.

An unintended consequence of the shift to managed care plans was that a very large share of the population became used to "first-dollar" coverage—that is, they paid only a nominal co-payment when they sought medical care and faced no other co-payment or deductible. Before managed care became so widespread, the vast majority of insured Americans had indemnity insurance coverage. Indemnity policies required the insured individual to pay out-of-pocket for the first $100 or more of medical care each year (the deductible) and then usually 20–30 percent of all allowed (insured) medical expenses above the deductible. A generation of the working age population has lost the idea of insurance as protection against catastrophic medical expenses. The result is that if they do not expect to use much medical care in the coming year, they view the current levels of premiums as being excessive. This is especially true among young and healthy individuals who have to pay most or all of the premium themselves because they are employees of small firms or are self-employed. It helps explain why people who used to be employed within companies but now are self-employed and working on contracts are not buying individual insurance.

More Reliance on Cost-Sharing of Medical and Insurance Costs

Since the pullback from relying on managed care to slow the growth in health care spending, employers have shifted their efforts toward imposing more costs of medical care on individuals and creating health plans that also involve more management of diseases and conditions. Almost all employers with more than 500 employees now are self-insured, and they have been especially active in developing plans that contain deductibles of $500 (or more) per person and payment incentives to the insurers if they meet benchmarks for preventive care and disease management. In addition, co-payments for office visits and emergency room visits have doubled since 2001 for most people with preferred provider organization (PPO) types of health plans (Claxton, Gabel et al. 2006). By increasing the use of deductibles (as well as the dollar amount of deductibles) and adopting higher co-payments for physician office visits and diagnostic tests, employers have likely prevented premiums from rising more than they did.[6]

Some employers also increased the fraction of the premium for which employees are responsible, particularly for family policies. While on average the employee shares of premiums for individual and family policies have not changed much since 2000, there is substantial variation in the fraction paid by employees. In 2006, the average employee share of premiums was 16 percent for individual coverage and 27 percent for family coverage. But, depending on the size of the firm someone works for and the fraction of workers who are low-wage within the firm, a worker can pay very different shares of the premium (Claxton, Gabel et al. 2006). Yet for all the efforts by employers to increase the cost-sharing by employees for health care costs, ESI premiums rose an average of 73 percent between 2000 and 2005 and an average of 68 percent between 2001 and 2006 (Claxton, Gabel et al. 2006; Gabel et al. 2005).

It is in this context that companies facing competition from abroad are especially concerned about their ability to continue to pay for health care costs. Although the European Union countries finance their health insurance systems with a combination of worker-individual premiums (or taxes) and employer contributions largely based on payroll taxes, a key point is that EU countries have significantly lower per capita health costs than the United States. Thus, employer payments for health insurance in the EU are lower than they are in the United States. With the exception of Japan, Asian and Latin American countries generally do not require employers to contribute much if anything to the health care costs of their workers. For many U.S. firms, the choice is therefore to move their operations to lower-wage countries—with far lower employer payments to health care costs—or to radically restructure their role with ESI here.

RIPPLE EFFECTS OF RISING HEALTH INSURANCE COSTS

While it is clear that companies facing direct competition from abroad are most sensitive to the increasing health insurance costs, the twin effects of rising health insurance costs and globalization are more nuanced and widespread among employers of all sorts in the United States.

Manufacturing Was the Beginning

Although manufacturing was the first industrial sector to be seen as losing to the lower wage workforces in Asia and Latin America, it slowly became apparent that what enabled goods to be made abroad was the expansion of relatively inexpensive and fast transportation. Containers that could be loaded up at the factory and then quickly loaded onto trucks, ships, or airplanes dramatically reduced shipping time between countries (Levinson 2006). Then, with the advent of the Internet and global computer communications by the early 1990s, suddenly shipping time for services that rely on electronic transmission was the same within the United States as across the world—and it wasn't just manufacturing that could be done more cheaply overseas. Many types of services can now be provided by people in other countries who are paid less than Americans. These services range from call centers taking reservations to software engineers who may be located 6–12 time zones from other workers but can take advantage of the time difference and the Internet to jointly work on new software programs.

Companies that have been most obviously affected by foreign competition are in manufacturing; many of these companies and industries had both aging production equipment and aging workforces (so-called legacy workforces)—automobiles, steel, durable appliances, and textiles/clothing are the prime examples. Those industries have been through several episodes of wrenching downsizing of their companies, and will experience more such downsizing in the coming decade.

Services Sector Industries and Small Firms

The growth in employment in the United States since the mid-1980s has been in construction and the services sector, especially financial services, professional and business services, education and health-related services, and entertainment and leisure services (Bureau of Labor Statistics n.d.; Council of Economic Advisers 2005; Swartz 2006, Figure 2.2, p. 22). Although some of these industries may seem insulated from foreign competition because they cater to individuals and sell their services to American companies, they are not insulated from the pressures to keep labor costs low. Rising health insurance costs are therefore a target in the efforts to keep labor costs competitive. Electronic transmission of information has enabled many service industries to ship or threaten to ship some of their jobs offshore, essentially reducing employee bargaining power in wage negotiations.

At the same time, while manufacturing was dominated by large companies until very recently, the dominant type of firm in construction and the services sector is small (fewer than 50 employees). Growth in employment in these industries explains why, since 1979, a rising share of the private sector workforce has been employed by firms with fewer than 50 workers.[7] In 2005, 43 percent of the private sector workforce was employed by small firms; in 1979 it was 37 percent.

For many years, small firms have been far less likely to offer ESI than large firms: 36 percent of firms with less than 10 employees offer ESI and 66 percent of firms with 10 to 24 employees offer ESI, compared with 95 percent of firms with more than 100 employees (Agency for Healthcare Research and Quality 2003, Table 1.A.2). Small firms face much higher premiums per person than do large firms because they have to buy policies underwritten by insurers; they do not have the financial resources to self-insure their employees' health care costs. Insurers have to account for the risk of adverse selection in the small group market when they price small group policies, and the risk increases as the size of the firm shrinks. Insurers' concern with adverse selection is that small firms that apply for coverage without buying other types of insurance (for example, life insurance) are more likely to be owned by someone who either has a health problem within his or her family or knows something about the health needs of a favorite employee. Until the 1990s, when a substantial fraction of large employers became self-insured, insurers could use their large-group insurance policies to cross-subsidize the higher risks in the small group insurance part of their business. Today, most insurers do not underwrite the health care costs of large employers; instead they are paid to be administrators of self-insured large companies. This change has helped drive up insurance costs for small firms even faster than the increase in premium equivalents among self-insured large firms. Thus, the last two decades' shift in private sector employment to the service sector and smaller firms coincided with a change in the insurance business that increased the costs of small firms' health insurance policies—at the very time that worries about foreign low-wage labor started rising.

Small businesses also typically have short lifetimes; many are small retail shops, restaurants, and service businesses that have an average tenure of two years. When any business starts up, it is short on cash—revenues lag behind start-up costs. Although many small businesses may want to offer health benefits, the more than doubling of premium costs since 2000 contributes to small firms' decisions not to offer insurance. They are reluctant to offer a benefit that they suspect they will not be able to afford within three years.

Finally, many service sector firms may not face direct competition from overseas but they supply services to companies that are facing foreign competition, which keeps up the pressure to reduce costs. Firms in the professional and business services, for example, work with companies that compete with international firms, and these service firms are constantly looking for ways to reduce their labor costs so they will not lose business. Among small professional services firms, it is not uncommon now to find "virtual" firms, where a person who has a reputation for client service obtains a contract for a service that actually requires several people to do the job, and then the person goes to other self-employed people he or she has worked with in the past and gives them contracts to work on the job at hand. A decade or more ago, these people would all have been in-house employees of large companies with ESI. But because the services they provide are not "core competency" functions, they now have to sell their services as independent contractors. Increasing numbers of people in software development, information technology in general, marketing consulting, advertising and writing, and a host of professional business support activities are such contract workers, and they do not have employer-group health insurance.

Service Companies with Large Numbers of Low-Wage Workers

A different type of ripple effect caused by fears of foreign competition exists in service industries with high numbers of low-wage and low-skilled workers—for example, the entertainment industry, protective services, food processing, and long-term care health services. Globalization has meant the movement of low-wage labor from other countries to these industries in the United States, in contrast with the movement of manufacturing to countries with lower-wage workers. Many service sector firms do not need to offer ESI to attract workers since there has been a steady supply of workers with the general skills needed for such firms. In the past, low-skilled workers might have organized to demand higher wages and fringe benefits such as ESI, but with a steady influx of immigrant workers willing to work for low wages, they have been reluctant to organize to demand higher wages and fringe benefits. Such workers know that other recent immigrants will be willing to take their place for the same low wages and lack of health insurance. Similarly, service-sector firms with low-wage workers know that if they were to provide ESI, they would be underbid in competition for contracts by firms with lower labor costs because they do not offer ESI.

Effects of Demographic Changes on Employers' Health Insurance Costs

The decline in ESI coverage, especially among workers in the 25–34-year-old and 35–44-year-old age cohorts, is coming at the same time that the demographics of the U.S. population are marked by the baby boomers in the older half of the workforce. The baby boomer cohort is currently 44–61 years old and consists of about 73.5 million people. The cohorts just behind them are 25–34 and 35–44 years old, and they include almost the same number of people: 70.3 million (U.S. Census Bureau n.d.b.). Roughly 10.5 million of the baby boomers are uninsured, but 18.3 million of the 25–44-year-olds are uninsured. With sharply smaller numbers of younger adults covered by ESI, the employers that do offer health benefits are facing higher premiums (or premium equivalents if they are self-insured) in part because so many younger workers are not part of the risk pool. When the baby boomers were younger, they had low levels of health care spending (as is typical of younger adults) and cross-subsidized the relatively smaller numbers of older workers in their firms. Today, that degree of cross-subsidization within firms no longer exists.

The demographic shift among workers also has reinforced companies' decisions to limit their financial obligations for retiree health benefits. (Abraham and Houseman [2008] have a more detailed discussion in Chapter 5 of how retiree health benefits are likely to change in the next decade.) Since 1988, the fraction of companies with 200 or more employees that are offering retiree health insurance has declined sharply, from 66 percent to 33–35 percent in 2005 and 2006 (Claxton, Gabel et al. 2006). The catalyst for this decline, most of which occurred by 1993, is widely believed to be a change in how the future costs of retiree benefits are to be accounted for in companies' financial statements. The non-governmental Financial Accounting Standards Board (FASB) required that companies show the expected future retiree health benefit costs as liabilities on their financial statements for fiscal years beginning after December 15, 1992. (As of 2007, larger state and local governments also are required to show liabilities for future benefits on statements; smaller government units have an additional two years to meet the new rules. These employers, too, are under financial strain because of inadequately funded future obligations and concerns about funding for current employees.[8]) Since 2000, the percentage of medium and large firms offering retiree health benefits has been vacillating between 33 and 38 percent, with most of those companies that do offer retiree benefits being large or older firms in particular industries. But because newer firms are particularly likely to have large shares of younger workers and have not offered retiree health benefits, their lower labor cost structure is putting pressure on those companies that do provide retiree health benefits. They are cutting back on retiree health benefit provisions for people who were hired within the last 10 years and/or limiting the company's financial obligations for such benefits in the future.[9] Recent surveys of employers and retirees also show that a rising number of companies are shifting the rising costs of retiree health benefits onto the retirees. Thus, over the last decade especially, companies became quite conscious of retiree health benefits costs and the adverse effects of having an aging workforce. The FASB accounting rules changes for retiree health benefits reinforced companies' unease about the rising costs of offering health benefits to active workers as well as retirees.

Large and long-standing companies are particularly likely to have high fractions of their workforces who are baby boomers. Much has been made of the Big Three automakers' legacy workforce (and retiree health benefits costs) and how foreign-owned car manufacturers that produce cars in the United States—with their younger American workers—have much lower health benefits costs per car made in the United States.[10] It is not surprising that many production workers at large companies are now hired on a contingent basis (Dey, Houseman, and Polivka 2007). They are paid on a lower pay-scale and are not permanent employees, so the companies do not pay benefits. For the large self-insured firms, this strategy allows output per worker to be obtained at a lower labor cost. But when these firms report the costs of health benefits per employee, they are focusing just on their aging workforce and do not include the contingent workers who would cost much less if they also had health benefits.

For smaller companies that are not large enough to self-insure, the decline in younger workers covered by true health insurance policies means that small group health insurance premiums are rising faster in part because the pool of people with such policies are aging. This further increases the pressures on small businesses to stop offering health benefits.

Thus, it would be incorrect to conclude that it is the large companies in the United States that have been most affected by the rising costs of health insurance and intensified competition due to globalization. Instead, the effects are widespread, with ripples expanding throughout the economy and with the greatest effects on younger adult cohorts. It is increasingly clear that our system of private health insurance built on employer-sponsored coverage is under pressure from rising health care costs and global competition and is unraveling in many directions.

RECONFIGURING HOW WE PAY FOR HEALTH INSURANCE: WHAT MIGHT EMPLOYERS PAY?

With employers moving to reduce their exposure to the costs of health care, it is increasingly likely that a large fraction of the U.S. workforce soon will not have ESI as we have known it in the second half of the twentieth century. People with highly sought-after skills may still obtain health insurance as a fringe benefit. But a rapidly increasing number of jobs that are currently considered good jobs will not have ESI as part of the compensation or will include only a defined contribution to help pay for health benefits.

This is a sea change in the American employment relationship.[11] The change provides an opportunity for reconfiguring the financing of health insurance so there can be more equity in how much people with the same income pay for health coverage. But the opportunity comes with an urgent need to devise a new financing structure quickly, ahead of the market changes being driven by companies' responses to increased globalization and rising health insurance costs.

As a starting place for restructuring the financing of health insurance, it is useful to see what several European countries have done recently to reconfigure their financing of health insurance. Many people in the United States regard other countries' health insurance systems, especially those in Europe, as being nationalized systems with a single payer and all health care providers as employees. This is not the case, however. A number of countries have private health insurance plans (or, as many Europeans call them, sickness funds) that compete with one another for enrollees. The countries collect funding for the insurance from a variety of sources and generally funnel the revenues to a central government fund that then disperses the funds to the health plans. The central government fund also is used to subsidize lower-income people's payments and in some cases to adjust the payments to reflect the expected higher costs of older or sicker individuals.

How Three Other Countries Finance Health Insurance

The Netherlands, Germany, and Switzerland are the three European Union countries with the highest percent of GDP spent on health care in 2003: Switzerland had 11.5 percent, Germany 11.1 percent, and the Netherlands 9.8 percent (Anderson et al. 2006). While they spend less per person than the United States (which spent 15 percent of GDP on health care in 2003 and 16 percent in 2005), all three countries changed their health insurance systems and financing structures within the past decade. They also all rely on private health insurance plans, providing useful examples of how we might consider alternative structures for financing U.S. health insurance.

The Netherlands implemented its changes on January 1, 2006 (De-Jong and Mosca 2006; Prinsze and van Vliet 2008). Everyone in the country is covered for basic services; people can purchase additional coverage if they want. There are 33 health insurers (some of which are for-profit) that compete for enrollment. They cannot turn away any applicant for basic services although they can deny coverage for supplemental policies. People can choose between plans that do and do not have deductibles; those with deductibles have lower premiums.[12] Everyone pays a nominal premium that depends on which plan they choose (in 2006, the average was 1,050 euros, or about $1,500). In addition to the premium, employers pay a payroll tax of 6.5 percent on their employees' income up to 30,105 euros (about $43,050), or a maximum tax of about 2,000 euros ($2,860) per year.[13] Self-employed people and retirees pay 4.4 percent of their income. Low-income people can apply for a subsidy, which is dependent on a person's income. About 30 percent (5 million people) of the population receive such subsidies. The health insurance costs of children under age 18 are viewed as the responsibility of the country, so parents do not explicitly pay for their children's health plans, although the children enroll in whichever plan the parents choose. The Dutch also reward people who have no medical expenses in a year with up to 255 euros in rebates.[14] The Dutch have long had a tradition of community-rated premiums, which continues under the revised health insurance system. To compensate insurers that might experience high numbers of enrollees with high medical costs, the Dutch are continuing their use of a risk adjustment mechanism that they have been expanding since 1992 and that provides risk-adjustments to the premiums. As a result, insurers receive a risk-adjustment from a central (federal) fund according to the risk characteristics of the people who enrolled in the plan. (The risk characteristics are a mix of simple demographic characteristics and recent medical care use factors.)

Germany requires that all people with annual incomes below about 47,250 euros ($67,570) participate; about 10 percent of the population is exempt from the social system. Employees pay 7.5 percent of their salaries (up to 47,250 euros) and employers pay 6.6 percent of their workers' salaries (up to 47,250 euros) for insurance. For the compulsory insurance, children and nonworking spouses are covered "free of charge"; there are no distinctions between individual and family policies. However, in the private insurance system, family members are charged separately. Private insurance premiums are set to reflect the expected risk of individuals, and the insurance companies can turn people down for coverage. (The insurance companies have full access to a person's medical records.) Germany is very concerned about stabilizing the financing of its health care system and reducing the costs of labor in order to increase German companies' competitiveness.

Switzerland implemented changes to its health insurance system in 1996. It now requires that everyone enroll in a health insurance plan. (Like the United States, there were fierce debates about mandating coverage, but since the law was passed, there has been widespread acceptance of the requirement [Noble 2007].) Insurance plans compete on premiums—like the Dutch system—but not on services provided. Like the Dutch, everyone has basic coverage and can purchase supplemental coverage if they want; they do not have to buy the supplemental and basic policies from the same insurance plan. (There were 93 insurance plans in 2004.) Premiums are community rated by canton for the mandatory basic package of benefits, and there is considerable variation in the premiums by canton. This has created disparities by income since people are restricted to buying their coverage within the cantons where they live. Insurers cannot reject someone who applies for the basic coverage but they can reject applicants for the supplemental policies. Most people have the same insurer for both plans, leading some to speculate that people are afraid to change basic plan insurers for fear that their premium for the supplemental policy might then increase significantly. To reduce the income consequences of per capita premiums, the federal government and the canton government subsidize the premiums for basic coverage through tax-financed, means-tested subsidies. Other than paying taxes to the federal and canton governments, companies do not pay for the financing of health insurance. In 1996, the expectation was that people would pay no more than 6 percent of their tax-adjusted income for health insurance, but it appears that a majority of people are now paying 8–10 percent of income.

Principles for Financing Health Insurance

The recent experiences of these three countries offer suggestions for how we might think about financing the costs of health insurance in the United States. Most importantly, they provide a set of principles that ought to govern how we share the costs among various interested parties. Three principles stand out. First, everyone is required to enroll in a health insurance plan that covers a basic set of services, and everyone pays at least a nominal premium. Second, the countries all subsidize lower-income people via taxes that flow to a central, federal fund. The Dutch further adjust the premium payments that go to the private insurance plans with risk adjustments based on a person's age, gender, and prior medical history. These risk adjustments also come from the taxes collected by the federal government. Third, companies help pay for the health insurance. Of the three countries, only Switzerland does not tax companies specifically for health insurance; however, the companies do pay taxes that are part of the general revenues used to subsidize lower-income people's premiums.

We could apply these same principles to a new financing system for health insurance in the United States. Requiring everyone to enroll in a health insurance plan and setting a nominal premium for every person implies that individuals have an obligation to participate in a social compact such as health insurance. Moreover, requiring everyone to contribute at least a small amount toward the costs of their health care reinforces the social compact of sharing risk for high health costs while simultaneously signaling that everyone is entitled to access to health care. Collecting additional revenues from individuals in proportion to their family income ensures that no person or family pays more than what is deemed an affordable percent of income, and that higher-income people contribute to the subsidization of lower-income people. Such a system also creates equity in that people with the same levels of income pay the same amount toward health insurance. Our current system does not have this equity. Premiums for health insurance depend primarily on the number and age distribution of a person's fellow workers.

Requiring companies also to contribute to the financing of health insurance is part of the social compact. Companies benefit tremendously from having a healthy workforce, and it seems reasonable therefore that they also should contribute to the financing of health care. Since (as we discussed earlier) not all companies actually hire people as their own employees, it is important that companies be the organizational entities that are required to contribute to the financing of health insurance and not just "employers." Companies might share in the financing of health care in a myriad of ways. For example, payments could be based on payroll, the number of employees (both those who are on the company's payroll and those who are there as temporary or contract workers), profits, or the value added by the company. Given our concern with the future of jobs in America, it is important that the financing mechanism for companies' contributions not contain incentives for companies to reduce the number of people working for them.

As we discussed earlier, the common perception is that employers pay most of the costs of health insurance. But as we also discussed, the costs are shared among workers, companies, consumers, and company stockholders, and the actual shares are determined by the markets for the labor used by the company and the product produced by the company. Embedded in the three principles are a notion of a social compact and a desire for equity in how the financing will be shared among individuals and companies. The social compact involves a responsibility to participate in the health insurance system—we all benefit from a system that ensures access to health care and we all have to contribute to that system. Further, subsidies to make sure people in weaker economic circumstances have a basic level of insurance are part of the social compact. Equity requires both that people in the same economic position pay the same amount and that companies contribute equally on whatever metric is chosen for determining company payments.

Note that these principles would permit basic health insurance coverage to be disconnected from where one works—basic insurance would be portable across jobs. This would increase the efficiency of the labor market in terms of sorting people to jobs where their talents might best be used. Although the Health Insurance Portability and Accountability Act of 1996 (HIPAA) was intended to minimize "job lock" caused by workers' concerns about losing health insurance if they changed jobs, people still have such concerns. Reconfiguring health insurance financing so that a person's benefits did not depend on a particular company would eliminate the inefficiencies in labor market sorting and increase overall labor productivity.

FUNDS NEEDED FOR U.S. HEALTH INSURANCE: HOW MIGHT THEY BE REAPPORTIONED?

We can do a back-of-the-envelope estimate of how health insurance financing would need to be distributed across all sources by examining recent health care expenditures by private health insurance and other private funds that financed care for the uninsured. Such expenditures would be covered by health insurance if we structure the financing such that everyone has health insurance. Note that almost all of this spending already is financed by employers and individuals, so in restructuring how we would pay for health insurance, we do not need to raise new monies other than what would be needed to cover the uninsured who need subsidies. Also, since we are interested in how we might restructure the financing for private health insurance, we will exclude health care spending paid for by Medicare and Medicare supplemental insurance, Medicaid, and the military health care system.

In 2005, the last year for which we have national health spending data, the United States spent a total of almost $2 trillion on health care (Catlin et al. 2007). We will use the financing sources in 2005 for our estimates, which are shown in Table 3.1. Of the $2 trillion, a little more than half (55 percent) was purchased with private funds (out-of-pock-

Table 3.1 Estimate of Health Care Spending That Would Have Been Paid by Private Insurance in 2005 for the Nonelderly Who Are Not Covered by Medicare, Medicaid, or the Military Health Care System, Using 2005 Health Care Expenditures (for illustrative purposes only)

Type of spending and assumption	$ (billions)
(1) Total U.S. health care spending	2,000
(2) Paid by private health insurance	700
Less 20% paid by Medicare supplemental	−140
(3) Paid by private health insurance for nonelderly	560
Plus administrative costs: 10–15% of revenues	+ 62 − 100
(4) Total private insurance costs for nonelderly	**622 − 660**
(5) Out-of-pocket spending	250
Retain as out-of-pocket spending	−150 − 200
(6) Would be covered by private insurance	**50 − 100**
(7) Other private funds	140
(8) Would be covered by private insurance	140
(9) Total (2005) spending that would have been covered by private insurance	**815 − 900**

et spending by consumers, private health insurance, and other private funds). Private health insurance accounted for almost $700 billion. This includes spending paid by Medicare supplemental health insurance policies, however. If we assume that 20 percent of the spending financed by private health insurance came from Medicare supplemental policies, then approximately $560 billion was paid by private health insurance for the nonelderly (line 3 of Table 3.1).[15] This does not include administrative costs associated with health insurance—it simply tells us how much private health insurance policies paid out for health care services. Since the costs of billing and insurance-related administrative activities need to be included in our estimate of insurance costs, we could estimate those costs as 10–15 percent of what is collected in premium revenues (Kahn et al. 2005). That is, the $560 billion of health care spending for the nonelderly paid by private insurance would equal 85–90 percent of premium revenues. This suggests that premium revenues for private insurance for the nonelderly were almost $622–$660 billion in 2005 (line 4 of Table 3.1).

Out-of-pocket spending on health care in 2005 was about $250 billion (line 5 of Table 3.1). Out-of-pocket expenditures are generated by people with and without health insurance. Uninsured people often pay for medical care when they use it (and sometimes they pay more than an insured person) (Anderson 2007). Insured people are responsible for out-of-pocket expenditures for co-payments (including for prescription drugs) and deductibles as well as expenditures for over-the-counter medications and medical equipment that are not covered by insurance. In addition, some medical services such as mental health or substance abuse care often are not covered by health insurance policies, so expenditures for such health care are paid out-of-pocket even by people with health benefits. We can assume that health insurance is likely to retain cost-sharing at the time of seeking medical care, and that a number of medical services such as mental health and substance abuse services would be covered with limits. Then perhaps between $50 and $100 billion of what were out-of-pocket expenditures in 2005 would be covered by health insurance if all the uninsured were covered (line 6 of Table 3.1). The $140 billion of health spending in 2005 paid by other private funds largely involves charity care, and we could assume that all of that spending would be covered by insurance under the new financing structure (line 8 of Table 3.1).

Taking all these spending estimates and assumptions together, the total amount of spending that we might have covered by private insurance and that we would have needed to pay for under a new financing structure in 2005 is between $815 and $900 billion (line 9 of Table 1). These expenditures would have been for people who were covered by private health insurance or were not insured; that is, they were for people who were not covered by Medicare, Medicaid, or military health coverage. In 2005, there were 203 million such people (out of a total population of 294 million) who generated these expenditures.[16] On a per capita basis then, the spending financed by insurance would have been approximately $4,000–$4,435.

Note that in thinking about how we might reconfigure the financing for health insurance, the new system of premiums and taxes would replace payments currently made by individuals and companies for health insurance. We would raise a modest amount more from premiums and taxes than we now obtain from premiums paid by workers and employers, but everyone not currently insured would be covered.[17]

Distributing the Financing for Health Insurance

How would we restructure the way we finance the $815–$900 billion (in 2005 dollars) for private health insurance? First, recall that these funds are not "new" or additional funds that have to be raised from individuals and companies. These funds were, in fact, spent on health care for the nonelderly in 2005. What we want to create is a new arrangement for how these same funds would be raised from a combination of premiums paid by individuals and taxes paid by individuals and companies. The new arrangement would substitute for the premiums individuals and companies are paying now for private insurance as well as other private funds that pay for medical care. In the aggregate, the amount could be split between workers, companies, people who are not employed for pay, and company stockholders, as well as other payers of collective taxes raised by the federal government. We can assume that anyone with an income below the poverty level would be enrolled in Medicaid (or be fully subsidized), and anyone eligible for Medicare would be enrolled in Medicare, so we are focused on restructuring how we finance the $815–$900 billion for private insurance. We might reallocate these costs along the following lines for individuals and companies.

Individuals

First, we could set a nominal annual premium of $1,000 per person; this would account for approximately $200 billion. Of course, not everyone would be able to pay such a premium—subsidies would have to be provided to people with family incomes between the poverty level and some threshold.[18] But $1,000 per year is less than $100 per month, and many people who are not eligible for Medicaid should be able to pay a sizeable portion of the $1,000. Moreover, the $1,000 per person per year is about what most people with employer-sponsored health insurance now pay out-of-pocket for their share of the premium, so it would not be a new burden for most people.

The remaining $615–$700 billion (plus whatever funds will be needed for the subsidies to the nominal premiums) would be paid by higher-income people (who include stockholders) and companies. Calculating how the members of these two groups might share the responsibility for the costs requires estimating sophisticated models of the distribution of income, profits and productivity, and taxes paid by individuals and companies. More to the point, the distributional consequences of new taxes for health insurance must be considered in conjunction with the effects of other taxes. It is unlikely that reconfiguring how we might finance health insurance would be considered without a general review of the current tax code.[19]

Nonetheless, we can use estimates of changes in tax rates to obtain rough estimates of how much money might be raised by changes in the tax rates. In thinking about these estimates, we need to recall that what people and companies are paying now for health insurance would be replaced by any new taxes and premiums. Thus, people's out-of-pocket contributions to the total premium for their employer-sponsored coverage would become their tax payments for health insurance. For our purposes here, we will make a simplifying assumption that premium payments (or premium equivalent payments) by companies for health insurance would not be paid as increased income to workers. By assuming this, we can ignore the increased tax payments that workers and companies would have to pay if such payments became taxable income. Moreover, as we discuss below, these payments will shift to payroll taxes (or some other tax) that the employers will pay.

Currently, for individuals, the lowest tax rate for ordinary taxable income is 10 percent and the highest rate is 35 percent (for income above $349,700 in 2007).[20] The Congressional Budget Office (2007) has estimated the change in revenues that would occur if small changes were made in a number of taxes. If all tax rates on ordinary income were increased by 1 percentage point, tax revenues would increase by $30.3 billion in 2010. If just the top ordinary tax rate were increased by 1 percentage point, revenues would go up by only $5.5 billion in 2010. Thus, it is clear that very small changes in the individual tax rates would not yield the magnitude of funds needed. A tax code change that would yield somewhat larger revenue increases is to limit the total of itemized deductions (for example, state and local income and property taxes, home mortgage interest payments, and contributions to charitable institutions) to 15 percent of a household's income. This would cause tax revenues to increase by $54.7 billion in 2010 and $90.3 billion in 2011. In contrast to these changes, if the tax cuts enacted since 2001 are made permanent, tax revenues will decline by $97.8 billion in 2011 and $174.7 billion in 2012. In the face of growing needs for federal dollars, these tax revenue losses could not easily be made up by small changes in the tax rates.

Clearly, for taxes on individuals to fund a substantial share of the $615–$700 billion for health insurance, the personal income tax cuts of 2001 will have to be rolled back and additional taxes imposed. But we are not expecting that individuals will pay all of the $615–$700 billion—the principles noted earlier include the principle that companies should pay substantial amounts of the health insurance costs, too. Moreover, since companies now are paying the majority of health insurance costs and we are simply working to restructure how the total costs are allocated, we would expect those same dollars to be coming into the financing system. The dollars will likely be distributed differently across all companies, however, because many companies do not now offer ESI as we discussed earlier. The question is, how should those dollars be apportioned?

Companies

Corporate income does not appear to be a good basis for taxing companies to finance health insurance—only about 8 percent of businesses currently pay corporate income taxes. In July 2006, corporate tax receipts for the nine months between September 2005 and June 2006 were $250 billion (Andrews 2006).[21] The corporate income tax has been a declining source of federal revenues since 1950. In 1952, corporate income tax receipts accounted for almost a third of federal tax receipts, but since the 1980s they have accounted for less than 10 percent (Friedman 2003).

Payroll taxes have replaced corporate income taxes as a substantial source of federal tax revenues. In 1952, they accounted for 10 percent of all federal tax receipts, but in 2003, the fraction was 40 percent (Friedman 2003). The second largest payroll tax paid by companies is that for the Medicare Part A Trust Fund, also known as the Medicare Hospital Insurance (HI) Trust Fund. The Medicare payroll tax is 1.45 percent and it applies to all employee earnings paid by an employer (there is no maximum on what is taxable income); individual workers also pay a tax of 1.45 percent on their wages and salary, so the combined Medicare HI tax rate is 2.9 percent of earnings.[22] In 2006, the Medicare HI payroll tax revenues were $211.5 billion—half paid by companies and half paid by workers (Social Security and Medicare Boards of Trustees 2007).

This provides an estimate of the amount of financing we could raise from employers if we were to use a payroll tax: a tax paid by employers of almost 3 percent of payroll in 2006 would have raised about $215 billion and a tax of 6 percent would have raised about $430 billion. To put this in perspective, a payroll tax of 6 percent would have raised at least 60 percent of the $615–$700 billion needed in 2005.

There are benefits and costs to using a payroll tax for obtaining company financing for health insurance. The costs are that a payroll tax raises the costs of labor, providing an incentive for companies to look for cheaper ways of producing their products, most likely involving less labor. However, the payroll tax needs to be seen in the context of how much many companies are now paying for ESI; a 6 percent payroll tax is on average what companies that provide employer-sponsored health insurance are paying now. Equally important, it is likely to be less expensive than what companies expect health insurance premiums will cost them later this decade. The other cost associated with using a payroll tax to collect health insurance financing from companies is that an increasing number of workers are not technically employees of a company—they are hired through temporary agencies or contract houses or are self-employed and have a contract to do a specific task. They are not part of the payroll for which companies pay taxes. If a payroll tax is used to obtain financing from companies, then it needs to apply to companies that hire people as contingent workers as well.

The primary benefit from using a payroll tax is that it redistributes the costs of employer financing of health insurance so that all employers are paying for health insurance. Large companies with legacy workforces will no longer be paying significantly more for ESI than their competitors with younger workforces. Further, the payroll tax creates a progressive tax across companies relative to company payrolls—companies with low-wage workers would pay less than companies with high-income workers, so companies with high margins would subsidize companies with low margins.

Summary of Distributing the Financing across Individuals and Companies

In sum, if we had been financing private health insurance for the nonelderly in 2005, we would have needed between $815 and $900 billion. An annual per person premium of $1,000 paid by everyone who was not enrolled in Medicaid or Medicare would have raised about $200 billion. The remaining $615–$700 billion would then have been shared by individual taxpayers and companies. If companies exchange what they are paying now for ESI for a payroll tax of 6 percent, revenues of about $430 billion would have been collected. The remaining $185–$270 billion would have to come either from increased taxes paid by individuals or a combination of individuals and a slightly higher payroll tax.

A SEA CHANGE AND THE NEED TO ACT QUICKLY

We are in the midst of a sea change in how private health insurance is financed for most Americans. The last half of the twentieth century was a period when employer-sponsored health insurance grew rapidly and became the source of private health insurance for as many as 70 percent of the nonelderly population. But in the last decade, the proportion of nonelderly with ESI has declined to about 60 percent, and employers are pulling back from paying for health insurance to the extent that they did even just five years ago. The twin forces behind this sea change are the global economy and the continuing high rates of increase in health care spending and insurance premiums. Looking to the near future, it is clear that we need to restructure how we pay for health insurance before the economic changes already under way cause a large fraction of the nonelderly to become uninsured.

Greater Equity and Efficiency

The need to restructure how we finance health insurance provides an opportunity for creating a financing system that is more equitable and more efficient than the current system of ESI and individually purchased coverage. Restructuring the system so everyone would have coverage and everyone would pay in proportion to their income is far more equitable than what we have now. Currently, whether a person has insurance at all and the premium that a person pays depend on where a person works, who else works for the company, and a person's own demographic characteristics and health history. Restructuring the financing so a company would pay only a tax rather than being involved in negotiating premiums and terms of a policy also is more efficient for employers. Companies would not have to pay for administrative costs associated with sponsoring health insurance. They also would not have to worry about possible adverse consequences to their premiums of hiring someone who has a medical condition (for example, diabetes or asthma). As a result, the labor market would operate more efficiently.

Restructuring the financing of health insurance also would create a safety net for everyone—something that is going to be increasingly important as the country goes through other significant changes affecting our economy and society in the next two decades. The global economy is forcing changes on how we manufacture and produce an increasing array of products, putting pressure on pensions and retiree health coverage as well as health insurance. The demographic changes and longer life expectancies are pushing people to rethink how long they need to work to have enough income in retirement. It is increasingly obvious that many Americans do not have sufficient savings to carry them through their old age. This is coming at a time when Medicare is in need of a financing restructuring, too. Finally, the age cohorts that are currently most affected by the lack of health insurance are also cohorts that are being squeezed by debts for higher education and the consequences of deficit spending over the past six years. Having a basic level of health insurance for everyone would provide a level of security that is going to be greatly needed if we are to avoid a general malaise.

Basic Insurance and the Need to Restrain Growth in Spending

The United States is not alone in struggling to slow the rate of increase in health care spending. All of the OECD countries and Japan are experiencing similar rates of increases in health care spending. This is good for American companies that are competing with companies in these countries since their health care costs are increasing at about the same rate as those in the United States. But at the same time, the similar rates of growth in spending mean that if we are to be successful competitors in a global economy, we need to restrain the rate of growth in the United States to keep our labor costs competitive. Particularly given the difficult transitions we are likely facing in the next decade or two, we simply cannot afford to have per capita spending on health care continue to rise at rates that far exceed productivity growth.

One way to restrain growth in medical spending is to finance only a basic package of health care services. This is the conclusion that the European Union countries have reached, although some allow people to purchase supplemental coverage if they wish. A basic package of health care services could include most if not all of the health care services that are now covered by most large companies. But in the future, new services would have to be shown to be cost-effective to be included in the basic package. This would provide an incentive for innovators to look for less costly ways of producing the same service.

Private Insurance Can Be Retained

Restructuring how we pay for health insurance does not have to be synonymous with a single-payer, national health insurance system. We can still have a system where people choose among private health insurance companies just as they do in the Netherlands and Switzerland. Financing funds are collected in these countries through a central agency, and then premium equivalent funds are sent to the insurers selected by individuals. However, in order to compensate insurers for enrolling individuals who may be likely to incur higher than average medical expenses, we also would want to adjust the premium payments for factors known to increase health care spending. As noted earlier, the Netherlands has a risk adjustment system that does this, and the risk adjustment models are very similar to those developed by Medicare and Medicaid for adjusting payments for enrollees who are in managed care plans. We also would need to understand more about why there are large regional differences in how much medical care people receive—specifically, how many different types of services are provided. To the extent that those differences are meaningful and justified, we also would need to adjust premiums on the basis of where one lives.

Finance Restructuring Must Be Done Quickly

The United States is experiencing a sea change in businesses' attitudes toward their role in financing and organizing health insurance for workers. Particularly because of the pressures from the global economy, companies feel they cannot compete if they cannot control spending for employee health benefits. Given the rapid rate of increase in premiums for ESI over the past six years especially, employers have reached a level of frustration where they no longer believe they can continue to pay for future costs of health coverage. Many also have decided that they do not need to offer ESI to attract or retain workers. This slippage in business support for ESI is likely to accelerate over the next decade, creating a crisis for millions of Americans as well as medical care providers.

This looming crisis could be mitigated or even avoided altogether if the country's public and private policy leaders move now to establish a new structure for financing health insurance for the nonelderly who are not enrolled in Medicaid or Medicare. There is an urgent need to start restructuring the financing—it will take time to agree on the different shares that workers, companies, people who are not employed for pay, and company stockholders will pay. And in the meantime, the market forces that are driving companies to decide they cannot afford to pay more for health insurance will continue to pressure businesses. As the percentage of companies that offer ESI gets closer to 50 percent, which it will within this next decade, we will arrive at a tipping point where large numbers of firms may choose to stop sponsoring health benefits. We need to structure a new way of paying for health insurance—with the help of business leaders, labor leaders, academics, and public policymakers—before we reach that tipping point.

America's challenge in the new global economy is to provide a safety net of social services—particularly health insurance—so that companies and workers will be able to use their imagination and skills to create new products that the world economy will purchase. Sharing the financing of these social services more equitably among companies and individuals will help ensure growth in the American economy—on which a future of good jobs and a strong nation depends.

Notes

I want to thank particularly Susan Houseman, Timothy Bartik, and Frank Levy for providing helpful comments on earlier drafts of the chapter; they are not responsible for any errors that remain.

1. Given the role that the country's largest companies—including General Motors—played in the decade right after World War II in establishing employer-sponsored group health insurance rather than supporting national health insurance, there is some irony in the leaders of the automotive industry now suggesting that the government should have a large responsibility for health care expenditures.

2. People who have studied the contingent workforce, including Susan Houseman, have raised concerns about the way respondents to the CPS may be answering questions about where they work and therefore whether the survey is picking up the full extent to which people are working as contract workers or as self-employed people.

3. Congress enacted section 106 of the Internal Revenue Code of 1954, which eliminated confusion arising from a 1953 IRS ruling that seemed to contradict its 1943 ruling that employer contributions to health insurance policies were tax-exempt.

4. In addition, an employer can pay more for ESI and thereby provide something more for all employees—but if the employer increases the wages of everyone in a certain position or rank, the employer then has to increase the wages of all the workers in more senior positions. This can be a far more costly proposition for companies.

5. Companies may choose to create different premium shares paid by employees based on income tiers—so higher-income employees pay more than lower-income workers—but the premium charged per employee by the insurer is the same within policy tier choice. Self-insured employers could set employee shares of premiums individually—perhaps on the basis of income, for example—but they have been reluctant to do this. One reason may be that companies have long stressed that ESI is a group benefit, and even self-insured firms are loathe to break the grouping bonds by setting employee shares of premiums that are highly tailored to individual workers' characteristics.

6. Note, however, that by shifting more of the lower level of medical expenses onto workers, people are bearing more of their medical expenses when they are sick or if they have chronic conditions.

7. Author's tabulations from the U.S. Department of Labor, Bureau of Labor Statistics, Office of Employment and Unemployment Statistics, Covered Employment and Wages (ES-202) data. See also Swartz (2006, Chapter 2, pp. 22–23).

8. State and local governments' accounting standards are set by the Governmental Accounting Standards Board (GASB), which in 2005 adopted rules similar to those of FASB. See also Freudenheim and Walsh (2005) and Carroll (2007).

9. Moreover, as employment growth has been occurring in firms that are new companies, a rising fraction of current workers do not have retiree health benefits as part of their benefits. This puts yet more pressure on those companies with aging workforces to reduce their labor costs by restricting their own obligations for retiree benefits for current workers.

10. The competition between the Big Three automakers and Toyota America offers a stark illustration of these differences. The Big Three contend that when wage, health care, retiree health care, and pensions are included, they pay UAW work-

ers $70–$75 per hour, whereas Toyota and the other Japanese automakers pay $40–$45 per hour for cars made at plants in the United States.

11. Momentum for this shift appears to be growing as rapidly as the shift from defined benefit pensions to 401(K) plans a decade ago and the move by employers to change their ESI benefits from indemnity health insurance plans to managed care plans at the end of the 1980s and early 1990s.

12. The highest deductible in 2006 was 500 euros (or about $715) per person. See the Royal Netherlands Government (2006). All dollar amounts in this chapter are based on the exchange rate as of October 18, 2007, which was $1.43.

13. Technically, the individuals pay the 6.5 percent tax on their income up to 30,150 euros, but employers are required to reimburse this amount to their employees.

14. In 2005, almost 4 million people received this rebate.

15. Author's assumption based on approximations from Keehan et al. (2004).

16. Author's calculations from census data contained in DeNavas-Walt, Proctor, and Lee (2006).

17. Of course, perhaps as many as 40 percent of the people currently uninsured would be covered by Medicaid or be fully subsidized for their health insurance premium because they are poor or near-poor.

18. We could assume that 22.8 million uninsured with incomes between one and three times the poverty level in 2006 would be subsidized on a sliding scale related to their incomes. If the average subsidy were $700 per person, such a subsidy would cost about $16 billion.

19. Three issues are particularly likely to cause the tax code to be revised. One is the fact that the country now has a large deficit. The second is that the alternative minimum tax (AMT) is not doing what it was intended to do and is instead affecting the taxes of increasing numbers of Americans. Third, there is increasing evidence that the very highest income earners in the country have benefited tremendously over the past two decades from the growth in productivity, but that the great bulk of people with incomes below the top 5 percent have not gained at all (see Levy and Temin 2007). Moreover, the changes in the tax code since 2001 have been highly regressive; if made permanent, they will become even more regressive. (If the tax cuts become permanent in 2011—as opposed to sunsetting at the end of 2010—the burden of federal taxes will shift onto middle-income taxpayers.) As the Urban Institute-Brooking Institution's Tax Policy Center (2006) estimates, taxpayers in the top 1 percent of the income distribution would see their share of the federal tax burden fall by 0.5 percentage points, while the share paid by households in the middle of the income distribution would increase by 0.1 percentage points. All of this suggests that before 2010, the country will at a minimum repeal the tax cuts for the highest income households, and then begin a serious overhaul of the tax code.

20. Income from long-term capital gains is taxed at lower rates, as is income from dividends (until 2010). The alternative minimum tax (AMT) will become the tax system for almost all people with incomes between $200,000 and $500,000 by 2010 if it is not changed; and the Urban Institute–Brookings Institution's Tax Policy Center (2006) estimates that almost half of all households with incomes

between $75,000 and $100,000 will pay the AMT by 2010 unless Congress acts to change current law. The AMT is extremely complicated, so comparing ordinary income tax rates with the AMT is not meaningful.

21. The $250 billion for the nine months was 26 percent larger than the amount raised a year earlier for the same nine months.

22. The primary payroll tax collected from companies is the tax for Social Security for Old-Age and Survivors Insurance (OASI)—what most people call Social Security. Employers pay a tax rate of 5.3 percent on earnings up to an annual maximum per person ($97,500 in 2007) for the OASI Trust Fund. Workers also pay 5.3 percent of their earnings up to the annual maximum so the combined payroll tax paid by employers and workers for OASI is 10.6 percent. There is a second Social Security payroll tax for the Disability Insurance (DI) Trust Fund; the DI payroll tax is 0.9 percent, which employers and workers each pay for a combined rate of 1.8 percent on earnings up to the annual maximum.

References

Abraham, Katharine, and Susan N. Houseman. 2008. "Removing Barriers to Work for Older Americans." In *A Future of Good Jobs? America's Challenge in the Global Economy*, Timothy Bartik and Susan N. Houseman, eds., pp. 161–202.

Agency for Healthcare Research and Quality, Center for Financing, Access and Cost Trends. 2003. "2003 Medical Expenditure Panel Survey—Insurance Component, Table 1.A.2." Washington, DC: U.S. Department of Health and Human Services. http://www.meps.ahrq.gov/mepsweb/data_stats/quick_tables_results.jsp?component=2&subcomponent=1&year=1&tableSeries=1&searchText=&SearchMethod=1&Action=Search (accessed October 17, 2007).

Anderson, G. 2007. "From 'Soak the Rich' to 'Soak the Poor': Recent Trends in Hospital Pricing." *Health Affairs* 26(3): 780–789.

Anderson, G.F., B.K. Frogner, R.A. Johns, and U.E. Reinhardt. 2006. "Health Care Spending and Use of Information Technology in OECD Countries." *Health Affairs* 25(3): 819–831.

Andrews, E.L. 2006. "Surprising Jump in Tax Revenues Is Curbing Deficit." *The New York Times*, July 9, 1:1.

Blumberg, L. 1999. "Who Pays for Employer-Sponsored Health Insurance?" *Health Affairs* 18(6): 58–61.

Bureau of Labor Statistics. n.d. "Employment and Earnings." Washington, DC: U.S. Department of Labor. http://www.bls.gov/ces/ (accessed October 18, 2007).

———. 2007. "Employer Costs for Employee Compensation—December

2006." *News*, March 29, USDL: 07-0453. Washington, DC: U.S. Department of Labor.

Burman, L. 1994. *The Tax Treatment of Employment-Based Health Insurance.* Washington, DC: Congressional Budget Office.

Carroll, M. 2007. "Health Care Costs Soar, Squeeze Localities." *Boston Globe*, May 13, A:1.

Catlin, A., C. Cowan, S. Heffler, B. Washington, and the National Health Expenditure Accounts Team. 2007. "National Health Spending in 2005: The Slowdown Continues." *Health Affairs* 26(1): 142–153.

Claxton, G., J. Gabel, I. Gil, J. Pickreign, H. Whitmore, B. Finder, B. DiJulio, and S. Hawkins. 2006. "Health Benefits in 2006: Premium Increases Moderate, Enrollment in Consumer-Directed Health Plans Remains Modest." *Health Affairs* 25(6): w476–w485.

Claxton, G., I. Gil, B. Finder, B. DiJulio, S. Hawkins, J. Pickreign, H. Whitmore, and J. Gabel. 2006. *Employer Health Benefits: 2006 Annual Survey.* Menlo Park, CA: Henry J. Kaiser Family Foundation, and Chicago: Health Research and Educational Trust.

Congressional Budget Office. 2007. *Budget Options.* http:www.cbo.gov/ftpdocs/78xx/doc7821/02-03-BudgetOptions.pdf (accessed July 30, 2007).

Council of Economic Advisers. 2005. *Economic Report of the President, 2005.* Washington, DC: U.S. Government Printing Office.

———. 2007. *Economic Report of the President, 2007*, Table B-49: Productivity and Related Data, Business Sector, 1959–2006, p. 288. Washington, DC: U.S. Government Printing Office.

De Jong, P.R., and I. Mosca. 2006. "Changes and Challenges of the New Health Care Reform in the Netherlands: What Should the Dutch Be Aware Of?" TILEC Discussion Paper DP 2006-026. Tilburg, The Netherlands: Tilburg Law and Economics Center, Tilburg University.

DeNavas-Walt, C., B.D. Proctor, and C.H. Lee. 2006. "Income, Poverty, and Health Insurance Coverage in the United States: 2005." U.S. Census Bureau, Current Population Reports, P60-231. Washington, DC: U.S. Government Printing Office. http://www.census.gov/prod/2006pubs/p60-231.pdf (accessed September 19, 2007).

Dey, M., S. Houseman, and A. Polivka. 2007. "Manufacturers' Outsourcing to Employment Services." W.E. Upjohn Institute Staff Working Paper no. 07-132. Kalamazoo, MI: W.E. Upjohn Institute for Employment Research.

Eberts, R. and J. Stone. 1985. "Wages, Fringe Benefits, and Working Conditions: An Analysis of Compensating Differentials." *Southern Economic Journal* 52(1): 274–280.

Friedman, J. 2003. "The Decline of Corporate Income Tax Revenues." Washington, DC: Center on Budget and Policy Priorities.

Freudenheim, M., and M.W. Walsh. 2005. "The Next Retirement Time Bomb." *The New York Times*, December 11, 3:1.

Fronstin, Paul. 2006. "Sources of Health Insurance and Characteristics of the Uninsured: Analysis of the March 2006 Current Population Survey." Issue Brief no. 298. Washington, DC: Employee Benefit Research Institute.

Gabel, J., G. Claxton, I. Gil, J. Pickreign, H. Whitmore, B. Finder, S. Hawkins, and D. Rowland. 2005. "Health Benefits in 2005: Premium Increases Slow Down, Coverage Continues to Erode." *Health Affairs* 24(5): 1273–1280.

Gruber, J. 1994. "The Incidence of Mandated Maternity Benefits." *American Economic Review* 84(3): 622–641.

Gruber, J. and A.B. Krueger. 1991. "The Incidence of Mandated Employer-Provided Insurance: Lessons from Workers' Compensation Insurance." In *Tax Policy and the Economy*, D. Bradford, ed. Cambridge, MA: MIT Press, pp. 111–143.

Haas, J., and K. Swartz. 2007. "The Relative Importance of Worker, Firm, and Market Characteristics for Racial/Ethnic Disparities in Employer Sponsored Health Insurance." *Inquiry* 44(3): 280–302.

Kahn, J.G., R. Kronick, M. Kreger, and D.N. Gans. 2005. "The Cost of Health Insurance Administration in California: Estimates for Insurers, Physicians, and Hospitals." *Health Affairs* 24(6): 1629–1639.

Keehan, S.P., H.C. Lazenby, M.A. Zezza, and A.C. Catlin. 2004. "Age Estimates in the National Health Accounts." *Health Care Financing Review* 1(1): 1–16.   http://www.cms.hhs.gov/NationalHealthExpendData/downloads/keehan-age-estimates.pdf (accessed July 30, 2007).

Klein, J. 2003. *For All These Rights: Business, Labor, and the Shaping of America's Public-Private Welfare State*. Princeton, NJ: Princeton University Press.

Levinson, M. 2006. *The Box: How the Shipping Container Made the World Smaller and the World Economy Bigger*. Princeton, NJ: Princeton University Press.

Levit, K.R., C.A. Cowan, H.C. Lazenby, P.A. McDonnell, A.L. Sensenig, J.M. Stiller, and D.K. Won. 1994. "National Health Spending Trends, 1960–1993." *Health Affairs* 13(5): 14–31.

Levy, F. and P. Temin. 2007. "Inequality and Institutions in 20th Century America." NBER Working Paper no. 13106. Cambridge, MA: National Bureau of Economic Research.

Marquis, S.H., and S.M. Long. 1999. "Trends in Managed Care and Managed Competition, 1993–1997." *Health Affairs* 18(6): 75–88.

Newhouse, J.P. 1992. "Medical Care Costs: How Much Welfare Loss?" *Journal of Economic Perspectives* 6(3): 3–21.

————. 1993. "An Iconoclastic View of Health Cost Containment." *Health Affairs* 12(Supplement): 152–171.

Noble, B.S. 2007. "Universal Coverage and Individual Mandate in Switzerland: Any Lessons for Massachusetts?" Harvard School of Public Health Paper. Boston: Harvard School of Public Health.

Prinsze, F.J., and R.C.J.A. van Vliet. 2008. "Health-Based Risk Adjustment: Improving the Pharmacy-Based Cost Group Model by Adding Diagnostic Cost Groups." *Inquiry* 44(4): 469–480.

Royal Netherlands Government. 2006. "The New Care System in the Netherlands." The Hague: Ministry of Health, Welfare and Sport. http://www.minvws.nl/en/folders/z/2006/the-new-health-insurance-system-in-three-languages.asp (accessed July 30, 2007).

Social Security and Medicare Boards of Trustees. 2007. "Status of the Social Security and Medicare Programs: A Summary of the 2007 Annual Reports." Baltimore, MD: Social Security Administration. http://www.ssa.gov/OACT/TRSUM/trsummary.html (accessed July 30, 2007).

Swartz, K. 2006. *Reinsuring Health: Why More Middle-Class People Are Uninsured and What Government Can Do*. New York: Russell Sage Foundation.

Tax Policy Center. 2006. "Tax Policy: Facts and Figures." Washington, DC: Urban Institute and Brookings Institution. http://www.urban.org/UploadedPDF/901006_taxpolicy.pdf (accessed July 30, 2007).

U.S. Census Bureau. n.d.a. "Historical Income Tables—Families," Table F-7: Type of Family, All Races by Median and Mean Income: 1947–2005. Washington, DC: U.S. Census Bureau. http://www.census.gov/hhes/www/income/histinc/f07ar.html (accessed July 30, 2007).

————. n.d.b. "Statistical Abstract of the United States, 2007." Washington, DC: U.S. Census Bureau. http://www.census.gov/compendia/statab/tables/07s0011.xls (accessed July 30, 2007).

Woodbury, S.A. 1983. "Substitution Between Wage and Nonwage Benefits." *American Economic Review* 73(1): 166–182.

4
Trade and Immigration

Implications for the U.S. Labor Market

Lori G. Kletzer

University of California, Santa Cruz, and
Peterson Institute for International Economics

In the United States, debate and concern about trade and immigration, two of the major components of globalization, have focused to date on low and moderately skilled workers. This focus is changing. As trade in services expands and as attention is directed to American technological leadership and a high-skill workforce, the more highly-skilled sides of trade and immigration are emerging as topical concerns for policy and politics. With the growth of services trade and the potential for services offshoring, the set of workers at risk of job displacement has broadened from a production and manufacturing focus to include professionals, office and administrative workers, and more generally the services sector. The migration of foreign-born skilled workers, particularly in the information technology sector, creates another outlet where more highly skilled domestic workers feel threatened by international forces. While it might be an overstatement to conclude that trade and immigration are two sides of the same coin in the sense of posing foreign competition to American workers, there are informative parallels for policy analysis. Importantly, international trade (as the flow of goods and services) and immigration and migration (as the flow of potential labor) are two sides of the same coin from the perspective of measured impact. In both cases, measured impact (net benefit) is a question of distribution: the net benefits of both are unevenly distributed. As Lowenstein (2006) notes, "Like any form of economic change, immigration causes distress and disruption to some" (pg. 71). Change one word, and the same sentence applies to trade.

On the political and policy side, 2008 is an important time, and the window of opportunity may be open only for a short period. President

Bush's trade promotion authority (TPA), formerly known as fast-track authority to negotiate trade agreements, expired at the end of June 2007, and TAA authorization expired that fall. It may not be an opportune time for the Bush administration to push for trade expansion. With the return of Congress to Democratic leadership following the midterm elections in November 2006, the ground has shifted on trade-related legislation. Passions about trade topics are running high, given the size of the current account deficit and the imbalance with China. The so-called social effects of trade are likely to get a louder hearing under Democrats. In particular, enforcing tougher labor standards for other countries within trade agreements will get some attention, which is due in no small part to strategic choices by organized labor. During the summer of 2007, Congress discussed (and ultimately failed to pass) a bipartisan immigration compromise—potential legislation addressing undocumented migrants, a guest worker program, border security, and a point system for green cards. All of this activity is taking place amid broadening anxiety over the impact of trade and immigration at home.

This chapter adds a focus on skilled migration, services trade, and offshoring to the existing assessment of the impact of trade and immigration on the labor market and domestic workers. I review recent studies of services trade and offshoring in the context of more established analyses of manufacturing trade and production-worker job loss. On the immigration side, I examine issues and concerns regarding high-skill migration that add complexity to the ongoing debate on the domestic labor market impact of immigration, particularly that of undocumented migration. A concluding section offers policy recommendations.

STARTING POINTS—A BRIEF SYNTHESIS OF THE LITERATURE

Trade: U.S. Gains from Global Integration; Trade-Related Job Loss

Almost without exception, economists view trade liberalization as a known and proven method of increasing national income. Comparative advantage, economies of scale, technological spillovers, and import competition are the main channels for (net) increases in national income. Production efficiencies result from all four of these channels. Import competition is the most controversial, in that when domestic firms lose market share or close, workers, firm owners, and communities lose sources of income and profits. It is widely agreed that the benefits are large and diffuse, and the costs relatively smaller and concentrated.[1]

There is a sizable literature quantifying the gains from trade and investment liberalization. Bradford, Grieco, and Hufbauer (2005) synthesize a large number of studies using different methods and assumptions. The various estimates reveal substantial gains—on the order of $1 trillion annually—from past integration. The estimates are notable in size: "The estimated gain in 2003 income is in the range of $2,800 to $5,000 additional income for the average person and between $7,100 and $12,900 for the average household" (pg. 68). Estimates of gains from future integration range from $450 billion to $1.3 trillion annually. Gains from future integration will be large because of the (likely) inclusion of agriculture and services. Readers interested in a more detailed discussion of gains (from product variety to firm productivity) should consult Bradford, Grieco, and Hufbauer (2005).[2]

Richardson (2004) provides a cogent summary of research detailing the unevenness of gains. Firms that are globally engaged, through exports, imports, investment, outsourcing, and licensing, share distinctive benefits. Some of these benefits include faster growth rates, lower risk of plant closure, and higher worker wages. The gains from import liberalization are broadly distributed.[3]

Recent attention has been drawn to free-trade skeptics, economists whose writings have been interpreted as noting second thoughts about free trade. Examples include Samuelson (2004), Blinder (2006), and Rodrik (2006). In all cases, the remarks are not really new; rather, the remarks represent a change in tone (emphasizing distributional aspects over aggregate welfare gains), or a highlight of points known for some time but largely ignored. Samuelson (2004) is a prominent example in his consideration of the timely issue of technological progress and human capital advancement in developing countries. Samuelson's basic point is that there are situations where free trade, in the context of changes in comparative advantage, is not always welfare-enhancing. He points out that in simple cases of (large) differences in labor productivity, free trade leads unambiguously to increases in national income for both countries. Yet in the case where a country (call it China) improves productivity in the goods it imports (and thus the goods that the United States exports), trade can be wiped out (if the productivity improvement is just enough to equalize wage ratios), robbing the United States of the benefits of trade it previously enjoyed. In other words, technical progress in China can reduce the potential benefits of trade experienced by the United States. For example, if China began producing aircraft (a good it imports and the United States exports), the United States would be made worse off by the direct change in the terms of trade.[4] As Panagariya (2004) notes, this point about productivity growth and technological change is not new; when the United States was growing faster than Europe in the 1950s, Europeans were concerned that U.S. growth might decrease their standard of living; when Japan was growing in the 1960s and 1970s, the United States was concerned about Japan's effects on American standards of living.[5]

In fairness to the aforementioned skeptics, none dispute the overall gains from trade. Rather, they take up reallocative costs and the uneven distribution of gains. Because traditionally the gains from free trade have played a much larger role in economic discourse than any discussion of the costs, there seems to be some notion of skepticism when influential scholars pick up the refrain that benefits are net, with often considerable gross costs. In part, this unevenness comes from the prominence of economic theory, where, as noted by Bhagwati, Panagariya, and Srinivasan (2004, pg. 111), "Popular economic models of trade, at least the basic ones . . . typically assume that workers who lose one job can readily find another. . . . In the real world, workers may suffer through a period of joblessness and displacement." These real-world questions are clearly empirical in nature. There are agents and units in the economy (workers, firms, and communities) that bear costs because of firm closure, job loss, or reemployment at lower earnings. Community futures are often tied to employment opportunities. Scaling up summaries of microdata outcomes reported in Kletzer (2001), Bradford, Grieco, and Hufbauer (2005) estimate that U.S. trade-displaced manufacturing workers lose $54 billion in lifetime earnings. Yet federal government spending on programs explicitly tied to trade liberalization (such as Trade Adjustment Assistance) is less than $2 billion annually, clearly far less than the worker costs and overwhelmingly smaller than the permanent gains from trade and investment liberalization.

The discussion here is hardly unique in noting the large and positive net benefits of free trade, and the corresponding ability of free trade's "winners" to compensate the "losers," based on the estimated sizes of benefits and costs. Within the economics literature, the presumption that the losers can be compensated (at least partially if not fully) is strong, and often seems to serve as adequate justification for promoting policies that advance free trade. These presumptions work well in the academic literature but are problematic in any policy or political context.

One key problem is that presumptions of an ability to compensate have only weakly translated into a record of compensation policies and programs. The record of trade liberalizations undertaken by the United States is not matched by a record of policies to compensate workers for their trade-related job losses. The creation of, and reforms to, Trade Adjustment Assistance (TAA) have some parallels to rounds of trade liberalization, but the important dimension is in results, and on this score there is little sense that TAA brings to workers any form of adequate compensation.[6]

The highly visible nature of job loss, along with the failure of current federal adjustment programs to compensate workers for their losses, clearly weakens popular support for the view that economic integration brings widespread benefits. Yet opinions about trade liberalization do become more favorable when it is linked to worker adjustment programs (Scheve and Slaughter 2001). The public sense remains strong that fairness dictates compensation for workers affected by trade. Access to a wider variety of goods, at lower prices, seems to be of little relief when accompanied by job insecurity.

Immigration

Similar to trade, immigration imparts both benefits and costs to the United States.[7] With the flow of people across borders, the benefit/cost calculations are even more political and emotional, given the complexities of race, ethnicity, class, language, and geography. But the questions remain distributional ones: how much is lost by native workers competing with immigrant labor; how much is gained by native workers complementary to immigrant labor; how much is gained by consumers of immigrant-produced goods and services (standard consumer benefit of a factor increase); and if immigration lowers the price of labor, what are the gains to employers?

Both academic and popular discussions of the impact of immigration on the employment opportunities of natives start with the basic textbook model of a competitive labor market where an influx of immigrant workers lowers the wage of competing (native) workers. (The earnings of complementary factors—whether labor or capital—increase.) That is, immigrants represent an outward shift of the labor supply curve, along a downward sloping labor demand curve. Given the widespread appeal of a simple demand and supply model, there is often surprise that the literature provides mixed results. Measured impacts vary considerably across studies, and it is commonly concluded that the estimated effects cluster around zero (Borjas 2003; Friedberg and Hunt 1995). More specifically, Friedberg and Hunt (1995, pg. 42) conclude strongly that "there is no evidence of economically significant reductions in native employment." On the wage side, estimated effects are truly small, with a 10 percent increase in the fraction of immigrants being associated with a 1 percent reduction in native wages.

Skill is very much the essence of the question about the impact of immigration, and skill is strongly associated with country of origin. The European dominance of migration to the United States, stemming from the national origin quotas of the Immigrant and Nationality Act of 1924, have given way to an Asian, Mexican, and Central American dominance, following the establishment of preferences for family reunification in the 1965 Immigration Act. Card (2005) reports, from the 2000 census, that both recent and more established migrants include a much larger fraction of people with low levels of educational attainment than is true for natives. About 40 percent of recent (less than five years) and more established (five-plus years) migrants are high school dropouts, as compared to 13 percent of natives. Card also notes that immigrants were 13 percent of the working-age population in the 2000 census, yet they made up 28 percent of the population having less than a high school diploma. Thus, from a relative supply perspective (the basis of the straightforward demand and supply model), natives with the lowest levels of education are seen as those facing the greatest labor market competition from migrants, and most studies have focused on this group. This group has also faced potentially adverse consequences from increasing manufacturing trade, from a stagnant minimum wage, and from declining unionization.

For economists, the debate about immigration is also methodological. Exploiting the presence of many local labor markets in the United States with different fractions of immigrants and therefore different relative supplies of skilled labor, one approach uses a cross-city research design.[8] If cities were closed economies, this approach might mimic the shift in labor supply associated with the textbook model. But cities are not isolated or closed; if natives respond to changes in price and wages, the impact of immigration may be diffused. In addition, migrants are not likely to be randomly distributed across cities, which means there is the potential for spurious correlations between migrant flows and changes in native employment opportunities. Recognizing the flow of goods and factors across local labor markets, the second approach is national, relating changes in relative outcomes to time-series changes in immigrant shares. This approach lacks a clear counterfactual (what would have happened without immigration), in part because of coincident time trends such as technological change.

Lewis (2005) takes on the interesting question of why local labor market outcomes of low-skilled natives are not much affected by relative supply shocks. Despite the large impact of immigrants on the relative supply of low-skilled workers, there is little impact on the wages of native low-skilled workers. He finds an absorption of unskilled immigrants within industries in high immigrant cities.[9]

MOVING UP THE SKILL LADDER: TRADE AND IMMIGRATION

Services Trade and Services Offshoring

Globalization, particularly globalized production, is evolving and broadening from manufacturing into services. Services activities have become increasingly tradable and now account for a larger share of global trade than in the past. Services trade has almost doubled over the past decade and a half: over the period 1990 to 2005, exports have increased from $189 billion to $353 billion, and imports have increased from \$143 billion to \$267 billion (GPO Access 2007, Table B-25). These changes, and their implications for American firms and workers, have attracted widespread attention.

That trade is now different can be seen simply in the phrase "knowledge industries." Knowledge industries are characterized by a focus on creating value from new ideas and concepts, a notion that is different from creating value from material inputs and physical labor. Firms have always had ideas and used knowledge, of course, but now the output is often information-based, intangible, or conceptual. Knowledge work and output includes areas such as software development, financial services, pharmaceuticals, engineering services, and biotechnology. Knowledge work need not be "new"; it can include new products, services, and processes within older and more established industries such as architectural and accounting services. Trade in knowledge industries and in information technology–enabled service activities have broadened services trade beyond the traditional areas of transportation, travel, and tourism.

The growth in services trade is seen in Figure 4.1, which shows net exports of services.[10] The United States is a net exporter of many services, most prominently financial services, business, professional and technical services, and education. The trade surplus in services is in contrast to goods trade, where imports exceed exports by a wide margin (Figure 4.2).

Services offshoring, which is the migration of jobs (but not the people performing them) across national borders (mostly from rich countries to poor ones), has received considerable attention since 2000. Fueled by the 2004 presidential race and continued slack in the labor market, the services-offshoring debate became headline material. The literature on services offshoring is expanding rapidly (see Jensen and Kletzer 2006 and Blinder 2006 for references).

The scope of the phenomenon is largely unknown because of a lack of data. Anxiety over services trade is often fueled by one simple statistic: the large share of employment in the services sector. As Figure 4.3 shows, services employment has been predominant in the United States for more than 30 years, and the services sector now accounts for 70 percent of total civilian employment (GPO Access 2007, Table B46). Most observers believe that the scope of services offshoring will be large,

Figure 4.1 U.S. Net Exports of Services, 1992–2005

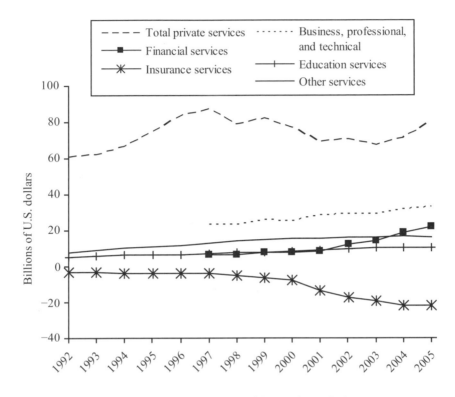

SOURCE: Department of Commerce, Bureau of Economic Analysis.

even huge. Here is an example, from the Web site of the U.S. House of Representatives Committee on Science and Technology:

> Recently, however, offshoring has begun to strike at the very high-tech jobs that we believed U.S. workers would move to fill as blue-collar opportunities shifted to other countries. A Cable News Network report in early March 2006 noted that 500,000 American jobs have migrated to India in recent years. That number is expected to triple in the next two years as American companies seek to cuts costs and streamline business. India is but one example of a country that seems to be gaining employment at the expense of American workers. Over the last six years, the U.S. has lost just under 3 million jobs due to offshoring.

Now, we are witnessing software engineering, computer design, research and development, radiology, architecture and design and other high-value-added positions moving offshore to low-wage markets such as India, China, Ireland, and Brazil (Committee on Science and Technology 2006).

Jensen and Kletzer (2006) developed a new empirical approach to identify, at a detailed level, service activities that are potentially exposed to international trade. The approach uses the geographic concentration of service activities within the United States to identify which service activities are traded domestically, then classifies activities that are traded domestically as *potentially* tradable internationally. With the tradability classification, we developed estimates of the number of workers who are in tradable activities for all sectors of the economy. The paper offers comparisons of the demographic characteristics of workers in tradable and nontradable activities and employment growth in traded and nontraded service activities. The tradability designation also allows an examination of the risk of job loss and other employment outcomes for workers in tradable activities.

Figure 4.2 U.S. Trade in Goods, 1992–2005

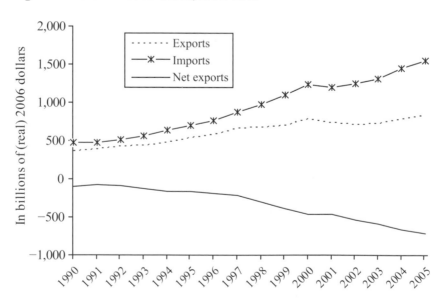

SOURCE: Department of Commerce, Bureau of Economic Analysis.

Figure 4.3 U.S. Employment by Aggregated Sector, 1970–2006

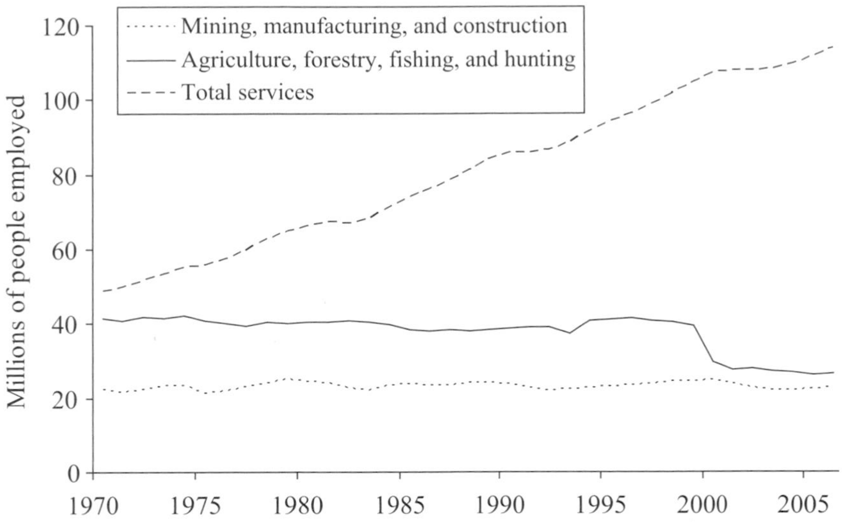

SOURCE: Bureau of Labor Statistics.

The Jensen and Kletzer methodology finds substantial employment in tradable service industries and occupations. Given the overall size of the services sector, it may not be surprising that more workers are employed in tradable industries in the services sector than in the manufacturing sector. Outside of education, health care, and personal care occupations, the typical white-collar occupation involves a potentially tradable activity. Workers in these industries and occupations are more highly skilled and have higher incomes than workers in the manufacturing sector and nontradable service activities. But the higher incomes are not solely a result of higher skill levels—in regressions controlling for observable characteristics, workers in select tradable service activities earn 16–17 percent higher incomes than similar workers in nontradable activities in the same sector.

There is little evidence that tradable service industries or occupations have lower employment growth than nontradable industries or occupations overall, though employment growth is negative for tradable services at the low end of the skill distribution. High-skill service activities have the highest employment growth rates.

While the share of employment in tradable services is large, this does not suggest that all or even most of these jobs are likely to move offshore. Just because an activity is tradable does not necessarily mean that the job will move to a lower-cost location. Tradable services are largely consistent with U.S. comparative advantage. While professional and business services are more skilled and higher paying than manufacturing in general, tradable services within these sectors are even more highly skilled and more highly paid than nontradable service activities. As technological and organizational change increases the potential for trade in services, economic activity within the United States will shift to activities consistent with comparative advantage. Because these activities are consistent with U.S. comparative advantage, it is possible that further liberalization in international services trade would directly benefit workers and firms in the United States.

Jensen and Kletzer (2007) extend the examination of tradable jobs with a focus on the task and activity content of jobs, in order to develop measures of the occupational job tasks, activities, and characteristics associated with potential offshoring. The literature on offshoring notes that movable jobs are those with the following characteristics: little face-to-face customer contact, high information content, and a work process that is Internet-enabled or telecommutable (Bardhan and Kroll 2003; Blinder 2006; Dossani and Kenney 2003). More informally, it is commonly believed that if the output of a job can be sent down a wire (or sent wireless), that job is offshorable.

The next step involves an operational assessment of how the basic principles of offshorability (high information content, remote from customer, Internet-enabled) match up to the characteristics of "real" jobs. Detailed information on the content and context of jobs (occupations) is available from O*Net, a U.S. Department of Labor database of 450 occupations. (O*Net is the successor to the well-known Dictionary of Occupational Titles.) For each of hundreds of occupations, O*Net contains detailed qualitative information on job tasks, work activities (interacting with computers, processing information), and work context (face-to-face discussions, work with others, work outdoors).

The Jensen and Kletzer index of offshorability (in which occupations are ranked based on a weighting of these characteristics) produces occupations that are "most tradable," such as credit authorizers, data-entry keyers, accountants, medical transcriptionists, market research analysts, bookkeepers, and account clerks. Occupations at the bottom of the list, the "least tradable," include crossing guards, massage therapists, manicurists, and barbers.

Blinder (2007) explores a subjective index based on various measures of face-to-face interaction: establishing and maintaining personal relationships, assisting and caring for others, performing for or working directly with the public, selling to others or influencing others, being aware of others' reactions and understanding why they react as they do (social perceptiveness). He concludes that an objective index does poorly in assessing offshorability (as compared to his subjective assessment, based on O*Net data). His subjective index does not incorporate any attributes related to amount of information content or to Internet enabling, nor does he consider the creativity or routineness of work.[11] Objective measures may well be preferred, given the number of occupations (more than 450) and the desire for replication. Using both production and nonproduction occupations, Blinder estimates that 30 to 40 million workers are currently in potentially tradable jobs, based on May 2005 employment levels.

An important question in moving forward is the time frame for the process of services offshoring. It is commonly believed (although untested) that a phenomenon that takes years to be fully realized will be less disruptive than a more rapid structural change.

Much more is yet to be learned about the scale, scope, and labor market costs of services offshoring. Until then, it remains to be seen whether Bhagwati, Panagariya, and Srinivasan (2004, pg. 94) were correct when they pronounced that "outsourcing is fundamentally just a trade phenomenon; that is, subject to the usual theoretical caveats and practical responses, outsourcing leads to gains from trade, and its effects on jobs and wages are not qualitatively different from those of conventional trade in goods."[12]

Services offshoring is one aspect of a larger concept that we might call "global operations." Briefly, global operations allow firms to access new markets and new sources of revenue, technologies, and ways of production. As firms globalize their business operations, there are implications for work and for workers. Much attention is paid to cost reduction (largely in the form of wages) as a motivator; other factors include proximity to global customers and enhanced abilities to meet customers' expectations that they should be able to reach a representative at any time of day or night. See Gereffi (2005) for a comprehensive introduction to research on global supply chains.

Skills and Immigration

The immigration debate is occurring at both ends of the skill spectrum. While headline coverage is often limited to undocumented (and lesser-skilled) migration, Web sites and the business press provide ample evidence of a heated debate about legally admitted, temporary, high-skill foreign workers. At the high-skill end, the real debate may be over whether or not a shortage exists of (legally residing, not necessarily native) computer programmers, systems analysts, and computer scientists. Claims of a shortage buttress arguments for more liberal H-1B caps.[13] These claims arose in the late 1990s, as the labor market tightened with strong economic growth and with the peak of the dot-com boom.

The United States is a net importer of the highly educated, particularly of scientists and engineers. There is little doubt that foreigners help the United States maintain its position at the technological frontier. "Leadership in science and technology gives the U.S. its comparative advantage in the global economy," writes Freeman (2006a, p. 124). "U.S. exports are disproportionately from sectors that rely extensively on scientific and engineering workers and that embody the newest technologies. . . . In a knowledge-based economy, leadership in science and technology contributes substantially to economic success."

Highly skilled immigrants play a prominent role in the economy. In 2003, the foreign-born accounted for about 13.0 percent of the population, 14.4 percent of the total adult workforce, and 17.2 percent of young adult workers (Figure 4.4). As Figure 4.4 illustrates, the share of foreign-born in the workforce has risen considerably since the late 1990s. The foreign-born are well-educated (particularly advanced degree holders). In 2002, they made up 16.2 percent of science, technology, engineering, and mathematical (STEM) occupations and 18.4 percent of core STEM (excluding social scientists and technicians) occupations (Figure 4.5). Foreign-born workers are particularly important in computer science occupations. Foreign-born STEM workers are more likely to have advanced degrees than natives, and the vast majority of both natives and foreign-born have degrees from U.S. institutions.

Figure 4.4 Percentage of Foreign-Born in the U.S. Workforce

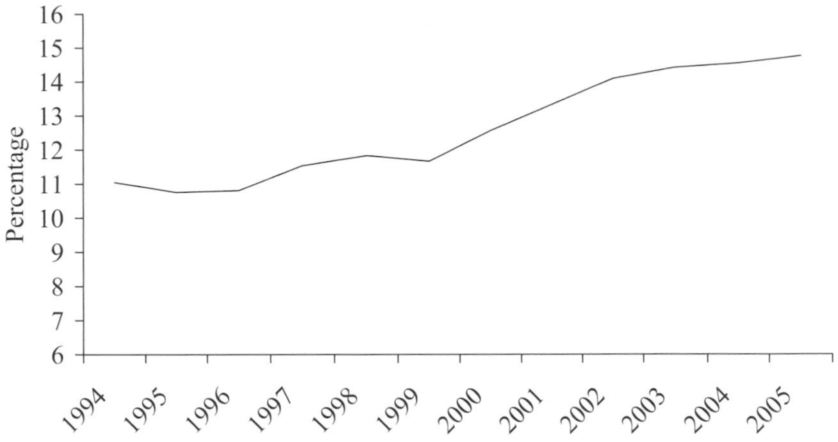

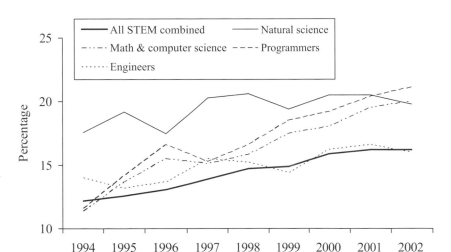

SOURCE: Bureau of Labor Statistics.

Figure 4.5 Foreign-Born as a Percentage of STEM Occupations, 1994–2002

SOURCE: Commission on Professionals in Science and Technology.

Saxenian (2002) notes the role of immigrants in Silicon Valley entrepreneurship. Wadhwa et al. (2007) update and expand that study and find that one-quarter of engineering and technology companies started between 1995 and 2005 had at least one foreign-born founder. Freeman (2006a) reports that 60 percent of the growth in the number of U.S.-based scientists and engineers over the decade of the 1990s came from the foreign-born. There is a critical question about maintaining U.S. comparative advantage in the absence of highly educated immigrants. With higher earnings, more domestic (or native) workers could be attracted to science and engineering fields, but this will take time. Without adequate supply, more research and development could be located offshore. Yet maintaining the flow of foreign-born scientists and engineers might lessen earnings growth, making it difficult to attract native students into science and engineering fields.

Since 1965, U.S. immigrant policy has been strongly based in family reunification. (Before 1965, immigrant admission was based on national origin.) The focus of the debate over skilled migrants is not about immigrant entry, but rather about nonimmigrant entry, the visa category of H-1B.

The H-1 nonimmigrant category was created under the Immigration and Nationality Act of 1952 to assist U.S. employers needing workers temporarily.[14] Nonimmigrants are foreign nationals who come to the U.S. on a temporary basis and for a specific purpose, such as schooling or work. The H-1B program was created by the Immigration Act of 1990, amending the 1952 Act. The H-1B program allows an employer to temporarily employ a foreign worker in the United States on a nonimmigrant basis in a specialty occupation or as "a fashion model of distinguished merit and ability." A specialty occupation requires the theoretical and practical application of a body of specialized knowledge and a bachelor's degree or the equivalent in the specific specialty (e.g., sciences, medicine and health care, education, biotechnology, and business specialties). The 1990 act, which is current law, limits the number of foreign workers who may be issued a visa or otherwise be provided H-1B status to 65,000 a year.

In 1998, Congress increased the H-1B cap to 115,000 for fiscal years 1999 and 2000. In 2000, Congress set the cap higher, at 195,000 for fiscal year 2001. That level was maintained for fiscal years 2002 and 2003. From fiscal year 2004 on, the cap has reverted back to 65,000.[15]

Under the H-1B Visa Reform Act of 2004, H-1B workers hired by institutions of higher education, nonprofits, and government research organizations are exempt from the cap. There is a separate 20,000 cap on H-1B petitions filed on behalf of aliens with U.S.-earned master's or higher degrees. An H-1B visa is generally valid for three years of employment and is renewable for an additional three years. From an H-1B visa, individuals may apply for permanent residency status.

To hire a foreign worker on H-1B visa status, the U.S. employer files a labor condition application (LCA) with the U.S. Department of Labor's Employment and Training Administration. On the application, the employer must attest to meeting the following four conditions: 1) paying at least the local prevailing wage, or the employer's actual wage, whichever is higher; 2) offering nonimmigrants benefits on the same basis as U.S. workers receive; 3) that employment of H-1B nonimmigrants must not adversely affect the working conditions of U.S. workers; and 4) that no strike or lockout exists in the occupational classification at the place of employment. In addition, the employer must attest to notifying employees, at the place of employment, of the intent to employ H-1B workers.

Employers who are "H-1B dependent"—that is, whose workforce is comprised of 15 percent or more H-1B employees—face additional requirements. These requirements include attesting to the following three conditions: 1) no U.S. workers displaced within a period of 90 days before or 90 days after filing an LCA petition; 2) good-faith steps were taken before filing the LCA to recruit U.S. workers and the job was offered to a U.S. applicant equally or better qualified than an H-1B worker; and 3) before placing the H-1B worker with another employer, the first employer inquired and has no knowledge as to that employer's action or intent to displace a U.S. worker within the 90 days before or 90 days after the placement of the H-1B worker with that employer.[16]

Information on worker characteristics is available from petitions to Citizenship and Immigration Service (CIS) for visas. These petitions are not, however, clear proxies for admission. Petitions are used to sponsor initial employment, continued employment, a change in employer (for someone already in the United States with H-1B status), or a change in location with the same employer. The total number of petitions therefore greatly exceeds the number of foreigners with nonimmigrant status. By country of origin, India, China, and Canada accounted for 58 percent of fiscal year 2005 petitions (44 percent, 9.2 percent, and 4.4 percent, respectively). Sixty-five percent of approved petitions were for workers between 25 and 34 years of age; 45 percent for workers with a bachelor's degree, 37 percent for those with a master's degree, 5 percent for those with a doctorate, and 12 percent for those with a professional degree. Forty-three percent went to those in computer-related occupations; 12 percent to those in architecture, engineering, and surveying; 10.9 percent to those in education (CIS 2006).

Hira (2007) argues that the above LCA conditions do not constitute a "labor market test," in the sense that employers can hire H-1B workers even (as worded by the U.S. Department of Labor) "when a qualified U.S. worker wants the job, and a U.S. worker can be displaced from the job in favor of the foreign worker" (pg. 2). Only H-1B–dependent employers face more stringent requirements about not displacing native (resident) workers. Hira also sees the following problems from the H-1B program and any proposed expansion: more offshore outsourcing of jobs, displacement of American technology workers, decreased wages and job opportunities for domestic workers, and discouragement of young Americans from entering science and engineering fields.

Hira's unique contribution to the debate is his assertion that the H-1B program promotes offshoring. He argues that the biggest users of H-1B visas are offshore outsourcing firms, and that these firms do not sponsor permanent resident status for their workers; rather, they train them in the United States and send those workers, along with the production, back to the country of origin. According to Hira's analysis of data from the U.S. Department of Labor's Office of Foreign Labor Certification (OFLC), the top 11 (and 15 of the top 20) H-1B requesters are firms that specialize in offshore outsourcing (Hira 2007, Table 1). These firms use H-1B (and L-1) workers as part of their knowledge transfer operations, rotating foreign workers to learn U.S. workers' jobs. H-1B workers also provide on-site (domestic) presence for these firms with their customers.[17]

Proponents of H-1B argue that nonimmigrant workers are vital because of systematic shortages of native (or resident) technology (science and engineering) workers. Yet standard labor market indicators yield little or mixed evidence of IT worker shortages. Wage or earnings growth is moderate (similar to that of other professionals); unemployment rates shot up in the dot-com bust and have now fallen. In a comprehensive survey, Lowell (2001a) found little evidence of shortages. Private (trade) surveys do often conclude that there are shortages, but there is little corroboration from public use data. The growth in H-1B visas alone is not evidence of a shortage; other factors include backlogs in the permanent visa application process, cyclical demand in main (IT) industries in the 1990s, strong U.S. economic growth, changes in global competition that create demand for foreign workers because of expansions of foreign markets, the growing importance of international students in U.S. institutions (students who stay in this country upon graduation and need to be transitioned from student visa status to a working visa). Healthy H-1B hiring, with an absence of clear evidence of shortages, is not a sufficient argument for an expansion of the H-1B program. Expanded H-1B caps will create problems for the permanent residency component of immigration (where there are already considerable backlogs).

Secondarily, proponents argue that the H-1B program is the point of entry for the world's best and brightest and essential for maintaining U.S. competitiveness. Existing separately from the H-1B debate, but clearly confounded with it, is the widespread concern that the United States faces a problem in maintaining its position as the scientific and technological leader in the world and that loss of leadership threatens the nation's future economic well-being and national security. Business, science, and education groups have issued reports that highlight the value to the country of leadership in science and technology. More specifically, numerous reports highlight the contribution of immigrants in innovative fields. In a report on the entrepreneurial economy, the Kauffman Foundation (2007) advocated an "entrepreneurial immigration policy" of raising H-1B quotas in the short term and eliminating them in the long term. There is also advocacy of new policies to increase the supply of scientific and engineering talent in the United States.[18]

A central charge is that employment of H-1B visa holders comes at a cost to older native-born workers, particularly engineers and technology (computer) workers, in terms of both wages and employment. Serious data limitations have prevented economists from doing much analysis on the question of the impact of H-1B visas on the wages and employment of U.S. workers.[19] The National Research Council (2001) concludes that the magnitude of a wage effect caused by the H-1B program is difficult to estimate. That report suggests that the H-1B program has an effect in keeping wages from rising as quickly as they might in the absence of an H-1B program (Lowell 1999, 2000a,b, 2001a,b). Zavodny (2003), using Department of Labor LCA data for fiscal year 2001 across states, found no relationship between share of H-1B workers and domestic earnings, earnings growth, or unemployment.[20]

As the fraction of doctoral degrees awarded to foreign students has risen (from 11.3 to 24.4 percent between 1976 and 2000), there is a natural question about labor market competition: do foreign student doctorates harm the economic opportunities of native doctorates? Borjas (2005a) estimates factor price elasticities and finds that an immigration-induced 10 percent increase in the supply of doctorates lowers the wages of competing workers by about 3 percent.

Thinking About Immigration Policy

A successful immigration policy is a challenge to build, given the lack of clear political alignments, contradictory empirical evidence, strong emotions, and conflicting political ideologies. It is easy to think of immigration as a "problem." But as Marshall (2007, pg. 1) advises,

> Immigration is not the problem: the United States is and will remain a nation of immigrants, who have contributed greatly to the vitality, diversity, and creativity of American life. Immigrants are particularly important to the U.S. economy, accounting for over half of the workforce growth during the 1990s and 86 percent of the increase in employment between 2000 and 2005. Because there will be no net increase in the number of prime-working-age natives (aged 25 to 54) for the next 20 years, the strength of the American economy could depend heavily on how the nation relates immigration to economic and social policy.

The most heated issues in the current immigration policy reform debate lie outside the boundaries of traditional economic policy thinking. Questions of culture, language, race, ethnicity, and geography trump economics now, and they could continue to do so. Current immigration policy is based on family unification, not economics. The small economic costs of immigration do not provide justification for an economics-based policy. As Borjas (1999a,b) argues, evidence alone (whether economic or not) cannot decide the course of immigration policy.[21] There needs to be an explicit understanding of national interest—what it is that Americans intend from an immigration policy. Borjas suggests consideration of three groups, whose interests may be in conflict: people living in the United States ("natives"), potential immigrants, and people who remain in the source countries. Most discussions attach the largest weight to the interests of natives. Even with this simplification, economic interests need to be defined: as Borjas asks, is it the size of economic pie (national income, or per capital income), or the splitting of the slices of the pie (distribution of income)?

This last question has a straightforward answer: like trade, the economic impact of immigration is distributional. The net impact is relatively small (a small increase in net national income), with losses (also small) concentrated among the less-skilled, and gains accruing to the skilled and owners of capital.[22] Borjas (1999b) states in plain terms, "The debate over how many and which types of immigrants to admit is best viewed as a tug-of-war between those who gain from immigration and those who lose from it" (p. 185). Yet, unlike trade, the policy "solution" for immigration is likely to involve regulation of the flow, while for trade the solution involves addressing adjustment costs. In this way, immigration policy stands out from trade and financial policy in the context of globalization. As countries have moved to liberalize flows of goods, services, and capital, the climate for liberalized movements of people has distinctly cooled. Freeman (2006a) notes that opinion surveys across the rich countries find majority support for more restrictive immigration.

An economics-based immigration policy may largely involve skill. Arguments for an entry system that favors skilled migrants include three considerations: 1) the skilled earn more, pay more taxes, and require fewer social services; 2) capital benefits from skilled migration (although Lewis [2005] sees production choices as endogenous to local relative skill supply, allowing capital to benefit from less-skilled migration as well); and 3) skilled migrants also contribute to innovation and entrepreneurship (Wadhwa et al. 2007). On the national competitiveness front, there is advocacy of a high-skill immigration policy that would permit unrestricted H-1Bs and automatic citizenship to foreign nationals earning science and engineering graduate degrees from U.S. institutions (Kauffman Foundation 2007).

Addressing the flow, presence, and impact of undocumented migrants dominates current public discourse on immigration policy reform. The "bipartisan immigration compromise," as it has been commonly termed, is the current template for public discourse. Highlights and contentious issues of that compromise include the following: border security, legalizing the residency of undocumented migrants, a guest worker program, and a point system for future immigrants that rewards skill (measured as educational attainment, occupational qualifications, and English-language proficiency). Other migration issues are also hotly contested, most prominently the H-1B visa program. Two bills were introduced in Spring 2007 to increase the allotment of H-1B visas while tightening the regulations regarding employer good-faith efforts to hire American workers first and strengthening USDOL enforcement capabilities.[23]

CURRENT WORKER ADJUSTMENT ASSISTANCE POLICY AND PROGRAMS; MOVING AHEAD ON POLICY

Regarding trade, the policy focus is on labor market adjustment programs. This section reviews the current policy landscape and looks ahead at possible reforms and expansions.

Current Policy Mix

The United States has a well-developed and broad set of labor market adjustment policies and programs, with unemployment insurance (UI) at the center. Other programs include advance notice for major layoffs, which is mandated by the Worker Adjustment and Retraining Notification (WARN) Act, and training and job search assistance, which is provided under the Workforce Investment Act (WIA). The Trade Adjustment Assistance (TAA) program, created in 1962, provides adjustment assistance to workers laid off as a result of international trade. The United States is unique among industrialized countries in providing special assistance to workers who have lost jobs because of increased imports or international shifts in the location of production.

The main benefits available through TAA are extended income support and training. The following summary comes from the GAO (2006a). By statute, the U.S. Department of Labor certifies groups of laid-off workers as potentially eligible for TAA benefits and services by investigating petitions filed on behalf of workers. Petitions can be filed by firms, unions, or groups of workers. Workers are eligible if laid off as a result of international trade and if they were involved in making a product, supplying component parts, or performing finishing work for directly affected firms. Historically, most eligible workers have lost jobs in the manufacturing sector.

Under the current TAA program, eligible participants have access to the following assistance:

- Training—up to 130 weeks, including 104 weeks of vocational training and 26 weeks of remedial training (such as ESL or language literacy). TAA-approved training must be full-time.

- Trade Readjustment Allowances (TRAs, or extended income support)—up to 104 weeks of extended income support, after the 26 weeks of standard UI is exhausted. By statute, the level of TRA support is set at the state's UI benefit level. The 104 weeks include 78 weeks while participating in vocational training and an additional 26 weeks if remedial training is necessary. During the first 26 weeks of TRA receipt, participants must be enrolled in training, have completed training, or have a waiver of the training requirement. Beyond the first 26 weeks, receipt of TRA support is conditional on training enrollment.

- Job search and relocation benefits.

- Health Coverage Tax Credit (HCTC). Eligible participants may receive an advanceable tax credit covering 65 percent of the health insurance premiums. To be HCTC-eligible, workers must be receiving TRA support, be eligible for TRA but still receiving standard UI (in both cases, in training), or be enrolled in ATAA (see below).

- Alternative Trade Adjustment Assistance (ATAA)—a targeted program of wage insurance, designed for workers aged 50 and older who forgo training, become reemployed within 26 weeks, and experience a reduction in earnings from the old job to the new job. If annual earnings on the new job are $50,000 or less, the benefit covers 50 percent of the difference between old and new job earnings, up to a maximum of $10,000 over two years.

The narrow focus of TAA on manufacturing, while historically appropriate given the predominance of goods (as opposed to services) in international trade, is becoming a serious point of contention. The U.S. Department of Labor follows a narrow interpretation in its eligibility determinations. The statute requires workers to prove that they lost their job from a firm that makes a product that is "similar to or like an imported good." The department's interpretation of the word "good" has resulted in many denials of eligibility. As services offshoring continues to capture attention, this conflict over interpretation will persist.

More generally, eligibility denial is a contentious issue. Workers, or worker groups, have appealed to the U.S. Court of International Trade, the court with jurisdiction over TAA. As noted by Kletzer and Rosen (2005), the Court is increasingly sharply critical of the Department of Labor's decisions on denials. The Court's opinion in the case of *Former Employees of BMC Software Inc. vs. U.S. Secretary of Labor* is illustrative, and worth quoting at length:

> Trade adjustment assistance programs historically have been—and today continue to be—touted as the *quid pro quo* for U.S. national policies of free trade.
>
> As illustrated by the history of virtually every TAA case filed with the court in recent years, the Labor Department's standard investigative modus operandi appears to be to target whichever element of a TAA claim the agency perceives to be the weakest, and—if the agency finds that that particular element is not satisfied—to deny the claim on that basis, with no investigation or analysis of the other elements of the claim.
>
> The TAA program is fundamentally broken, as evidenced by a number of key indicators, particularly the . . . extraordinarily high percentage of cases in which the agency reverses itself on appeal. Those statistics are a scathing indictment of the Labor Department's administration of the TAA program.
>
> In short, "there is something fundamentally wrong with the administration of the nation's trade adjustment assistance programs if, as a practical matter, workers often must appeal their cases to the courts to secure the thorough investigation that the Labor Department is obligated to conduct by law."

The literature assessing TAA performance is limited, in large part because of the Labor Department's paltry release of outcome and performance data. Decker and Corson (1995) is perhaps the most commonly cited study, and it was based not on (the nonexistent) publicly available data, but on data obtained through Mathematica's contracted evaluation of TAA in 1993. The 2002 Trade Act mandated an evaluation, with data collection beginning in 2005 and a final report to be issued by the end of 2008. GAO (2004) offers a preliminary assessment, based on contact with state workforce agencies, of the 2002 reforms. Kletzer and Rosen (2005) also offer an assessment, based on publicly available information, and with an eye to policy reform. In the context of program evaluation, GAO (2006b) notes serious administrative concerns about the collection of TAA program performance data, and of data on outcomes such as employment and earnings. As that GAO report concludes,

> since the passage of the TAA Reform Act of 2002, the TAA program has evolved to become one of the most important means to help the workers affected by our nation's trade policies rejoin our nation's workforce. The program has seen substantial increases in the population it serves and in the funds available to serve them. Unfortunately, efforts to monitor the program's performance have not kept pace with the program's development. Four years after the passage of the reforms, we still do not know whether the program is achieving what lawmakers intended.

In the current budgetary environment, with many claims on limited discretionary funds, it is increasingly important to have performance data and assessments.

Two of the 2002 reforms, the health care tax credit and wage insurance (ATAA), have received considerable recent attention (Andrews 2007). A number of recent policy-related studies and articles address the costs and benefits of wage insurance (Brainard, Litan, and Warren 2006; Kletzer and Rosen 2006; Kling 2006). While these debates are a vital component of policy discourse, it is frustrating to note that virtually nothing is known about the efficacy of these two program additions. Kletzer and Rosen's (2005) study predates any real numbers on ATAA take-up, and surprisingly little has been learned since late 2004. GAO (2006a) concludes that

> while few workers took advantage of training and long-term income support through the TAA program, even fewer made use of two new benefits under the TAA program—health insurance assistance and wage insurance for older workers. Workers who knew

about the benefits sometimes told us that the benefit levels were not high enough to get them to participate. But relatively large numbers were simply not aware of the benefits, and some said they might have applied for the benefits had they known about them. Sometimes workers admitted to being overwhelmed by the prospect of losing their jobs and by the wealth of information they initially received. However, states' efforts to inform workers about and explain these benefits have been mixed at best—some trained their case managers to answer questions from workers, while others did not see that as their role. Despite Labor's efforts to encourage states to make this information more widely available, many workers still do not know about these benefits and, as a result, cannot make use of them. Without better information, these workers may not have the opportunity to avail themselves of benefits that could ease their transition to reemployment.

MOVING AHEAD ON POLICY—SHORT-TERM PROSPECTS

A Democratically controlled Congress facing a lame-duck Republican administration, and a costly war in Iraq, are impediments to the goal of progress on the globalization policy agenda. Public skepticism about the benefits of trade expansion further complicates the picture. With all these complexities, it may not be possible to set out an economically defensible policy plan that is also politically feasible. Thus the discussion here will focus on the former, and leave the latter to political professionals.[24]

Any policy discussion must recognize the highly dynamic nature of the U.S. labor market, in which millions of jobs are created and lost each year. A flexible labor market can benefit an economy, especially when workers are able to move from low- to high-productivity jobs. Young workers benefit from turnover, since they gain skills and experience and find productive matches with a sequence of employers. At the same time, labor market flexibility can impose significant costs on workers and their families. Workers can experience prolonged unemployment, and once reemployed they may experience large and persistent earnings losses. In a rapidly changing economy, workers lose jobs for many reasons (domestic competition, technological change, plant or office relocation), and, as shown in Kletzer (2001), there is very little variation in the reemployment earnings consequences: losing a job is costly, regardless of reason. Analysis of data from the Dislocated Worker Survey reveals that only two-thirds of unemployed workers find a new job within one to three years after layoff. More than 40 percent of workers experience earnings losses. Only about one-fourth of workers experience no earnings loss or an improvement in earnings after reemployment. Preliminary evidence on the reemployment consequences of services job loss, as reported in Jensen and Kletzer (2006), suggests little reason to temper this conclusion on costly job loss. The numbers of workers facing job displacement are significant: over the 2003–2005 period, 1.8 million workers were displaced from manufacturing industries, and 3.7 million workers were displaced from services industries (down from the 2001–2003 period, when 2.9 million workers were displaced from manufacturing and 4.9 million were displaced from services).[25]

Calls for reform are timely, based on workers' needs, which are unmet by current programs. It may, however, be time to reconsider the usual ways of advocating assistance policy. Consider the legislative history of TAA. President Kennedy and Congress established the Trade Adjustment Assistance (TAA) program in 1962 to provide assistance to workers who lose jobs because of increased import competition. The unique manner in which international trade policy is conducted in the United States, along with the modest level of existing adjustment assistance, played a role in the establishment of TAA. Congress must transfer, temporarily, authority to the president in order for the administration to participate in trade negotiations. This transfer of authority (now called trade promotion authority) gives Congress an opportunity to influence the negotiating agenda. Just as importantly, Congress gets a chance to pass legislation to compensate workers adversely affected by changes in foreign competition associated with trade agreements. As a result, expansions of TAA programs have been highly correlated with efforts to liberalize trade. This is the framework in which TAA has been seen as a quid pro quo for congressional support of trade-liberalizing legislation. As noted by Kletzer and Rosen (2005), reforms to TAA in the 1980s, the creation of NAFTA-TAA, and the 2002 reforms to TAA all fit into this framework of mustering votes to pass trade legislation.

There is a view that little additional gain accrues from assistance programs targeted at trade-displaced workers. TAA does not receive much support from organized labor. On a practical basis, unions do work to ensure that workers receive assistance, yet their political support is tepid out of fear that out-and-out support will weaken unions' priority position against trade liberalization. With TAA as assistance after job loss (and modest levels of assistance at that), the program is often sarcastically referred to as "burial insurance" among union leaders. The same arguments exist for organized labor's lukewarm response to wage insurance (Andrews 2007). As analyzed by Destler (2005), the 2002 reforms to TAA, as part of the Trade Act of 2002 that granted trade promotion authority to the president, gained little additional Democratic support. TAA is viewed by many as "a backwater government program that gets attention only when an administration needs votes for trade legislation" (Destler 2005, p. 328). A broad program of assistance to all displaced workers is more justifiable on the economic costs of job loss and is likely to more broadly address public anxieties about job insecurity. In addition, a general program of adjustment assistance avoids politicizing (or demonizing) any one particular cause of job loss, such as free trade and globalization.

In turning to a broad program of assistance to all displaced workers, we should recognize that a comprehensive reform strategy starts with reforming UI. Unfortunately, political will does not currently seem to exist to significantly reform UI. Short of UI reform, the next best alternative would be to continue expanding TAA eligibility to include more workers, specifically those adversely affected by the various aspects of globalization. An expanded TAA program would be in addition to the existing UI system. Rosen (2007) suggests the following parameters, in a program that would be renamed Globalization Adjustment Assistance (GAA).

Eligibility

The existing eligibility test, i.e., the association between 1) an increase in imports or a shift in production and 2) a decline in output and employment, is tedious, difficult to implement, and subject to judicial objection. In addition the USDOL currently does not consider workers who are employed in the service sector as producing "an article" and thus deems them ineligible for TAA. The problem of covering service workers is exacerbated by the absence of detailed service import data, which makes it difficult to show that a decline in output and employment is associated with an increase in service imports.

One alternative would be to move toward more qualitative eligibility criteria. Criteria would be developed to determine if an entire industry, occupation, or region was considered to be under distress. Once this determination was made, any worker losing a job from that industry, occupation, or region would only need to prove membership in any of these groupings in order to receive assistance under the revised program. This reform would reduce the discrimination between similar workers and also significantly reduce the bureaucratic burden associated with administering the program.

Criteria to determine industry distress could include some combination of declines in sales and output, increases in imports, and job loss throughout the entire industry or occupation, not just a single firm. The addition of occupations as a potential eligible grouping is necessary due to the task-oriented (or occupation-oriented) nature of services offshoring. High unemployment, plant closings, and vacancies could be used to identify regions under distress.

Financial Assistance

The current system of providing 78 weeks of income maintenance at the UI rate if a worker is enrolled in training (a provision that goes well beyond the traditional 26 weeks of UI) would continue to be the central aspect of the program. The adjustment burden of workers changing industry or occupation is high (Kletzer 2001). Longer duration of income maintenance enables workers to enroll in significant training and thereby make a serious adjustment. In the case of regional distress, income maintenance payments can help stimulate the local economy.

Training

Training funds are inadequate, and many states exhaust their allocation before the end of the year. Income maintenance payments under TAA are an entitlement—i.e., Congress must appropriate enough money to provide income maintenance payments to all eligible workers. In contrast, appropriation of training funds is considered a "capped entitlement," for which Congress sets an appropriation cap on the amount of total funding for training. It is inconsistent to make entitled income maintenance payments conditional on (limited) training enrollment.[26] In addition, given the training appropriation cap, all workers may not receive the same amount or quality of training. Raising the training appropriation cap would begin to address this problem.

Health Coverage Tax Credit

Currently, workers participating in TAA can receive a 65 percent advanceable, refundable tax credit to help cover the cost of maintaining health insurance during the period of unemployment. Anecdotal evidence suggests that workers find the Health Coverage Tax Credit (HCTC) to be the most valuable form of assistance offered under the TAA program. On the other hand, the GAO (2006a) finds that many workers claim they cannot afford to pay the remaining 35 percent in order to maintain their health insurance. To remedy this, the HCTC could be increased to 75 percent. In addition, states could be encouraged to offer some assistance, thereby reducing workers' out-of-pocket expenditures even more.

Wage Insurance

Wage insurance offers assistance that is tailored to actual earnings losses. In order to be effective, wage-loss insurance must be a complement to traditional UI, since it only assists those workers who find new jobs. Under the program, eligible workers would receive some fraction— perhaps half—of their weekly earnings loss over a specific period.

For example, between 1979 and 2001, the average weekly wage before layoff for workers displaced from manufacturing industries was $396.88. At the same time, the average weekly wage for those laid off from nonmanufacturing jobs was $368.65. For those workers who found new jobs, the average percentage loss in earnings was 29.2 percent for manufacturing workers and 18.6 percent for nonmanufacturing workers. Had a wage-loss insurance program been in place, manufacturing workers would have received approximately $6,000 over a two-year period, which is 15 percent of their prelayoff wage. Nonmanufacturing workers would have received approximately $3,600 over a two-year period, which is equal to 9 percent of their prelayoff wage.

Despite its benefits, wage insurance is not a perfect solution to addressing the costs associated with unemployment. Structuring a program with a relatively short eligibility period, which would start with the date of job loss, creates a reemployment incentive and addresses one of the most commonly expressed UI concerns, but it also limits the compensatory nature of the program. Displaced worker earnings losses are long-term (earnings losses exist for five to six years after job loss), well beyond the two years covered by ATAA.

The cost of a wage insurance program depends on the number of eligible workers, the earnings losses of those reemployed at lower pay, and the duration of unemployment prior to reemployment. Other critical program characteristics include the duration of wage insurance payments, the annual cap on program payments, and the replacement rate. It has been estimated that the cost for a program with a two-year duration, a 50 percent replacement rate, and a $10,000 annual cap for all dislocated workers would be around $4 billion.

The Trade Act of 2002 established a wage insurance program, formally called Alternative Trade Adjustment Assistance (ATAA). ATAA encourages and provides financial assistance to workers who return to work within 26 weeks after separation. It is possible that their new employers may provide on-the-job training, which is seen by many as more effective than classroom training.

Financing an Expanded Program

The Office of Management and Budget reports that current spending on TAA is approximately $1 billion a year. Kletzer and Rosen (2005) estimate that making all workers that have been displaced from import-competing manufacturing industries eligible for TAA would cost approximately $3 billion a year. Including service workers could potentially double the price tag. Increasing the HCTC and reducing the wage insurance age requirement could add another $1 billion to the total cost. These estimates are very tentative, but total spending on an assistance program sketched here could be in the range of $6–$7 billion a year.

One immediate proposal for financing the additional costs would be to raise the maximum taxable wage base currently used in calculating the UI payroll tax (the Federal Unemployment Tax Act, or FUTA). In addition to raising revenue to offset the additional expense associated with expanding the program, raising the maximum taxable wage base would also make the UI tax more progressive. The maximum wage base has been fixed at $7,000 for more than 20 years. Adjusting the base to $45,000, over time, could be expected to raise an additional $9 billion, enough to finance a program expansion.

A More Expansive Policy Reform

Should the political will exist (or be found) to engage in a more comprehensive reform of the nation's worker assistance programs, the first step would be UI reform.[27] The original UI program was designed to offset income losses during cyclical periods of temporary involuntary unemployment. In contrast, current workers face long-term structural unemployment. The existing UI system is inadequate in responding to these current labor market conditions.

The current UI system does not assist workers who seek part-time employment, workers who voluntarily leave one job in order to take another, or workers who experience long-term unemployment. New entrants and reentrants into the labor market are not currently eligible for UI, since these two groups of unemployed do not fit well with one of the program's original objectives, i.e., insuring against the risk of involuntary job loss. Covering these workers would raise issues concerning the amount and duration of assistance, since they may not have relevant work experience.

Underlining these macroeconomic changes to the U.S. labor market is a shift from traditional employer-based full-time employment to an increased reliance on contingent and part-time employment. The shift to these nontraditional forms of employment reflects additional shortfalls in the current UI program. A system designed to provide income support during temporary layoffs for workers who were permanently attached to a single employer is not well designed for a labor market with considerable self-employment and contingent, part-time, and low-wage employment.

Although there clearly remain some differences in local labor market conditions, the current pressures on the U.S. labor market are becoming more national. State differences in the incidence and experience of unemployment have narrowed considerably. Local labor market conditions primarily affect the prospects for reemployment. Given the increasingly national nature of the labor market, UI would be better able to meet its original objectives if the federal government played a more prominent role in this state-federal partnership.

In addition to inequities created by disparate rules across states, a significant downside of the current federal-state partnership is the states' real or perceived fears that program generosity will result in adverse changes to their business environment. Increased federal leadership would avoid interstate competition and a race to the bottom in program benefits.

An increased leadership role for the federal government would be characterized by expanding standards for eligibility, duration, and level of benefits, and for financing the program. Recommendations include the following:

- Standardize the base period for determining eligibility to the past four complete calendar quarters prior to job loss. This change, already implemented by a number of states, updates the operational definition of labor market attachment and reflects the reduced time needed to report earnings.

- Use hours rather than earnings in determining eligibility. Shifting the determination of eligibility to hours instead of earnings would bring more low- and moderate-wage workers—who often most need help during periods of unemployment—into the system.

- Harmonize nonmonetary eligibility standards. The patchwork of nonmonetary eligibility criteria, in which some states consider voluntary separations for good cause while others do not, creates unnecessary complexity and inequities in the system.

- Enable reentrants to the labor force, if it is determined retroactively that they were eligible at the time of job loss or separation, to be eligible to receive the benefits they would have received at the time of job loss. In a fluid labor market, many workers may leave the labor force for some time (e.g., to care for a child or parent) and then return. If the workers were eligible for UI when they separated from their previous job but did not claim them at that time, they should be eligible for benefits when they return to the labor force.

- Amend the work test to allow job search for part-time employment. Part-time work is a common feature of the current labor market, accounting for 16 percent of employment in July 2006, and unemployed workers should not be disqualified from receiving benefits because they are searching for part-time work.

The share of unemployed workers who actually received assistance under the UI program averaged 37 percent between 1980 and 2005. The proposals outlined above are designed to increase the number and share of unemployed workers eligible to receive assistance. Table 4.1 reports estimates for the costs associated with raising the recipiency rate in increments to 50 percent.

A more comprehensive reform would bring the fuller set of assistance programs into the twenty-first century. The basic structure of current UI was designed for a system of single employers, full-time work, and cyclical temporary layoff. The workforce today faces permanent job loss, part-time or contingent work, and self-employment. In addition, technological change and intensified competition from globalization create increased pressures and anxieties.

CONCLUSION

The U.S. debate about trade and immigration is broadening to include higher skilled workers. The growing services trade potentially broadens the group of workers at risk of displacement. Migration and immigration of skilled workers also may be perceived as a threat to higher skilled U.S. workers.

Trade-displaced manufacturing workers may lose over $50 billion in lifetime earnings, and there are additional service workers' losses. Federal spending on Trade Adjustment Assistance is less than $2 billion annually, due in part to restrictions on workers' eligibility. Because the TAA statute refers to "imported goods," virtually all displaced service workers are deemed ineligible for TAA.

Most reviews conclude that immigration's effects on native U.S. workers are small, in terms of wages and employment. High skill immigrants help the U.S. maintain technological leadership.

Table 4.1 Estimated Costs Associated with Increasing the Recipiency Rate

Recipiency rate	Increase in number of workers eligible (thousands)[a]	Increase in total benefits paid (billions $)[a]
0.40	220	1.6
0.45	620	4.5
0.50	1,000	7.4

[a] Increase in workers and costs (benefits paid) relative to 25-year average.
SOURCE: Kletzer and Rosen (2006).

Strengthening programs of adjustment assistance is essential for maintaining any significant level of public support for globalization efforts. Eligibility for Trade Adjustment Assistance should be expanded to include services workers, and additional training dollars should be made available to program participants. The wage insurance program started in 2002, which provides trade-displaced workers over age 50 with up to half the difference between their old and new wages, should be evaluated, with the possibility of expanding eligibility to workers in their 40s. Reforms to the unemployment insurance (UI) system should include allowances for reentrants and part-time employment and the addition of wage-loss insurance for all displaced workers.

Skilled migration is critical for U.S. innovation. Ensuring that temporary migrant workers have basic labor market rights, such as free mobility, may help lessen problems from more open immigration.

Openness to flows of goods, services, people, and investment brings economic benefits to Americans. The same flows are also associated with economic costs, especially for competing workers, firms, and communities. Thus, it is the distribution of benefits and costs that is contentious and controversial. While the academic debate remains lively on the distributional questions and can be expected to continue, there is a clear need to strengthen the programs and policies in place to assist workers who are confronting job and income losses and the uncertainties created by globalization and other structural change.

Notes

Financial support from the Labor and Employment Research Fund of the University of California Office of the President is gratefully acknowledged. Lauren Malone provided excellent research assistance. I am grateful to Susan Houseman and Timothy Bartik for their comments and suggestions.

1. Gains to all countries do not necessarily follow on theoretical grounds. In addition, trade liberalization is only guaranteed to enhance welfare under certain limited theoretical conditions (including that the home economy is small, relative to world markets).
2. Broda and Weinstein (2005) examine in more detail the gains from expanded varieties of goods.
3. Gresser (2002) showed that textile tariffs apply disproportionately to lower-end garments, purchased mainly by lower-income consumers.
4. Gomory and Baumol (2000) present a model with similar outcomes, where gains from trade can shrink as competitors gain technological expertise.
5. See Rodrik (2006) for other skeptical thoughts on the benefits of free trade. He sees the evidence of the past 15 years as yielding no one single recipe for developing country growth, including policies of open trade.
6. TAA has held center stage in the limited mix of worker adjustment policies since the mid-1970s. Overlapping with the evaluation literature, a number of papers consider the evidence on TAA and training for displaced workers. See Decker and Corson (1995) and Leigh (1990).
7. The two-sides-of-the-same-coin analogy fits well in economy theory. In models of international trade based on differing factor endowments across countries, trade in goods and services or movements of factors of production can equalize prices and earnings. In an essay on international labor mobility, Freeman (2006b) notes that Mundell (1957) provides a model of substitutability between commodity movements and factor movements. If country A has more labor relative to capital than country B, A can send labor to B directly through immigration or indirectly through the export of labor-intensive goods. Immigration restrictions should therefore result in an increase in trade.
8. Grossman (1982) was the first in this approach. Card (2005) provides an updated summary.
9. Most of the immigration literature focuses on impacts on lesser-skilled workers. Friedberg (2001) studied mass migration from the former Soviet Union to Israel, finding little effect on the earnings and employment of natives. The H-1B literature is even thinner, given data limitations.
10. Net exports (of either services or goods) is the difference between the value of exports and the value of imports—i.e., exports (in $) minus imports (in $).
11. The routineness of work, or the codification of tasks, is a characteristic emphasized by Autor, Levy, and Murnane (2003).
12. Bhagwati, Panagariya and Srinivasan (2004) seem to mean "offshoring" when

they use "outsourcing." Their outsourcing is arms-length and located in a foreign country.

13. As discussed in more detail below, the H-1B nonimmigrant work visa allows employers to temporarily employ foreign workers in the United States in a specialty occupation.

14. GAO (2006c) is the source of information for this section.

15. Over the recent past, employer demand for H-1B visas has greatly exceeded the cap. For fiscal 2007, the application cap was reached in May 2006. For fiscal 2008, first-day applications exceeded the cap, and Citizenship and Immigration Services (CIS) received a record 150,000 applications as of late afternoon on April 2, 2007. For the first time, applications will be placed in a computer-generated lottery (Marcucci 2007).

16. As noted in GAO (2006c), these additional requirements applied from January 19, 2001, to September 30, 2003. The provision requiring these attestations expired, and was only reinstated on March 8, 2005. From October 1, 2003, to March 7, 2005, H-1B–dependent employers and willful-violator employers were able to hire H1-B workers even if U.S. workers were displaced, and they did not have to undertake efforts to hire U.S. workers.

17. The L-1 nonimmigrant visa is for intracompany transfers.

18. Freeman (2006b) proposes tripling the number of NSF graduate fellowships and increasing the size of the award to encourage advanced study in science and engineering fields.

19. See Matloff (2003) for a survey.

20. The problem with LCA data is that observations are applications, not actual visa issuances for workers. Wage information is the submitted prevailing wage, not the wage paid.

21. Chapter 1 of Borjas (1999b) contains a thoughtful discussion on the framing of a U.S. immigration policy.

22. Focusing on California, Peri (2007) finds that immigrants are imperfect substitutes for natives with similar education and age and that immigrant flows stimulated, rather than harmed, the demand for—and the wages of—most U.S. native workers.

23. The two bills are "The H-1B and L-1 Visa Fraud and Abuse Prevention Act of 2007," introduced by Senators Dick Durbin (D-IL) and Chuck Grassley (R-IA) and "The Skilled Worker Immigration and Fairness Act of 2007," introduced by Senators Joe Lieberman (I-CT) and Chuck Hagel (R-NE).

24. See Destler (2005) for a broader discussion of a desirable direction for American trade policy.

25. Based on author's estimates from the 2004 and 2006 Displaced Worker Surveys. Overall manufacturing employment has declined by nearly 18 percent since 2000, while employment in the services sector has grown by 5.4 percent.

26. Workers can apply for a waiver to excuse them from the requirement of enrolling in training in order to receive income maintenance payments.

27. This section borrows heavily from Kletzer and Rosen (2006).

References

Andrews, Edmund L. 2007. "Economic View: Why Wage Insurance Is Dividing Democrats." *New York Times*, March 18, C:6. http://www.nytimes.com/2007/03/18/business/yourmoney/18view.html (accessed July 11, 2007).

Autor, David H., Frank Levy, and Richard J. Murnane. 2003. "The Skill Content of Recent Technological Change: An Empirical Exploration." *Quarterly Journal of Economics* 118(4): 1279–1334.

Bardhan, Ashok Deo, and Cynthia A. Kroll. 2003. "The New Wave of Outsourcing." Fisher Center Research Report No. 1103. Berkeley, CA: Fisher Center for Real Estate and Urban Economics, University of California, Berkeley.

Bhagwati, Jagdish, Arvind Panagariya, and T.N. Srinivasan. 2004. "The Muddles over Outsourcing." *Journal of Economic Perspectives* 18(4): 93–114.

Blinder, Alan S. 2006. "Offshoring: The Next Industrial Revolution?" *Foreign Affairs* 85(2): 113–128.

———. 2007. "How Many U.S. Jobs Might Be Offshorable?" CEPS Working Paper No. 142. Princeton, NJ: Princeton University.

Borjas, George J. 1999a. "The Economic Analysis of Immigration." In *Handbook of Labor Economics*, Orley C. Ashenfelter and David Card, eds. Vol. 3A. Amsterdam: Elsevier, pp. 1697–1760.

———. 1999b. *Heaven's Door: Immigration Policy and the American Economy*. Princeton: Princeton University Press.

———. 2003. "The Labor Demand Curve *Is* Downward Sloping: Reexamining the Impact of Immigration on the Labor Market." *Quarterly Journal of Economics* 118(4): 1335–1374.

———. 2005a. "The Labor Market Impact of High-Skill Immigration." NBER Working Paper No. 11217. Cambridge, MA: National Bureau of Economic Research.

Bradford, Scott C., Paul L.E. Grieco, and Gary Clyde Hufbauer. 2005. "The Payoff to America from Global Integration." In *The United States and the World Economy: Foreign Economic Policy for the Next Decade,* C. Fred Bergsten and the Institute for International Economics, eds. Washington, DC: Institute for International Economics, pp. 65–109.

Brainard, Lael, Robert E. Litan, and Nicholas Warren. 2006. "A Fairer Deal for America's Workers in a New Era of Offshoring." In *Brookings Trade Forum 2005: Offshoring White-Collar Work*, Susan M. Collins and Lael Brainard, eds. Washington, DC: Brookings Institution, pp. 427–456.

Broda, Christian, and David Weinstein. 2005. "Are We Underestimating the

Gains from Globalization for the United States?" *Current Issues in Economics and Finance* 11(4): 1–7.

Card, David. 2005. "Is the New Immigration Really So Bad?" NBER Working Paper No. 11547. Cambridge, MA: National Bureau of Economic Research.

Citizenship and Immigration Services (CIS). 2006. *Characteristics of Specialty Occupation Workers (H-1B): Fiscal Year 2005*. Washington, DC: U.S. Department of Homeland Security, Citizenship and Immigration Services.

Committee on Science and Technology. 2006. *Globalization and the American Workforce*. Washington, DC: Committee on Science and Technology, U.S. House of Representatives. http://sciencedems.house.gov/investigations/investigations_detail.aspx?NewsID=1167 (accessed July 30, 2007).

Decker, Paul T., and Walter Corson. 1995. "International Trade and Worker Displacement: Evaluation of the Trade Adjustment Assistance Program." *Industrial and Labor Relations Review* 48(4): 758–774.

Destler, I.M. 2005. *American Trade Politics*. 4th ed. Washington, DC: Institute for International Economics.

Dossani, Rafiq, and Martin Kenney. 2003. "Went for Cost, Stayed for Quality? Moving the Back Office to India." Berkeley Roundtable on the International Economy Working Paper No. 1020. Stanford, CA: Asia-Pacific Research Center, Stanford University.

Freeman, Richard B. 2006a. "Does Globalization of the Scientific/Engineering Workforce Threaten U.S. Economic Leadership?" In *Innovation Policy and the Economy*, Adam B. Jaffe, Josh Lerner, and Scott Stern, eds. Vol. 6. Cambridge, MA: National Bureau of Economic Research, pp. 123–157.

———. 2006b. "People Flows in Globalization." *Journal of Economic Perspectives* 20(2): pp. 145–170.

Friedberg, Rachel M. 2001. "The Impact of Mass Migration on the Israeli Labor Market." *Quarterly Journal of Economics* 116(4): 1373–1408.

Friedberg, Rachel M., and Jennifer Hunt. 1995. "The Impact of Immigrants on Host Country Wages, Employment and Growth." *Journal of Economic Perspectives* 9(2): 23–44.

Gereffi, Gary. 2005. *The New Offshoring of Jobs and Global Development*. Seventh ILO Social Policy Lecture. Geneva: International Institute for Labour Studies and International Labour Office.

Gomory, Ralph E., and William J. Baumol. 2000. *Global Trade and Conflicting National Interests*. Cambridge, MA: MIT Press.

Government Accountability Office (GAO). 2004. *Trade Adjustment Assistance: Reforms Have Accelerated Training Enrollment, but Implementation Challenges Remain*. GAO-04-1012. Report to the Committee on Finance, U.S. Senate. Washington, DC: GAO.

———. 2006a. *Trade Adjustment Assistance: Most Workers in Five Layoffs Received Services, but Better Outreach Needed on New Benefits.* GAO-06-43. Report to Congressional Requesters. Washington, DC: GAO.

———. 2006b. *Trade Adjustment Assistance: Labor Should Take Action to Ensure Performance Data Are Complete, Accurate, and Accessible.* GAO-06-496. Report to the Committee on Finance, U.S. Senate. Washington, DC: GAO.

———. 2006c. *H-1B Visa Program: Labor Could Improve Its Oversight and Increase Information Sharing with Homeland Security.* GAO-06-720. Report to Congressional Requesters. Washington, DC: GAO.

GPO Access. 2007. *Economic Report of the President: 2007 Report Spreadsheet Tables.* Washington, DC: Government Printing Office. http://www.gpoaccess.gov/eop/tables07.html (accessed July 30, 2007).

Gresser, Edward. 2002. "Toughest on the Poor: Tariffs, Taxes and the Single Mom." Policy Report. Washington, DC: Progressive Policy Institute.

Grossman, Jean Baldwin. 1982. "The Substitutability of Natives and Immigrants in Production." *Review of Economics and Statistics* 64(4): 596–603.

Hira, Ron. 2007. "Outsourcing America's Technology and Knowledge Jobs: High-Skill Guest Worker Visas are Currently Hurting Rather than Helping Keep Jobs at Home." EPI Briefing Paper No. 187. Washington, DC: Economic Policy Institute

Jensen, J. Bradford, and Lori G. Kletzer. 2006. "Tradable Services: Understanding the Scope and Impact of Services Offshoring." In *Brookings Trade Forum 2005: Offshoring White-Collar Work*, Susan M. Collins and Lael Brainard, eds. Washington, DC: Brookings Institution, pp. 75–116.

———. 2007. "Measuring Tradable Services and the Task Content of Offshorable Services Jobs." Unpublished manuscript. University of California, Santa Cruz, and Peterson Institute for International Economics, Washington, DC.

Kauffman Foundation. 2007. *On the Road to an Entrepreneurial Economy: A Research and Policy Guide.* Kansas City, MO: Kauffman Foundation.

Kletzer, Lori G. 2001. *Job Loss from Imports: Measuring the Costs.* Washington DC: Peterson Institute for International Economics.

Kletzer, Lori G., and Howard Rosen. 2005. "Easing the Adjustment Burden on U.S. Workers." In *The United States and the World Economy: Foreign Economic Policy for the Next Decade*, C. Fred Bergsten, ed. Washington, DC: Institute for International Economics, pp. 313–342.

———. 2006. "Reforming Unemployment Insurance for the Twenty-First Century Workforce." Hamilton Project Discussion Paper 2006-06. Washington, DC: Brookings Institution.

Kling, Jeffrey R. 2006. "Fundamental Restructuring of Unemployment Insurance: Wage-Loss Insurance and Temporary Earnings Replacement Accounts." Hamilton Project Discussion Paper 2006-05. Washington, DC: The Brookings Institution.

Leigh, Duane E. 1990. *Does Training Work for Displaced Workers? A Survey of Existing Evidence.* Kalamazoo, MI: W.E. Upjohn Institute for Employment Research.

Lewis, Ethan G. 2005. "Immigration, Skill Mix, and the Choice of Technique." FRB Philadelphia Working Paper No. 05-8. Philadelphia: Federal Reserve Bank of Philadelphia.

Lowell, B. Lindsay. 1999. "Skilled Temporary Specialty Workers in the United States." *People and Place* 7(1): 24–32.

———. 2000a. "The Demand and New Legislation for Skilled Temporary Workers (H-1Bs) in the United States." *People and Place* 8(4): 29–35.

———. 2000b. "H-1B Temporary Workers: Estimating the Population." CCIS Working Paper No. 12. La Jolla, CA: Center for Comparative Immigration Studies, University of California, San Diego.

———. 2001a. "The Foreign Temporary Workforce and Shortages in Information Technology." In *The International Migration of the Highly Skilled: Demand, Supply, and Development Consequences in Sending and Receiving Countries*, Wayne A. Cornelius, Thomas J. Espenshade, and Idean Salehyan, eds. La Jolla, CA: Center for Comparative Immigration Studies, University of California, San Diego, pp. 131–160.

———. 2001b. "Skilled Temporary and Permanent Immigrants in the United States." *Population Research and Policy Review* 20(1–2): 33–58.

Lowenstein, Roger. 2006. "What Is She Really Doing to American Jobs and Wages?" *The New York Times Magazine*, July 9, pp. 36–43.

Marcucci, Michele R. 2007. "H-1B Demand Exceeds Limit: Lottery Will Determine Which Requests from Employers are Accepted." *San Jose Mercury News*, April 4, C:1.

Marshall, Ray. 2007. "Getting Immigration Reform Right." EPI Briefing Paper No. 186. Washington, DC: Economic Policy Institute.

Matloff, Norman. 2003. "On the Need for Reform of the H-1B Non-Immigrant Work Visa in Computer-Related Occupations." *University of Michigan Journal of Law Reform* 36(4): 1–99.

Mundell, Robert A. 1957. "International Trade and Factor Mobility." *American Economic Review* 47(3): 321–335.

National Research Council. 2001. *Building a Workforce for the Information Economy.* Washington, DC: National Academies Press.

Panagariya, Arvind. 2004. "Why the Recent Samuelson Article is NOT about Offshore Outsourcing." Policy Paper. New York: Columbia University School of International and Public Affairs. http://www.columbia.edu/

~ap2231/Policy%20Papers/Samuelson%20JEP%20(Summer%202004) _Not %20on%20Outsourcing.htm (accessed July 11, 2007).

Peri, Giovanni. 2007. "Immigrants' Complementarities and Native Wages: Evidence from California." NBER Working Paper No. 12956. Cambridge, MA: National Bureau of Economic Research.

Richardson, J. David. 2004. "Some Measurable Costs and Benefits of Economic Globalization for Americans." In *Globalization and Its Outcomes*, John O'Loughlin, Lynn Staeheli, and Edward Greenberg, eds. New York: Guilford Press, pp. 182–192.

Rodrik, Dani. 2006. "Goodbye Washington Consensus, Hello Washington Confusion? A Review of the World Bank's Economic Growth in the 1990s: Learning from a Decade of Reform." *Journal of Economic Literature* 44(4): 973–987.

Rosen, Howard F. 2007. "The Case for Globalization Adjustment Assistance." Unpublished manuscript. Peterson Institute for International Economics, Washington, DC.

Samuelson, Paul A. 2004. "Where Ricardo and Mill Rebut and Confirm Arguments of Mainstream Economists Supporting Globalization." *Journal of Economic Perspectives* 18(3): 135–146.

Saxenian, AnnaLee. 2002. "Silicon Valley's New Immigrant High-Growth Entrepreneurs." *Economic Development Quarterly* 16(1): 20–31.

Scheve, Kenneth F., and Matthew J. Slaughter. 2001. *Globalization and the Perceptions of American Workers*. Washington, DC: Peterson Institute for International Economics.

Wadhwa, Vivek, AnnaLee Saxenian, Ben Rissing, and Gary Gereffi. 2007. *America's New Immigrant Entrepreneurs*. Durham, NC: Pratt School of Engineering, Master of Engineering Management Program, Duke University. http:// memp.pratt.duke.edu/downloads/americas_new_immigrant_entrepreneurs .pdf (accessed July 11, 2007).

Zavodny, Madeline. 2003. "The H-1B Program and Its Effects on Information Technology Workers." *Federal Reserve Bank of Atlanta Economic Review* Third Quarter(2003): 1–11.

5
Removing Barriers to
Work for Older Americans

Katharine G. Abraham
University of Maryland and *NBER*

Susan N. Houseman
W.E. Upjohn Institute

Over the next dozen years, as the baby boomers age, the share of the population aged 55 and older is projected to grow dramatically, from 21.4 percent in 2000 to 25.1 percent by 2010 and 29.5 percent by 2020. Over the same period, the share of the population aged 25–54—the age group that historically has been attached most strongly to the labor market—is projected to fall from 43.4 percent in 2000 to 40.8 percent in 2010 and 37.7 percent in 2020 (U.S. Census Bureau 2002). Among other anticipated consequences, the aging of the population threatens the solvency of both the Social Security and the Medicare systems. Reflecting concerns over these trends, there is a growing consensus that increased employment among older Americans would be in the public interest.

Congress already has taken several important steps to encourage work at older ages. Recent changes to the law allow Social Security beneficiaries to earn more money without having their benefits reduced and permit workers under the normal retirement age to phase into retirement by collecting pension benefits while working a reduced schedule. Congress also has raised the age at which workers may collect full Social Security benefits—in effect making benefits less generous—and this too can be expected to increase older Americans' desire to work. Developments in the private sector, most notably the shift from defined benefit retirement plans to less generous defined contribution plans and the shrinking share of employers who offer retiree health benefits, have reinforced the effects of public policy changes. Americans are not saving enough to compensate for the reduction in public and private retirement benefits. If they wish to maintain their standard of living, many Americans will need to work later in life.

Although recent changes to federal policy have altered financial incentives in ways that should make it more attractive for older Americans to work, these policies have not addressed the barriers to finding suitable employment that older workers frequently face. Survey evidence shows that a high percentage of older Americans already wish to remain employed rather than withdrawing fully from the labor market, but many want or need to work fewer hours or to find less physically demanding jobs. Our research indicates that the need to make a job transition, particularly a job transition that involves a change of employer, is a major impediment to continued employment for seniors. In addition, as job stability has declined and the incidence of worker dislocation has risen over the last 20 years, a growing number of older Americans have found themselves involuntarily out of work and searching for a new job late in life. Many are unsuccessful in their search.

Although labor force participation among older women has grown in the last two decades, it has declined among men in their fifties. The decline in employment among older, less-educated men has been precipitous: labor force participation among men in their fifties with less than a high school education fell by 11 percentage points over the last two decades. The current low rate of labor force participation among men in their fifties—traditionally a group considered to be of preretirement age—does not portend well for increasing the labor force participation of these cohorts as they age.

Why is it so difficult for many older Americans, particularly the less educated, to transition to new employment? Part of the explanation may be that older workers—especially those who have worked for a single employer for an extended period and thus have no recent experience with having to find a job—do not have a clear idea about how to search for employment. Employer reluctance to hire older workers is another factor. Unwarranted stereotyping accounts for some of this reluctance to hire older workers, but more legitimate concerns about older workers as potential employees play a role as well. Lack of technical skills, low perceived returns to training, and high health insurance costs are among the most common reservations that employers cite about hiring older workers.

Job training and employment programs, currently funded under the Workforce Investment Act (WIA) and, to a lesser degree, the Trade Adjustment Assistance Act (TAA) and the Older Americans Act (OAA), are the primary active labor market programs through which the federal government seeks to overcome impediments to employment faced by workers. In real terms, federal funding for these programs has fallen significantly over the last decade. Moreover, services to older workers have been deemphasized under WIA compared to what they were under the Job Training Partnership Act (JTPA), WIA's predecessor, despite the fact that the population is aging and older workers' needs for such services likely have risen. Some states and private organizations have begun to take steps to address the impediments to employment that older workers face. Many of these initiatives have focused on public relations efforts to reduce what program managers perceive to be widespread discrimination by employers against older workers. Some state and private initiatives also have sought to improve the delivery of employment and training services to older job seekers, but funding for these initiatives has been limited.

Failure to develop and implement effective programs to retrain older workers and place them in jobs has high public costs. Among other concerns is the fact that many of those who fail to find work end up on public assistance in the form of Social Security Disability Insurance (SSDI), at least in some cases not because they cannot work but because they are unable to *find* work. Partly as a result, the costs of the SSDI program are soaring. Although the difficulties that older workers experience as they seek to transition to new jobs will not be easy to overcome, we propose the following five policy steps in order to begin to address the problem seriously:

1) Increase funding for employment and training programs that serve older workers.

2) Modify performance standards for WIA service providers to eliminate disincentives to serve older workers.

3) Experiment with promising approaches to serving an aging workforce more effectively, including

   • Improving outreach to seniors and to their potential employers,

- Posting older-worker specialists who are knowledgeable about the employment and training issues seniors often confront at "one-stop" centers, and

- Providing specialized technical skills training for seniors.

4) Evaluate promising initiatives using rigorous methodologies to determine whether and to what extent they improve older workers' employment prospects and would be cost-effective if adopted nationally.

5) Reform health care financing to reduce disincentives to hiring older workers.

We elaborate upon these proposals later in the chapter.

RECENT TRENDS IN THE LABOR FORCE PARTICIPATION RATES OF OLDER AMERICANS

Various researchers have noted the increasing rate of labor force participation among older Americans in recent decades (Burtless and Quinn 2002; Munnell and Sass 2007; Purcell 2005; Quinn 1999). Although the share of men aged 55 and older who were active in the labor force fell from the early 1900s through the mid-1980s, labor force participation rates leveled off beginning in 1985 and have risen slightly since the mid-1990s. Among women, the pre-1985 trend towards earlier retirement was offset by rising labor force participation overall, with the result that labor force participation rates among women 55 and older were relatively flat from the mid-1960s through the mid-1980s. Since the mid-1980s, labor force participation among older women aged 55 and older has trended upwards (Federal Interagency Forum on Aging-Related Statistics 2006).

These aggregate trends mask important differences, however, in trends across education groups and across more refined age categories. Although labor force participation rates have increased since the 1990s among older women in all age groupings (Figure 5.1), the increase in male labor force participation in recent years has occurred only among men over age 60 (Figure 5.2B) and has been most pronounced among men over age 65 (Figure 5.2C). As shown in Figure 5.2A, labor force participation among men in their fifties—men traditionally considered to be of preretirement age—has actually continued to fall.

One possible explanation for the decline in labor force participation among men in their fifties could be that their financial situation has improved, either because their lifetime earnings have risen or because their wives are now more likely to be employed, making earlier retirement a more viable option. Examination of labor force participation trends by education level suggests that this is not what has happened. The labor force participation rate for college-educated men in their fifties has been fairly stable over the last 20 years but has declined for those with lower levels of education, especially those with less than a high school education. Between 1984 and 2005, the labor force participation rate for men aged 50–59 with less than a high school education dropped by 11 percentage points, and the decline for men aged 50–54 was almost as large as that for men 55–59. This drop can be explained neither by rising income levels (real wages for less-educated men have fallen) nor by increased spousal employment (labor force participation rates for women with less than a high school education have been stagnant). Below we discuss some of the factors that underlie these trends and the special policy challenges they pose.

AMERICAN WORKERS WILL WANT OR NEED TO WORK LATER IN LIFE THAN IN THE RECENT PAST

For the past few decades, the health of older Americans has been improving, while changes in the mix of occupations associated with the growth of the service economy, as well as technological advances affecting many blue-collar jobs, have made work less physically demanding. In addition, life expectancies have increased steadily, increasing in turn the financial resources required to maintain individuals' standard of living over their lifespan (Munnell and Sass 2007; Technical Panel on Assumptions and Methods 2003). In the past, rising incomes and generous public and private retirement benefits made it attractive for Americans to retire at younger ages despite their increased life expectancy (Costa 1998). In the future, however, financial incentives are likely to make it more attractive for Americans to keep working longer.

Figure 5.1 Trends in Labor Force Participation Rates of Older Americans, 1984–2005, by Gender and Age (Women)

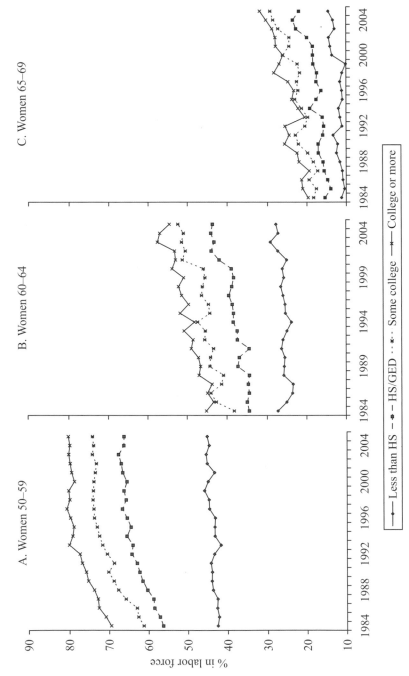

A. Women 50–59

B. Women 60–64

C. Women 65–69

% in labor force

—◆— Less than HS   – ■ – HS/GED   ··✻·· Some college   —✕— College or more

Figure 5.2 Trends in Labor Force Participation Rates of Older Americans, 1984–2005, by Gender and Age (Men)

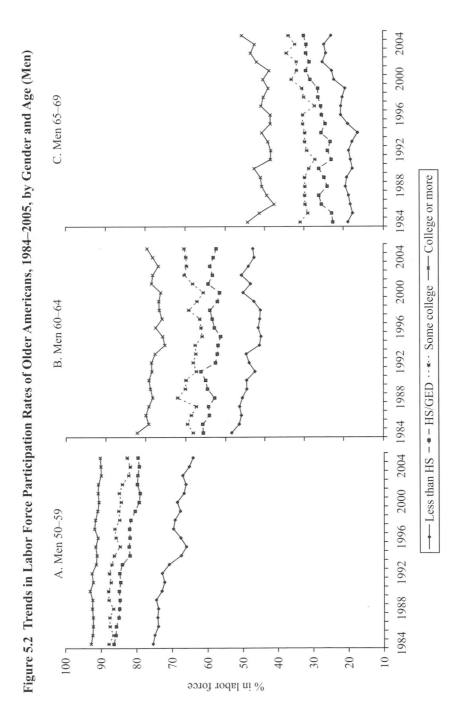

Social Security Reforms

Several features of the Social Security system discouraged work at older ages in the past. Recent changes have greatly reduced if not eliminated these disincentives. First, the Social Security earnings test, which determines any reduction in current monthly benefits for those with earnings from employment, has been liberalized for those between age 62 and the normal retirement age and eliminated for those above the normal retirement age. These changes allow beneficiaries to earn more without experiencing a reduction in their current Social Security benefits. Although under previous law those whose benefits were reduced because of the earnings test could expect to receive higher future benefits, this fact seems to have been poorly understood by benefit recipients, and consequently the liberalization of the earnings test appears to be one of the factors responsible for the recent increase in labor force participation at older ages (Munnell and Sass 2007).

Second, new rules regarding the delayed retirement credit are being phased in. When fully implemented in 2008, these rules will approximately equate the actuarial present value of Social Security benefits received by those who choose to delay receipt of benefits to the value for those who begin collecting benefits at the normal retirement age. By reducing the penalty previously imposed on those who chose to continue working past the normal retirement age, the delayed retirement credit appears already to have increased work among those age 65 and older (Munnell and Sass, 2007).

A third change whose full effect has not yet been felt is the scheduled increase in the normal retirement age—the age at which individuals may begin to receive full benefits—from 65 to 67. Although workers still may retire and begin to collect Social Security benefits at 62, their monthly benefit amount will be proportionately lower than would have been true in the past, reflecting the larger actuarial reduction needed to equate the expected present value of lifetime benefits for a person retiring at age 62 to that for someone retiring at age 67 as opposed to age 65. This is a reduction in benefits that should increase the number of Americans who want to work at older ages (Munnell and Sass 2007; Thompson 2004).

Changes to Private Sector Retirement Plans

Roughly half of workers of retirement age are covered by an employer pension plan, but the character of those plans has changed a great deal. Data from the Survey of Consumer Finance show that the share of those with a pension covered by a defined benefit plan fell from 87 percent to 44 percent between 1983 and 1998; over the same time period, the share covered by a defined contribution plan rose from 40 percent to 79 percent (Friedberg and Webb 2005). Analysis of data collected from employers by the Bureau of Labor Statistics (BLS) shows that the shift away from defined benefit plans towards defined contribution plans continued through 2005. In addition, many employers offering defined benefit plans have converted them to cash balance or pension equity plans that in important respects are more like a defined contribution plan than the traditional defined benefit plan (Costo 2006).

The ongoing shift in employer-sponsored retirement plans from defined benefit to defined contribution plans is providing additional financial incentives to workers to retire at an older age. The traditional defined benefit plan imposes a significant financial penalty for working past a certain age; in contrast, the present value of retirement benefits under a defined contribution plan continues to grow so long as the individual continues to work (Friedberg and Webb 2005). Further, although this would not have to be the case, defined contribution plans tend to be less generous than defined benefit plans in practice. Ghilarducci and Sun (2006) find that employers contribute significantly less per capita under defined contribution plans than under defined benefit plans. Similarly, the cash balance plans offered by employers who have converted from traditional defined benefit plans generally have been less generous than the plans they replaced (Government Accountability Office 2005a). Research has concluded that participants in defined contribution plans retire later on average—perhaps as much as two years later—than participants in defined benefit plans and that the shift towards defined contribution plans has been an important reason for the recent increases in labor force participation at older ages (Friedberg and Webb 2005; Munnell, Cahill, and Jivan 2003).

New rules regarding phased retirement plans included in the Pension Protection Act of 2006 also may increase the share of older individuals who choose to work.[1] The new rules allow in-service distributions from defined benefit pension plans to employees aged 62 and older, meaning that they are allowed to reduce their hours on the job while beginning to collect pension benefits, something that had not previously been permitted for employees below the normal retirement age specified in their employer's pension plan.[2]

Falling Retiree Health Benefit Coverage

Paralleling these changes in pension benefits has been a decline in the coverage and generosity of retiree health insurance. As medical-care costs have risen, so too have the costs of retiree health insurance. In addition, the rules that govern how firms must account for those costs have changed in a way that makes it less attractive for firms to offer a retiree health insurance plan. Federal Accounting Standards Board (FASB) Statement of Financial Accounting Standards (SFAS) No. 106, issued in 1990, requires companies to report retiree health insurance benefits as a liability on their financial accounting statements.

Issuance of this standard is widely believed to have triggered a reduction in the coverage of such plans. Data from employer surveys sponsored by the Kaiser Family Foundation show that the fraction of companies with 200 or more employees offering retiree benefits fell from 66 percent in 1988 to 36 percent in 1993 and has fluctuated between 35 and 40 percent since that time, except for a dip in 2005 (Johnson 2007; McCormack et. al 2002). Other data from the Medical Expenditure Panel Survey Insurance Component (MEPSIC), an employer survey that covers both large and small employers, show that the share of private sector employees who work for an employer with a retiree health plan fell between 1997 and 2003 (Buchmueller, Johnson, and Lo Sasso 2006). Furthermore, in recent years a growing share of firms with plans have closed them to new retirees (Eibner, Zawacki, and Zimmerman 2007). In coming years, all of these changes can be expected to reduce significantly the share of retirees with employer-sponsored health coverage. In addition, the premium contributions that eligible workers must pay to be covered have risen sharply (Buchmueller, Johnson, and Lo Sasso 2006). Increases in the cost of coverage may strain the finances of older individuals and also may reduce take-up rates, further depressing the share of retirees with employer-provided health insurance coverage.

Inadequate Savings Rates

The ongoing shift away from defined benefit plans and anticipated declines in retiree health insurance coverage imply that fewer Americans will enjoy generous company-provided benefits in the future, and hence that they will need to save more to ensure adequate income in retirement. Yet a recent survey of adults conducted by the Employee Benefit Research Institute (EBRI) shows that many do not fully understand how these changes affect their retirement security, and, among those who do, few have altered their savings behavior to compensate for the decline in generosity of retirement income provided by employers. EBRI found that large numbers of adults grossly underestimated the amount of savings they would need to cover expected medical expenses in old age and overestimated their chances of receiving traditional defined benefit pension plans (Helman, Copeland, and VanDerhei 2006).

More generally, recent studies have highlighted the fact that many individuals are not saving sufficiently to maintain living standards in old age (Congressional Budget Office 2003). One effective method of increasing retirement savings would be to change default options to require employees who do not wish to participate in 401(k) and similar retirement plans to opt out rather to require those who wish to participate to opt in (Madrian and Shea 2001). The Pension Protection Act creates a safe harbor for such automatic enrollment plans in the form of minimum employer contribution schedules that, if adopted, exempt the employer from the usual nondiscrimination tests otherwise required to ensure that 401(k) plans do not offer disproportionate benefits to highly paid employees (Deloitte 2006). This safe harbor provision should encourage more employers to adopt an automatic enrollment default. Another proposed reform would replace incentives for retirement savings that operate by making contributions to retirement plans tax deductible—an incentive that is worth considerably more to high-income households than to low- or middle-income households because of their higher marginal tax rates—with a plan that matches contributions up to some threshold amount (Gale, Gruber, and Orszag 2006).

It is unclear how effective such reforms can be in increasing retirement savings for the typical American. Their adoption would not change the fundamental fact that wages for middle- and lower-income Americans have been stagnant or falling, and that many feel they have limited slack in their household budgets to set aside money for retirement. This problem is implicit in the analysis of Scholz, Seshadri, and Khitatrakun (2006), who challenge the conventional wisdom that Americans are not saving optimally for retirement. For individuals with low or modest incomes, "optimal" savings may be at or near zero with standard discount rates. Instead of relying on savings, many Americans, because of declining Social Security and pension benefits, may need to delay full retirement to maintain their living standards.

THE PROBLEM: OLDER WORKERS MAY HAVE DIFFICULTY FINDING SUITABLE EMPLOYMENT

The premise that there will be a growing supply of older Americans who want to work seems uncontroversial. Recent Social Security and pension policy reforms, coupled with inadequate retirement and savings income and the decline in retiree health benefits, will give more older Americans an incentive to postpone retirement or reenter the labor force. By itself, an increase in the number of older workers seeking employment will put downward pressure on their wages or, if wages do not adjust smoothly, will result in involuntary or disguised unemployment.

Employer Demand for Older Workers

Some have argued that any increase in the supply of older Americans seeking employment will be matched or exceeded by an increase in demand among employers seeking to hire them. Many policy analysts predict that, faced with massive retirements among the baby boom generation, employers soon will face serious labor shortages. This, they believe, will induce employers to work harder to retain their existing workforce and to recruit more actively among the pool of retirees (AARP 2006; Dychtwald, Erickson, and Morison 2006; Ernst and Young 2006; Judy and D'Amico 1997). These analysts predict that employers' need for older workers will lead them to be more accommodating both of older workers' physical limitations and of their desires for more flexible employment, including part-time or part-year work. Under this scenario, older workers will find it relatively easy to arrange flexible, phased retirement with their existing employer or to land an attractive job with a new employer.

Other researchers are more skeptical that the future will be this rosy for seniors. Although the baby boom generation already has started to retire, existing research finds little evidence that companies are moving to establish broad-based worker retention programs (AARP 2006; Ernst and Young 2006; Government Accountability Office 2005b). A large employer survey about phased retirement options offered to white-collar workers found that such programs were uncommon and that, when these programs were offered, employers typically operated informally, choosing to make special arrangements for the most valued employees (Hutchens 2007). Dychtwald, Erickson, and Morison (2006), who make a strong case that employers will need to retain employees to avoid shortfalls in the near future, also acknowledge that employers will want to be selective in whom they retain. For this reason, they advocate liberalization of "nondiscrimination tests for flexible retirement plans so that employers [can] more easily customize work arrangements and offer them to employees with exceptionally valuable skills and experience without breaking antidiscrimination laws and uniformity mandates" (p. 62). Low-skilled workers, who are the most vulnerable to cuts in Social Security and in the worst position to increase their own savings for retirement, arguably are the least likely to benefit from any growth in employer retention programs. Freeman (2006) also has criticized the labor shortage hypothesis, arguing that employers will meet any shortages with immigration and offshoring. Again, the least skilled workers are of greatest concern, because they tend to be the most adversely affected by pressures from immigration and offshoring.

Evidence on the Difficulty Older Workers Face in Finding New Work

Many older Americans work long hours or in physically demanding jobs and would like to cut back on their hours or change the type of work they do as they age. Although much of the literature on retirement transitions discusses the prevalence of so-called bridge jobs, it appears that far more individuals would like to work in later years than in fact do so. For example, 73 percent of workers aged 51 to 61 surveyed in the 1992 Health and Retirement Study (HRS) said that they would like to continue paid work following retirement (AARP 1998). Other surveys have yielded similar findings. Yet actual employment rates among older Americans are far lower than one might expect from these survey responses. In 2001, when those interviewed for the 1992 HRS would have been aged 60 to 70, only 57 percent of men and 44 percent of women aged 60 to 64, and only 32 percent of men and 21 percent of women aged 65 to 69 were employed either part-time or full-time. Other data show that among men aged 55 to 64 who received pension or retirement-plan income in 2002 just over a third were working in March 2003, and the corresponding share among men 65 and older was only 12 percent (Purcell 2005).

Although there are multiple reasons why the number of individuals who plan to work in later years is substantially higher than the number who, in fact, realize their plans, our research suggests that the difficulty older workers experience with transitioning to new jobs is a significant factor. We draw on panel data from the Health and Retirement Study. The HRS panel includes a representative sample of Americans born in the years 1931 to 1941. Seven waves with interviews conducted biennially from 1992 to 2004 are currently available. In each wave, survey participants answer detailed questions about many aspects of their health, work, and finances. We use questions about future plans for work and retirement that were asked of individuals employed at the time of the survey. We then exploit the panel structure of the data to examine whether individuals followed through on these plans.[3]

Among those with definite future work or retirement plans, a minority (39 percent) indicated that they planned to stop work altogether, and almost as many indicated that they planned to work fewer hours (29 percent) or change the type of work they do (7 percent) (Table 5.1). Exploiting the fact that the HRS reinterviews the same individuals at two-year intervals, we examine the degree to which individuals followed through on these work and retirement plans. Specifically, we identify the subset of individuals who indicated during the interview that they planned to stop work altogether, cut back on their hours, or change the type of work they do within the following two years. We then look at whether what they are doing at the subsequent two interviews—which take place about two years and about four years later—is consistent with their stated plans. We classify people as having reduced their weekly hours if the sum of weekly hours worked on all jobs dropped by

Table 5.1 Plans for Work and Retirement

	Percent of observations for which plan reported	
Plan	Including "Don't know"	Excluding "Don't know"
Stop work altogether	24.5	39.3
Work fewer hours	18.6	29.8
Change type of work	4.5	7.3
Never stop work	7.8	12.4
Other	7.0	11.2
Don't know	37.7	n.a.

SOURCE: Authors' calculations from waves 1–7 of the Health and Retirement Study (1992–2004), based on 18,758 reports of individuals' work and retirement plans. All estimates constructed using HRS sample weights.

eight hours or more between waves. Whether individuals have changed the type of work they do is somewhat subjective, and there is no clean measure of such a work change in the HRS. We consider anyone who changed occupation to have changed the type of work they were doing. Because our measure of work and retirement plans groups those who plan to change their type of work with those who plan to begin working for themselves, we also treat those who move from employee to self-employed status, or the reverse, as having changed their type of work.

Table 5.2 compares individuals' work and retirement plans with what they were actually doing when next interviewed two years later. Most interesting is the fact that those with near-term plans to stop work altogether were much more likely to follow through on those plans than were individuals who planned to reduce their hours of work or change the type of work they do. Whereas about 65 percent of those who planned to retire fully were not working at the next interview about two years later, only 35 percent of those who planned to reduce their hours and 24 percent of those who planned to change the type of work they do followed through on their plans. Roughly half of those who failed to realize plans to reduce their hours or change their type of work made no changes in their employment situation and roughly half stopped working altogether. Although various factors, such as an unanticipated worsening of health status, may help explain why relatively few follow through on these stated plans, analysis we have done suggests that, for many older workers, the need to change jobs is an

Table 5.2 Labor Market Outcomes among Those with Near-Term Plans to Stop Work, Work Fewer Hours, or Change Type of Work (%)

Change planned within 2 years	Work or retirement outcome after 2 years						
	Realized plan	Reduced hours of work	Changed type of work	Reduced hours and changed type of work	Stopped work	No changes	N
Stop work altogether	64.8	9.7	2.5	8.6	64.8	14.5	751
Work fewer hours	34.9	25.5	6.9	9.4	27.7	30.5	569
Change kind of work	24.4	12.3	6.5	17.9	33.9	29.5	123

SOURCE: Authors' calculations from waves 1–7 of the Health and Retirement Study. Calculations based on reports from individuals who indicated that they planned to stop work or make significant changes to hours worked or job held within two years and who were interviewed in the following wave. Information on plans collected in waves 1 through 6; information on outcomes collected in following wave. All estimates constructed using HRS sample weights. In computing the percent distribution of work and retirement outcomes for people with given plans, we excluded a small number of cases (2 percent or fewer) for which the outcome could not be determined.

important impediment to reducing hours and changing the type of work they do. In Abraham and Houseman (2005) we show that, among the employed, those who reported that their employer allowed employees to reduce work hours were much more likely to plan to reduce work hours and, if they had such plans, were much more likely to realize their plans to reduce hours than were individuals whose employers did not allow such flexibility.

Because it may take more time than initially anticipated to make a planned change, especially when the change entails finding a new job, we also examine whether individuals realized their stated plans either by the next wave interview, about two years later, or by the subsequent interview, about four years later.[4] When examined over this longer period, a higher percentage of individuals realized plans to reduce their work hours or change their type of work. Even over this longer horizon, however, only half of those planning to reduce their hours and a third of those planning to change the type of work they do appear to have followed through on their plans, compared to about 80 percent who followed through on plans to stop work altogether. Four years after stating plans to reduce their hours or change their type of work, those who failed to realize these plans were roughly twice as likely to have stopped working altogether as they were to be still working.

In analysis not reported here, we find that adults with low education levels have the most difficulty making such job transitions, as is consistent with prior research on dislocated workers discussed below. Less-educated individuals were significantly less likely to formulate plans to reduce their hours of work or change the type of work they do, and, conditional on having such plans, were significantly less likely than more-educated workers to follow through on those plans. We estimate that those who have not completed high school were 11 to 17 percentage points less likely to follow through on plans to reduce their hours and 10 to 17 percentage points less likely to follow through on plans to change the type of work they do.[5]

Declining Job Stability and Its Consequences

The apparent decline in job stability in recent years poses a further obstacle for older workers who wish to continue working. Although long-term jobs are still quite common among older workers (Stevens

2006), recent evidence suggests that they are less common than they used to be. In a detailed look at trends in employment over the last 50 years, Farber (2006) finds that mean and median job tenure among men have declined for all age groups, as has the incidence of being in a long-lasting job (one that lasts at least 10 or 20 years). The largest declines have been among older men. Comparing men born in the 1930s to those born in the 1950s, for example, Farber shows that median job tenure at age 50 decreased by more than two years, from 11.9 years to 9.7 years. In addition, Farber finds some evidence of job churning (which he defines as jobs lasting less than a year) among men in their thirties. Men in their twenties always have experienced a lot of job turnover, a fact interpreted to mean that they were trying out various jobs before settling in to long-term employment. The fact that job churning has increased significantly among men in their thirties suggests that men today may be having more difficulty finding a suitable long-term job than were men in previous generations.

Research evidence suggests that at least some of the decline in job stability among older workers is associated with layoffs. While the incidence of layoff is lower among older than among younger workers, the gap has narrowed in recent recessions (Farber 2005), and, conditional on tenure in the job, workers aged 45 to 64 have become substantially more susceptible to job loss (Farber 2007).

The narrowing gap between the dislocation rates of younger and older workers may be related to an aging workforce in sectors—like manufacturing—that are especially sensitive to business cycles and that have experienced large secular declines in employment in recent years. Case study evidence also suggests that business perceptions about the desirability of retaining older workers when there is a layoff may be changing. Historically, layoffs generally occurred in inverse seniority order, even in the absence of union contracts dictating such layoff rules (Abraham and Medoff 1984). This pattern has been widely interpreted to imply that employers value the skills and experience of their long-tenure employees, though other research has indicated that the higher pay of more senior workers cannot be fully justified on the basis of their higher productivity (Medoff and Abraham 1980, 1981; Hellerstein and Neumark 2007). Recent high-profile cases involving Wal-Mart and Circuit City indicate that at least some employers have concluded that the extra pay long-tenure employees typically receive exceeds any additional productivity garnered from their experience and have adopted policies that some allege discourage long-term employment (Greenhouse and Barbaro 2006; Leonhardt 2007). Besides wages that arguably rise faster than productivity, the high cost of providing health insurance for older workers provides an incentive to companies to lower the average age at the workplace.

Taken as a whole, the evidence of a decline in job stability implies that older workers will be less able to rely on long-term jobs that last until retirement and more likely to need to search for new jobs, possibly in new fields, late in their working life. Yet research on dislocated workers—defined as those who have lost their job for economic reasons—unambiguously shows that older workers have an especially difficult time making job transitions. Using data from the Health and Retirement Study, Chan and Stevens (2001) find large and long-lasting adverse effects of job loss on employment among older workers. Only 61 percent of men and 55 percent of women who involuntarily lose their jobs are reemployed two years following job loss. Compared to similar workers who do not lose their jobs, individuals who experience job loss at age 55 are an estimated 20 percentage points less likely to hold a job at age 59. Farber (2005) finds similarly low levels of reemployment among older, displaced workers. He also finds much lower reemployment rates among less-educated workers. Among displaced workers who become reemployed, older displaced workers, who on average had longer tenure and were earning more on the job they lost, also experience substantially higher earnings losses.

What happens to older dislocated workers who fail to find new jobs? Many appear to wind up in the Social Security Disability Insurance (SSDI) program, collecting benefits from SSDI until they qualify for regular, age-related Social Security benefits. The fraction of the U.S. adult population on SSDI has grown dramatically over the last 20 years, increasing from 2.2 percent of 25-to-64-year-olds in 1985 to 4.1 percent in 2005. The largest increases have occurred among older, less-educated subgroups. Using data from the Survey of Income and Program Participation (SIPP), Autor and Duggan (2006) estimate that between 1984 and 2004 the rate of SSDI receipt rose from 14.8 to 19.7 percent among male high school dropouts aged 55 to 64 and from 9.1 to 12.7 percent among female high school dropouts of the same ages. The approximately 5-percentage-point increase in disability coverage among high school dropout men aged 55 to 64 compares to an 8-percentage-point decline in the labor force participation rate in this age group over the same period. Autor and Duggan point to increases in the generosity of benefits and to changes that have made it easier to qualify for benefits when an individual has difficulty finding employment—not true increases in the incidence of disability—as explanations for the dramatic growth in the program. They argue cogently that SSDI has become a program for the unemployable.

WHY DO OLDER WORKERS OFTEN HAVE DIFFICULTY FINDING NEW JOBS?

The above evidence indicates that older workers, particularly less skilled and less educated workers, have difficulty transitioning to new jobs. Part of the problem undoubtedly is that many of these workers do not know how to go about looking for a job. And even before they start, many are convinced that employers simply are not interested in hiring older workers, which itself may discourage active search (Government Accountability Office 2005b).

An audit study conducted by Lahey (2008) provides perhaps the best research evidence to date of employer discrimination against older workers applying for entry-level jobs. In her study, Lahey sent resumes of women to be considered for entry-level positions to prospective employers in Boston, Massachusetts, and St. Petersburg, Florida. The resumes were carefully written to appear nearly identical, except that information on the resumes indicated that some applicants were relatively young (age 35 or 45), while others were older (age 50, 55, or 62). Younger applicants were more than 40 percent more likely than older applicants to be called in to interview for the position. Two commonly offered reasons why employers, all else being the same, might prefer younger to older workers are that older workers lack necessary skills, especially technical skills, and that their wage and benefits costs are too high.

Lack Necessary Skills

Although skills and experience are much-touted assets of older workers (see, for instance, AARP 2005), years of work experience may benefit an older worker primarily in the job in which he or she accrued that experience. Unless the skills from one job are readily transferable to another job, years of accrued experience provide an older worker with little advantage when those workers want or need to change jobs. Moreover, businesses indicate one problem they have with hiring older workers is that they often lack up-to-date technical skills (Arizona Mature Worker Initiative 2006). Older workers themselves sometimes acknowledge their lack of computer skills (Government Accountability Office 2005b). Employers may be reluctant to invest in training older workers given the relatively short time that they can be expected to continue working (Arizona Mature Worker Initiative 2006). Perceptions that older workers are more rigid and slower to learn may reinforce employers' unwillingness to hire older workers who require training (Bendick, Jackson, and Romero 1996).

Beyond lacking technical skills, older job applicants may not possess physical or social attributes that are important in some jobs. Older workers may no longer have the physical stamina or dexterity to handle certain jobs, particularly jobs in low-skilled manual occupations in which many less-educated individuals historically have been employed. In addition, employers believe that some older workers would find it difficult to accept being part of an ethnically or culturally diverse workforce, meaning that their presence could undermine effective communication and smooth functioning in many workplace settings (Arizona Mature Worker Initiative 2006).

High Wage and Benefits Costs

Based on analyses of personnel records for the salaried workforces of several large companies, Medoff and Abraham (1980, 1981) find that senior workers receive higher pay than equally productive junior workers. Hellerstein and Neumark (2007) find that manufacturing workers aged 55 and over are less productive than younger workers, but this lower productivity is not matched by lower earnings. The high earnings of older workers relative to their productivity is widely seen as an impediment to the hiring of older workers in many developed countries (OECD 2006). Recent high-profile cases in the United States suggest that relatively high pay for workers with long job tenures is becoming an important human resources issue for cost-conscious corporations. A memorandum by a top Wal-Mart executive to its board of directors, for instance, outlined a proposed policy to increase turnover and thereby reduce the average tenure of its stores' employees, which it calls associates, by setting wage caps on certain positions and requiring staff to work nights and weekends. The memo noted that the cost of an associate with seven years of tenure was 55 percent more than the cost of an associate with one year of tenure, yet the productivity of the two was the same. Similar concerns at Circuit City led to dismissals of about 8 percent of its employees who were deemed overpaid so that these employees could be replaced by lower-cost workers (Leonhardt 2007).

Although human resource practices that reward employee performance with pay raises that exceed employees' productivity growth may be coming to an end, the apparent pervasiveness of the practice points to another reason why employers are reluctant to hire older workers as new employees. According to one survey, employers believe that many older workers expect higher salaries than those that come with the jobs for which they are applying (Arizona Mature Worker Initiative 2006). A corollary is that employers fear that, if older workers take a job with lower wages than they feel entitled to, they may view the relatively low wages as unfair; consequently they may have low morale and perform poorly on the job. Thus, employers may be reluctant to hire a person who has earned significantly higher wages in the past, even if that individual indicates a willingness to accept the job.

Older workers also are more expensive to insure. Health insurance has become the most costly worker benefit (Government Accountability Office 2006a), and according to analysis by Towers Perrin for the AARP (AARP 2005), on average, workers aged 50 to 65 have medical expenses that are 1.4 to 2.2 times higher than workers in their thirties and forties, translating into significantly higher health insurance costs. One of the leading obstacles to hiring older workers, according to employer surveys, is the high cost of providing them with health insurance (Arizona Mature Worker Initiative 2006). One study found that employers with health benefit plans are significantly less likely to hire persons aged 55–64 than are employers who do not offer health insurance

(Scott, Berger, and Garen 1995). And the issue of high health insurance costs generally does not go away once the older worker reaches age 65 and thus qualifies for Medicare coverage. Under existing Medicare rules, if an employee aged 65 or over working for an employer with 20 or more employees is covered by employer-provided health insurance, in most cases that insurance policy, not Medicare, is the first payer for any claim that may be made.

POLICIES

The aging of the American population is expected to place severe strains on the Social Security and Medicare systems in the coming decades and has led to a broad consensus that it is in the public interest to increase employment among older Americans. The perceived need to increase employment among older Americans comes at a time when their job tenure is on the decline and job loss is on the rise. Although labor force participation among older women has risen in recent decades and labor force participation among men over age 65 has edged up since the mid-1990s, labor force participation among men in their fifties—i.e., men in their immediate preretirement years—has declined over the last two decades. The decline has been particularly marked for less-educated men.

As discussed earlier in the chapter, selected policies designed to provide greater incentives for older Americans to work have been adopted. Most notably, the age at which individuals will qualify to retire with full Social Security benefits is rising from age 65 to age 67. For those with traditional defined benefit pensions, reforms to ERISA will facilitate workers' participation in phased retirement programs within their company. Still, for many workers, whether because they seek a change in hours or job duties or because they are forced out of their jobs, continued employment at older ages will require a change of employers. The failure by many to make these job transitions has significant, if hidden, public costs, which include growing dependence of older Americans on the Social Security system and other forms of public assistance. Policies that provide financial incentives to older Americans to work, we believe, must be supplemented by policies that ease job transitions and remove some of the substantial barriers to being hired that older Americans face. Below we review federal employment and training programs that serve older workers and recent initiatives that some states have taken to facilitate employment among older Americans. We conclude by outlining policies that we believe are needed to fill existing gaps.

Federal Programs

The Senior Community Services Employment Program (SCSEP) is the only federal employment program that specifically targets older Americans. SCSEP serves approximately two-thirds of individuals aged 55 and over who receive federal employment and training services (General Accounting Office 2003). Funded under the Older Americans Act of 1965, the SCSEP program provides subsidized part-time and community service employment for individuals aged 55 and older who have incomes below 125 percent of the poverty level. Historically, moving participants to unsubsidized employment was not a stated goal of the program. Although this was changed in 2000, placement rates into unsubsidized employment remain relatively low (Government Accountability Office 2006b). According to official program statistics, in recent years SCSEP has served around 100,000 seniors nationwide (Table 5.3), most of them over age 65. The U.S. Department of Labor estimates that this represents fewer than 1 percent of the eligible population (Government Accountability Office 2006b). Program funding has been stagnant in current dollars and, as shown in Figure 5.3, has been falling in real terms since the late 1990s.

The Work Force Investment Act (WIA) is the country's primary employment and training services program, although the number of older workers who are served by WIA programs is considerably smaller than the number served by SCSEP (Table 5.3).[6] WIA provides basic labor market information and preliminary job skills services to any adult 18 or over who seeks them. More intensive job search assistance and training services are limited to individuals enrolled in one of three funded WIA programs: the adult, dislocated worker, and youth programs. Older Americans are served under the first two programs. Priority for enrollment in the WIA adult program is given to individuals on public assistance and others in low-income households. Enrollment in the WIA

**Figure 5.3 Trends in Real Spending on Employment and Training
Programs (2006 constant dollars)**

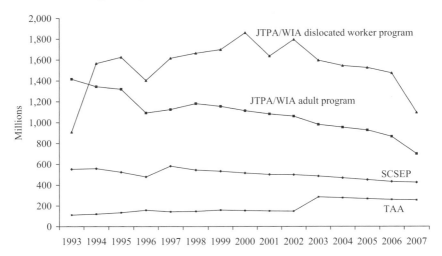

SOURCE: Budget numbers from U.S. Department of Labor, Employment and Training Administration, Training and Employment Programs Budget Authority. PY 1984–
2004, http://www.doleta.gov/budget/tepbah.pdf. The authors deflated all budget figures using the CPI Series CUUROOOOSAO.

dislocated worker program is reserved for individuals permanently laid
off from jobs.

In July 2000, the WIA adult and dislocated worker programs replaced similar programs funded under the Job Training Partnership
Act (JTPA). The JTPA dislocated worker program enjoyed funding increases that offset declines in funding for the JTPA adult program over
much of the 1990s, but under WIA, funding for both programs has been
stagnant in current dollars and falling in real dollars. In constant dollars,
total funding for the WIA adult and dislocated worker programs was 35
percent lower in 2007 than funding for the comparable JTPA programs
had been ten years earlier, and the decline has been even steeper relative
to the size of the working-age population. Within this funding context,
official program statistics show that the absolute number of workers
over age 55 served by WIA programs has been lower than the number
served under the corresponding JTPA programs and that older workers
have declined as a fraction of all adults served.[7]

Table 5.3 Data on Program Exiters, JTPA, WIA, and SCSEP Programs, 1997–2004

	Program year							
	1997	1998	1999	2000	2001	2002	2003	2004
SCSEP program								
Program exiters								
N						96,852	105,829	93,000
As % of population 55–64						0.38	0.38	0.32
JTPA/WIA adult programs								
Program exiters								
N	159,389	163,223	142,147	109,868	193,518	261,544	229,607	225,683
As % of population	0.10	0.10	0.09	0.07	0.11	0.15	0.13	0.13
Program exiters age 55+								
N	14,823	15,180	14,073	6,922	11,418	14,385	13,776	13,541
As % of population 55–64	0.07	0.07	0.06	0.03	0.05	0.06	0.05	0.05
As % of all exiters	9.30	9.30	9.90	6.30	5.90	5.50	6.00	6.00
JTPA/WIA dislocated worker programs								
Program exiters								
N	266,112	240,896	205,637	99,491	147,715	200,264	194,425	178,446
As % of population	0.16	0.15	0.12	0.06	0.09	0.12	0.11	0.10
Program exiters age 55+								
N	26,611	24,812	22,826	11,441	16,692	22,229	21,970	21,592
As % of population 55–64	0.12	0.11	0.10	0.05	0.07	0.09	0.08	0.07
As % of all exiters	10.00	10.30	11.10	11.50	11.30	11.10	11.30	12.10

JTPA/WIA adult plus dislocated worker programs							
Program exiters							
N	425,501	404,119	347,784	209,359	341,233	461,808	424,032	404,129
As % of population	0.26	0.24	0.21	0.12	0.20	0.27	0.24	0.22
Program exiters age 55+								
N	41,434	39,992	36,898	18,363	28,109	36,614	35,746	35,133
As % of population 55–64	0.19	0.18	0.16	0.08	0.12	0.14	0.13	0.12
As % of all exiters	9.74	9.90	10.61	8.77	8.24	7.93	8.43	8.69
Trade adjustment assistance programs								
Program exiters								
N					26,363	24,883	30,047	
As % of population					0.01	0.01	0.02	
Program exiters age 55+								
N					3,045	2,924	3,933	
As % of population 55–64					0.01	0.01	0.01	
As % of all exiters					11.55	11.75	13.09	

SOURCE: Data on programs from Social Policy Research Associates (PY 1997–2000), the 2001 WIASRD Data Book, http://www.doleta.gov/performance/results/PY_2001_WIASRD_Databook.pdf (PY 2001), and the corresponding data books and links for PY2002 through PY2004.

Under JTPA, states were required to set aside 5 percent of their adult program allotment for older workers. This provision was dropped in WIA and, as can be seen in Table 5.3, the share of those in the adult program who are aged 55 and over declined from about 9 percent in the JTPA adult program to about 6 percent in the WIA adult program. Although one might hypothesize that eliminating the quota on spending for older workers in WIA resulted in a more efficient allocation of resources, recent government reports have raised concerns that the federal performance standards used to evaluate organizations that administer the WIA programs have resulted in a bias against serving older workers. Until 2005, the performance standards for WIA service providers included measures of participants' postprogram earnings relative to their preprogram earnings. Some observers think that this created a disincentive to serve older workers, many of whom have considerable prior work experience and may wish to transition from full-time to part-time employment (General Accounting Office 2003). In an attempt to address this problem, revised performance standards introduced in 2006 substitute a measure of postprogram earnings for the previous earnings change measure (Employment and Training Administration 2006). However, even this new measure may discourage providers from serving older workers, who are likely to seek part-time work and thus have relatively low earnings.

Older workers also may receive job search assistance and training under Trade Adjustment Assistance programs, which are reserved specifically for workers displaced by foreign trade. Fewer than 4,000 TAA-qualified workers—about 13 percent of all participants in TAA training and placement programs—were 55 or older in 2003. The Trade Act of 2002 wrote into law a five-year demonstration program under which eligible workers aged 55 and older who agree to forgo TAA-funded training and are able to find jobs within 26 weeks that pay less than their previous earnings (and less than $50,000) are eligible for a wage subsidy of up to $10,000 cumulatively to supplement their earnings. States moved slowly to implement the demonstration program and, as was the case with a similar Canadian program in place from 1995 to 1998 (Levine 2007), take-up of the TAA wage subsidies has been relatively low. In addition to a lack of awareness of the program and not wishing to forgo the possibility of training, eligible workers who did not participate cite the difficulty of finding a job within six months as required by program rules (Government Accountability Office 2006c).

Recent State Initiatives

Although the federal government has taken no major policy initiative for older workers in recent years, a few states are beginning to take steps to address what is perceived as a growing need for employment services among this population. To identify innovative policies at the state level, we conducted an informal survey of relevant state workforce agencies through their national association (the National Association of State Workforce Agencies). Although most states do not have older worker programs besides the federally funded SCSEP, 10 states responded to our survey with information on initiatives they are currently taking or planning. In some instances, the AARP has worked with states to plan and implement initiatives. In addition, the National Governors Association has selected eight states to participate in a policy academy designed to develop model programs to meet the needs of mature workers (National Governors Association 2007).

These state initiatives generally fall into three broad categories. The first is employer outreach and education. Several states have initiated programs to advise employers on how to accommodate an aging workforce. Initiatives also include information campaigns to combat what are regarded as inaccurate and damaging stereotypes of older workers with the aim of reducing discriminatory practices against those workers. These public relations efforts emphasize positive attributes of older workers relative to young workers, such as reliability and good social skills. Patterned in part on an AARP program, efforts in several states also feature or are planning to feature employers who evidence a commitment to hiring and promoting older workers. The idea behind these programs is at one level to help seniors connect with employers who are willing to hire them, but at a deeper level to provide positive public relations for the identified companies and advance the notion that hiring older workers is a good business practice.[8]

A second area involves outreach and better delivery of existing services to older workers. One of the most common initiatives adopted by states is to place an older worker specialist in the one-stop centers, which serve as the central clearinghouse for all workforce development programs under WIA. This specialist would be able to better direct older workers to services meeting their specific needs and, some think, make older workers feel more welcome at one-stops. The concern that older workers are often reluctant to go to one-stop centers was expressed by a number of state workforce representatives, some of whom consequently planned outreach efforts at senior centers and other places where seniors might congregate. Such outreach may also involve providing access to job listings at these remote sites.

A third area involves tailoring programs to meet specific needs of older workers. One program, for instance, emphasizes peer counseling, networking, life planning seminars, and other resources targeting those over 50 who are changing jobs and even careers. In addition to having special planning and counseling needs, older individuals often lack basic technical and computer skills that are needed for many jobs, and, indeed that may be needed even to find a job. Training in Internet job search and in the basic computer skills required on many jobs is widely recognized as a prevalent need among older workers. Arizona, for instance, is planning the development of a Web-based mechanism for posting jobs and resumes that would be technologically friendly for older workers and efficient for businesses. Some states offer free or reduced tuition to older adults who wish to advance their skills at public postsecondary institutions.

In sum, states are experimenting with a variety of approaches to increase workforce participation among seniors. These efforts involve changing employer perceptions of older workers and hence receptiveness to hiring them, reaching out to older individuals who may be unaware of work opportunities, and tailoring programs to meet the special needs of older workers. We are aware of no serious effort to evaluate any of these initiatives, which, given the lack of federal funding or other resources available, are all modest in scope.

Policy Recommendations

Several circumstances, discussed above, serve as a backdrop for our policy recommendations: 1) there is a public interest in increasing employment among older Americans, 2) many older workers will need to make job changes late in life in order to remain employed, 3) older workers face significant impediments to finding new employment, and

4) public funding for employment and training programs that help older workers has been low and is falling. These facts lead us to make the following recommendations:

Increase funding for employment and training programs to help smooth employment transitions for older workers. While the population of older workers is growing and many in this population will need to make job transitions to remain employed, overall funding for the major government programs designed to help workers prepare for and find employment has fallen by over a third in real terms in the last decade, and older workers have received a shrinking share of that shrinking pie. The chances that an older person who leaves or loses a job will reenter employment are low unless the individual transitions to a new job in a reasonably short period of time. Because many who fail to find jobs end up collecting Social Security disability payments or some other form of public assistance, it is critical to have effective programs to help older workers transition to new jobs.

To put the funding of workforce programs for older workers in some perspective, in 2004 about 0.1 percent of the adult population aged 55 to 64 participated in a WIA adult or dislocated worker program.[9] In the same year, about 9 percent of those aged 55 to 64 were collecting SSDI, at an average annual cost per participant of two-and-a-half to three times that of the average cost per participant of serving someone in a WIA program. Although by no means does everyone who drops out of the labor force qualify for SSDI, individuals who fail to find employment are much more likely to receive other forms of public assistance, such as food stamps, Medicaid, and public housing. Even a return-to-work program with a modest success rate could save taxpayer dollars.

In the absence of better information on the return-on-investment to be expected from increased expenditures on such programs, history may provide some useful context. Returning real expenditures on the employment and training programs that serve older workers (SCSEP, the WIA adult program, the WIA dislocated worker program, and the TAA program) to the level of a decade ago would require an increase in total spending of about 40 percent. Taking into account the growth in population that has occurred over the past 10 years and returning spending per working age adult (aged 25–64) to its 1997 level would require an increase in spending of about 48 percent.

Modify WIA performance standards to eliminate disincentives to serve older workers. The performance standards currently used to evaluate the federally funded WIA programs include a measure of the subsequent earnings of participants taken from state unemployment insurance quarterly wage records data. Because these data record only total earnings in a quarter, not hourly wages, and because older workers are more likely than younger workers to want part-time employment, this performance standard creates an unintended disincentive for program operators to serve older workers. Although it is an improvement upon the previously used measures that compared postprogram earnings to preprogram earnings, the WIA earnings performance standard requires further modification to eliminate this disincentive. One straightforward way to do this would be to develop different standards to be applied to clients of different ages. For instance, performance measures for employment services programs operating in the United Kingdom and Australia explicitly take into account the fact that some individuals face more serious barriers to employment than others; thus, service providers receive more credit for placing clients with significant employment barriers, such as older workers, into jobs (OECD 2006).

Tailor programs to meet needs of older workers. As a general proposition, it is important that programs be designed appropriately to meet the needs of special populations, including older workers. Experimentation with initiatives for older workers such as those recently taken or planned by some states should be encouraged. Promising approaches include outreach and education efforts directed towards both employers and seniors, placing older-worker specialists in one-stop employment centers, and developing job-search assistance programs and job training courses that address skill deficiencies common among seniors, such as deficiencies in basic computer skills. Experiences in Australia suggest that older people particularly benefit from intensive assistance that includes a personal coach and career counseling (OECD 2006).

Rigorously evaluate older-worker initiatives. While we are confident that program providers can do a better job of serving older workers and helping them to find employment, it must be emphasized that relatively little is known about how this can best be done. Rigorous evaluation of new initiatives at the state level to assess their effectiveness and their suitability as models for the national level must be an integral part of any new funding for such programs. In the same spirit, the planned evaluation of the wage subsidies for older workers, introduced as part of the Trade Adjustment Assistance program, should be completed. Programs that prove to be cost-effective should be promoted and expanded.

Reform health-care financing to reduce disincentives to hiring older workers. The high cost of providing health insurance for older workers is a major impediment to reemployment in good, full-time jobs for older workers. For those aged 65 and older, making Medicare rather than the employer insurance policy the first payer in the event of a claim would help address this problem. However, such reform will not help the bulk of older workers, who are under age 65 and thus not yet eligible for Medicare. A growing consensus of experts agrees that "the employer-sponsored system of benefits in its current form may not be sustainable, largely because productivity growth is unlikely to support rising benefit costs" (Government Accountability Office 2006a, p. 26). Health insurance reform of a more comprehensive nature, as addressed in detail by Swartz (2008), is needed to remove this serious barrier to employment for other older workers.

CONCLUSION

Over the coming decades, work for pay is likely to be increasingly important to the financial well-being of many older Americans. Higher rates of employment at older ages also could help with addressing the long-term funding problems faced by the Social Security and Medicare systems.

To date, public policy initiatives intended to increase employment among older Americans have focused primarily on monetary incentives. Recent changes to the Social Security system that allow Social Security recipients to earn more without having their benefits reduced, that make the present value of benefits roughly independent of the age of retirement rather than favoring those who retire early, and that raise the age at which recipients qualify for full benefits should make employment significantly more attractive to older Americans. Furthermore, trends in private-sector benefits should reinforce the incentives associated with these recent changes in the Social Security system. In particular, the marked shift from defined-benefit pension plans to less generous defined-contribution pension plans and the sharp declines in the coverage of retiree health insurance plans, together with the fact that savings for retirement have not risen to offset the reduction in the generosity of the pension and health benefits available to retirees, should provide additional encouragement for Americans to work at older ages.

Although the altered financial incentives associated with recent policy and labor market changes unquestionably will be important in promoting employment among older Americans, we have argued in this chapter that policies designed to make work more attractive financially should be accompanied by policies designed to improve the functioning of labor markets for older workers. Our research as well as research by others points to the special challenges to remaining employed that older individuals face, even when they possess the ability and the desire to continue working. These problems are particularly acute for low-educated workers and for older individuals who attempt to transition to new jobs.

We have advocated policies to help ensure that older workers who wish to remain employed are able to do so. The measures we propose should make it easier for older workers to search for a job and should help to address some of the legitimate concerns that employers have about hiring older workers. Although these measures are unlikely to address fully the problems we have diagnosed, they would make an excellent start and seem likely to have a significant societal payoff.

Notes

This paper was prepared for A Future of Good Jobs: America's Challenge in the Global Economy, a conference sponsored by the W.E. Upjohn Institute held in Washington, DC on June 22, 2007. We have benefited from conversations with many individuals, including Linda Levine, Blake Naughton, Debra Whitman, and Julie Whittaker of the Congressional Research Service; Dianne Blank, Barbara Bovbjerg, Mindy Bowman, Alicia Cackley, and Sigurd Nilsen of the Government Accountability Office; and Emily Allen, Dalmer Hoskins, Sara Rix, and Jim Seith of AARP. Richard Hobbie of the National Association of State Workforce Agencies kindly assisted us with an informal survey of association members. We are also grateful to Lillian Vesic-Petrovic for excellent research assistance.

1. For a description of these rules, see Deloitte (2006).
2. Although the share of older individuals who work should increase, the effect of this change on total hours of work is ambiguous. Total hours of work could increase if those choosing phased retirement would otherwise have quit working altogether, or they could decrease if those choosing phased retirement would otherwise have worked full time. Although the context is somewhat different, the analysis reported by Gustman and Steinmeier (2007) of the effects of eliminating the Social Security earnings test for those below normal retirement age suggests the former effect may dominate.
3. This work updates research reported in Abraham and Houseman (2005). That paper contains a more detailed discussion of the HRS and the questions pertaining to future work and retirement plans that we use.
4. For instance, consider an individual who stated in the 1992 interview that he planned to reduce his work hours by 1994. We count that individual as having realized his stated plans if he was working at least eight fewer hours per week either at the 1994 or at the 1996 interview. Because we only observe work hours at the point in time of the interview, we do not know if an individual who is observed to be working the same hours as before or who has stopped working altogether reduced hours between interviews.
5. These estimates come from multivariate regression analyses that control for age, gender, and time period in addition to education level. This analysis is available from the authors on request.
6. We do not consider the Employment Service programs, which provide free labor exchange services to job seekers and employers but do not offer the more intensive counseling, job placement, or training services of the other federal programs discussed in this chapter.
7. Figures for program year 2000 were affected by the transition from JTPA to WIA and do not reflect true changes in the population served. More generally, the accuracy of data on the number of exiters from JTPA and WIA programs has been questioned because states have discretion in defining whom to count as an exiter (General Accounting Office 2004; Government Accountability Office 2005c). As long as how states define exiters has not changed significantly over time, these data should be indicative of broad trends both in the total number served and in the number of older individuals served.
8. Public information campaigns and employer guidelines to combat discrimination against older workers have been a leading strategy used in many countries to try to increase the hiring of older workers (OECD 2006).
9. This figure comes from Table 5.3. For the purpose of the calculations reported there we have assumed that all program exiters aged 55 and older were aged 55–64.

References

AARP. 1998. *Boomers Approaching Midlife: How Secure a Future?* Washington, DC: AARP. Public Policy Institute. http://assets.aarp.org/rgcenter/econ/d16687_boomers.pdf (accessed September 12, 2007).

―――. 2005. *The Business Case for Workers Age 50+: Planning for Tomorrow's Talent Needs in Today's Competitive Environment.* A Report for AARP Prepared by Towers Perrin. http://assets.aarp.org/rgcenter/econ/workers_fifty_plus.pdf (accessed August 8, 2007).

―――. 2006. *Business Executives' Attitudes Toward the Aging Workforce: Aware But Not Prepared?* Report on Survey Conducted by BusinessWeek Research Services for AARP. Rev. ed. Washington, DC: AARP. http://assets.aarp.org/rgcenter/econ/aging_workforce.pdf (accessed August 8, 2007).

Abraham, Katharine G., and Susan N. Houseman. 2005. "Work and Retirement Plans among Older Americans." In *Reinventing the Retirement Paradigm*, Robert L. Clark and Olivia S. Mitchell, eds. New York and Oxford: Oxford University Press, pp. 70–91.

Abraham, Katharine G., and James L. Medoff. 1984. "Length of Service and Layoffs in Union and Nonunion Work Groups." *Industrial and Labor Relations Review* 38(1): 87–97.

Arizona Mature Worker Initiative. 2006. *Year One Outcomes and Recommendations.* A Report to Governor Janet Napolitano. Phoenix: Arizona Mature Worker Initiative. http://www.nga.org/Files/pdf/0611SENIORWEBCASTSTARNS.PDF (accessed August 8, 2007).

Autor, David H., and Mark G. Duggan. 2006. "The Growth in the Social Security Disability Rolls: A Fiscal Crisis Unfolding." *Journal of Economic Perspectives* 20(3): 71–96.

Bendick, Marc Jr., Charles W. Jackson, and J. Horacio Romero.1996. "Employment Discrimination Against Older Workers: An Experimental Study of Hiring Practices." *Journal of Aging and Social Policy* 8(4): 25–46.

Buchmueller, Thomas, Richard W. Johnson, and Anthony T. Lo Sasso. 2006. "Trends in Retiree Health Insurance, 1997–2003." *Health Affairs* 25(6): 1507–1516.

Burtless, Gary, and Joseph F. Quinn. 2002. "Is Working Longer the Answer for an Aging Workforce?" Issue in Brief No. 11. Boston: Center for Retirement Research at Boston College.

Chan, Sewin, and Ann Huff Stevens. 2001. "Job Loss and Employment Patterns of Older Workers." *Journal of Labor Economics* 19(2): 484–521.

Congressional Budget Office. 2003. *Baby Boomers' Retirement Prospects: An Overview.* Washington, DC: Congressional Budget Office. http://www.cbo

.gov/ftpdocs/48xx/doc4863/11-26-BabyBoomers.pdf (accessed August 8, 2007).

Costa, Dora L. 1998. *The Evolution of Retirement: An American Economic History, 1880–1990.* Chicago: University of Chicago Press.

Costo, Stephanie. 2006. "Trends in Retirement Plan Coverage Over the Last Decade." *Monthly Labor Review* 129(2): 58–64.

Deloitte. 2006. *Securing Retirement: An Overview of the Pension Protection Act of 2006.* Washington, DC: Deloitte.

Dychtwald, Ken, Tamara J. Erickson, and Robert Morison. 2006. *Workforce Crisis: How to Beat the Shortage of Skills and Talent.* Boston: Harvard Business School Press.

Eibner, Christine, Alice Zawacki, and Elaine Zimmerman. 2007. "Older Workers' Access to Employer-Sponsored Retiree Health Insurance, 2000–2004." Center for Economic Studies Discussion Paper CES 07-12. Washington, DC: U.S. Census Bureau, Center for Economic Studies.

Employment and Training Administration. 2006. "Common Measures Policy for the Employment and Training Administration's (ETA) Performance Accountability System and Related Performance Issues." Training and Employment Guidance Letter No. 17-05. Washington, DC: U.S. Department of Labor, Employment and Training Administration.

Ernst and Young. 2006. *The Aging of the U.S. Workforce: Employer Challenges and Responses.* New York: Ernst and Young.

Farber, Henry S. 2005. "What Do We Know about Job Loss in the United States? Evidence from the Displaced Workers Survey, 1984–2004." Working Paper No. 498. Princeton, NJ: Industrial Relations Section, Princeton University.

———. 2006. "Is the Company Man an Anachronism? Trends in Long Term Employment in the U.S., 1973–2005." Network on Transitions to Adulthood Research Network Working Paper. Philadelphia: Network on Transitions to Adulthood. http://www.transad.pop.upenn.edu/downloads/farber%20with%20cover%20sheet.pdf (accessed August 8, 2007).

———. 2007. "Job Loss and the Decline of Job Security in the United States." Working Paper No. 520. Princeton, NJ: Industrial Relations Section, Princeton University.

Federal Interagency Forum on Aging-Related Statistics. 2006. *Older Americans: Key Indicators of Well-Being.* Update 2006. Hyattsville, MD: Federal Interagency Forum on Aging-Related Statistics. http://www.agingstats.gov/agingstatsdotnet/Main_Site/Data/2006_Documents/OA_2006.pdf (accessed September 17, 2007).

Freeman, Richard B. 2006. "Is a Great Labor Shortage Coming? Replacement

Demand in the Global Economy." NBER Working Paper No. 12541. Cambridge, MA: National Bureau of Economic Research.

Friedberg, Leora, and Anthony Webb. 2005. "Retirement and the Evolution of Pension Structure." *Journal of Human Resources* 40(2): 281–308.

Gale, William G., Jonathan Gruber, and Peter R. Orszag. 2006. "Improving Opportunities and Incentives for Saving by Middle- and Low-Income Households." Hamilton Project Discussion Paper 2006-2. Washington, DC: Brookings Institution.

General Accounting Office. 2003. *Older Workers: Employment Assistance Focuses on Subsidized Jobs and Job Search, but Revised Performance Measures Could Improve Access to Other Services.* Report to the Ranking Minority Member, Subcommittee on Employer-Employee Relations, Committee on Education and the Workforce, House of Representatives. GAO-03-350. Washington, DC: U.S. General Accounting Office.

———. 2004. *Workforce Investment Act: States and Local Areas Have Developed Strategies to Assess Performance, but Labor Could Do More to Help.* Report to Congressional Requesters. GAO-04-657. Washington, DC: U.S. General Accounting Office.

Ghilarducci, Teresa, and Wei Sun. 2006. "How Defined Contribution Plans and 401(k)s Affect Employer Pension Costs." *Journal of Pension Economics and Finance* 5(2): 175–196.

Government Accountability Office. 2005a. *Private Pensions: Information on Cash Balance Pension Plans.* Report to Congressional Requesters. GAO-06-42. Washington, DC: U.S. Government Accountability Office.

———. 2005b. Older Workers: *Labor Can Help Employers and Employees Plan Better for the Future.* Report to Congressional Requesters. GAO-06-80. Washington, DC: U.S. Government Accountability Office.

———. 2005c. *Workforce Investment Act: Labor and States Have Taken Actions to Improve Data Quality, but Additional Steps Are Needed.* Report to Congressional Requesters. GAO-06-82. Washington, DC: U.S. Government Accountability Office.

———. 2006a. *Employee Compensation: Employer Spending on Benefits Has Grown Faster Than Wages, Due Largely to Rising Costs for Health Insurance and Retirement Benefits.* Report to Congressional Requesters. GAO-06-285. Washington, DC: U.S. Government Accountability Office.

———. 2006b. "Senior Community Service Employment Program: Labor Has Made Progress Implementing Older Americans Act Amendments of 2000, but Challenges Remain." Testimony before the Special Committee on Aging, U.S. Senate. GAO-06-549T. Washington, DC: U.S. Government Accountability Office.

————. 2006c. *Trade Adjustment Assistance: Most Workers in Five Layoffs Received Services, but Better Outreach Needed on New Benefits*. Report to Congressional Requesters. GAO-06-43. Washington, DC: U.S. Government Accountability Office.

Greenhouse, Steven, and Michael Barbaro. 2006."Wal-Mart to Add Wage Caps and Part-Timers." *New York Times*, October 2, A:1.

Gustman, Alan L., and Thomas Steinmeier. 2007. "Projecting Behavioral Responses to the Next Generation of Retirement Policies." NBER Working Paper 12958. Cambridge, MA: National Bureau of Economic Research.

Hellerstein, Judith K., and David Neumark. 2007. "Production Function and Wage Equation Estimation with Heterogeneous Labor: Evidence from a New Matched Employer-Employee Data Set." In *Hard-to-Measure Goods and Services: Essays in Honor of Zvi Griliches*, Ernst R. Berndt and Charles M. Hulten, eds. Chicago: University of Chicago Press, pp. 31–71.

Helman, Ruth, Craig Copeland, and Jack VanDerhei. 2006. "Will More of Us Be Working Forever? The 2006 Retirement Confidence Survey." EBRI Issue Brief No. 292. Washington, DC: Employee Benefit Research Institute.

Hutchens, Robert. 2007. "Worker Characteristics, Job Characteristics, and Opportunities for Phased Retirement." IZA Discussion Paper No. 2564. Bonn, Germany: Institute for the Study of Labor.

Johnson, Richard W. 2007. "What Happens to Health Benefits after Retirement?" Issue in Brief. Work Opportunities for Older Americans, Series 7. Boston: Center for Retirement Research at Boston College.

Judy, Richard W., and Carol D'Amico. 1997. *Workforce 2020: Work and Workers in the 21st Century*. Indianapolis: Hudson Institute.

Lahey, Joanna. 2008. "Age, Women and Hiring: An Experimental Study." *Journal of Human Resources* 43(1): 30–56.

Leonhardt, David. 2007. "One Safety Net Is Disappearing. What Will Follow?" *New York Times*, April 4, C:1.

Levine, Linda. 2007. *Older Displaced Workers in the Context of an Aging and Slowly Growing Population*. CRS Report for Congress RL33054. Washington, DC: Congressional Research Service.

Madrian, Brigitte C., and Dennis F. Shea. 2001. "The Power of Suggestion: Inertia in 401(k) Participation and Savings Behavior." *Quarterly Journal of Economics* 116(4): 1149–1187.

McCormack, Lauren A., Jon R. Gabel, Nancy D. Berkman, Heidi Whitmore, Kay Bailey Hutchison, Wayne L. Anderson, Jeremy Pickreign, and Nathan West. 2002. "Retiree Health Insurance: Recent Trends and Tomorrow's Prospects." *Health Care Financing Review* 23(3): 17–34.

Medoff, James L., and Katharine G. Abraham. 1980. "Experience, Performance, and Earnings." *Quarterly Journal of Economics* 95(4): 703–736.

————. 1981. "Are Those Paid More Really More Productive? The Case of Experience." *Journal of Human Resources* 16(2): 186–216.

Munnell, Alicia H., Kevin E. Cahill, and Natalia A. Jivan. 2003. "How Has the Shift to 401(k)s Affected the Retirement Age?" Center for Retirement Research Issue in Brief No. 13. Boston: Center for Retirement Research at Boston College.

Munnell, Alicia H., and Steven A. Sass. 2007. "The Labor Supply of Older Americans." Paper prepared for the Federal Reserve Bank of Boston summer conference "Labor Supply in the New Century," held in Boston, June 18–20.

National Governors Association. 2007. "NGA Center Eyes Increasing Employment and Volunteer Opportunities for Retirees: Eight States Invited to Policy Academy on Civic Engagement." News release, May 24. Washington, DC: National Governors Association. http://www.nga .org/portal/site/nga/menuitem.6c9a8a9ebc6ae07eee28aca9501010a0/ ?vgnextoid=9b3a084726fb2110VgnVCM1000001a01010aRCRD   (accessed August 8, 2007).

OECD. 2006. *Live Longer, Work Longer.* Ageing and Employment Policies Project. Paris: Organisation for Economic Co-operation and Development.

Purcell, Patrick. 2005. "Older Workers: Employment and Retirement Trends." In *Reinventing the Retirement Paradigm*, Robert L. Clark and Olivia S. Mitchell, eds. New York and Oxford: Oxford University Press, pp. 55–70.

Quinn, Joseph F. 1999. "Has the Early Retirement Trend Reversed?" Paper presented at the first annual joint conference of the Social Security Administration's Retirement Research Consortia, held in Washington, DC, May 20–21.

Scholz, John Karl, Ananth Seshadri, and Surachai Khitatrakun. 2006. "Are Americans Saving 'Optimally' for Retirement?" *Journal of Political Economy* 114(4): 607–643.

Scott, Frank A., Mark C. Berger, and John E. Garen. 1995. "Do Health Insurance and Pension Costs Reduce the Job Opportunities of Older Workers?" *Industrial and Labor Relations Review* 48(4): 775–791.

Stevens, Ann Huff. 2006. "The More Things Change, the More They Stay the Same: Trends in Long-Term Employment in the United States, 1969–2002." NBER Working Paper 11878. Cambridge, MA: National Bureau of Economic Research.

Swartz, Katherine. 2008. "Revising Employers' Role in Sponsoring and Financing Health Insurance and Medical Care." In *A Future of Good Jobs? America's Challenge in the Global Economy*, Timothy J. Bartik and Susan N. Houseman, eds. Kalamazoo, MI: W.E. Upjohn Institute for Employment Research, pp. 81–118.

Technical Panel on Assumptions and Methods. 2003. *Report to the Social Security Advisory Board*. Washington, DC: Social Security Advisory Board. http://www.ssab.gov/2003TechnicalPanelRept.pdf (accessed August 8, 2007).

Thompson, Lawrence H. 2004. "Social Security Reform and Benefit Adequacy," Retirement Project Brief No. 17. Washington, DC: Urban Institute.

U.S. Census Bureau. 2002. "Projections of the Total Resident Population by 5-Year Age Groups and Sex, with Special Age Categories: Middle Series, 1999–2010." Summary Table NP-T3, National Population Projections. Washington, DC: U.S. Census Bureau.

6

Improving Job Quality

Policies Aimed at the Demand Side
of the Low-Wage Labor Market

Paul Osterman
Massachusetts Institute of Technology

The last decades have been anxious ones for U.S. employees. The sources of worry are not hard to identify: for most workers, wages have not grown even at the pace of productivity gains, health and pension benefits are harder to obtain, and job security seems increasingly shaky. For many employees, stress levels and work/family pressures have ratcheted up as the job market becomes increasingly difficult to navigate. In addition, at the bottom of the labor market, too many adult Americans continue to find themselves in jobs that pay poverty wages and provide little in the way of a future.

There are diverse explanations of these trends, some of which are well beyond the scope of this chapter. But one central concern is the decisions firms make about how to organize their work. As we will see, employers have alternative choices regarding their employment and human resource systems, and these choices have significant implications for the quality of jobs. With this in mind, it is worthwhile to think about what kinds of policy interventions might succeed in tilting those choices in the direction of better quality employment. Unlike traditional employment and training programs that focus on the supply side, that is, on changing the characteristics of individual workers, this chapter takes up policies that operate on the demand side to influence firms.

The chapter begins by briefly laying out the facts regarding trends in job quality. It then develops a framework for thinking about interventions on the demand side of the market. The remainder of the chapter discusses various policy options. These include efforts to assist firms to improve the quality of the work they offer, as well as interventions intended to develop a set of standards and constraints regarding the nature of work that can be offered.

TRENDS IN JOB QUALITY

How many adults work in what might be termed "bad" jobs? The answer to this question obviously depends on definitions, and there is no common standard. One simple and compelling approach is to focus on wages since these are obviously the most important single consideration. In 2006, the percentage of adults in the private sector who were working for poverty-level wages or less was 18.4 percent, a figure that is strikingly high, particularly given the strength of the job market and the widespread view that this standard is too low an estimate of what it takes to live a decent life.[1] Among government workers (who represented 18.3 percent of employment), the rate was a surprisingly high 10.3 percent (a finding that points directly to a policy recommendation). For men in the private sector the rate was 12.4 percent, and for women 22.1 percent. These numbers change only marginally if they are weighted by the number of hours each person works.[2] This order of magnitude is confirmed by a quite different data source, the National Compensation Survey of Occupational Wages. Conducted in 2001, it surveyed firms as well as state and local governments. In these data, 21.6 percent of all hours worked were in jobs that paid less than two-thirds of the median wage and 16.3 percent were in jobs that paid less than $8.00 an hour (Bernstein and Gittleman 2003).

Unfortunately, recent evidence suggests that the fraction of jobs that are in the lower end of the earnings distribution is growing. The shape of the wage distribution is thinning in the middle and growing at each of the two tails. In one study, Autor, Katz, and Kearney (2006) ranked occupations by their median earnings for the period 1980–2000. For the first 10 years (1980–1990) they find that employment grew most rapidly in higher paid occupations. However, for the second decade they identify a polarization: employment grew rapidly in both the best and the worst paid occupations while it declined in the middle range. Other studies find a similar pattern (Acemoglu 1999).

Adding to the concern is evidence that adults who find themselves in low-wage employment have difficulty moving to higher rungs of the labor market. One study found that among low earners in six years starting in the early 1990s, a period of remarkable economic strength, only 27 percent raised their incomes enough to rise consistently above the poverty line for a family of four (Holzer 2004). A more recent study using the Panel Survey on Income Dynamics came to a similar conclusion. Looking at low earners in the years 1995–2001, the researchers found that 6 percent of those working full time and 18 percent of those working part time in any year had dropped out of the labor force by the next year. Among those who did stay in the workforce, 40 percent experienced either a decrease or no change in their earnings (Theodos and Bednarzik 2006). The experience of welfare reform suggests a similar pattern: the earnings for mothers who leave welfare and enter the job market remain very low over time (Acs and Loprest 2004).

There is also reason to be worried about what is happening further up the distribution in the middle range of jobs that seem to be disappearing. Many of these jobs are located in manufacturing, although other sectors are also experiencing losses. To get a flavor of the problem, consider recent reports of changes at Caterpillar, one of the nation's largest manufacturers. In the past, a typical worker received a package that averaged about $25 an hour in pay; with benefits included the package was valued at $40 an hour. Under the new contract, new employees would receive $12 an hour and an additional $9 per hour in benefits. Explaining this shift, a group president at the firm commented that, "There is a balance that must be struck between being competitive and being middle class" (Uchitelle 2006).

The loss of these good manufacturing jobs is obviously due to a range of forces, notably trade and technology, which are beyond the purview of this chapter. These are highly charged economic and political issues, and there is considerable divergence of opinion regarding this trajectory and what to do about it. However, as we will see, there are possible labor market interventions that might prove helpful in improving the job growth and retention picture in this sector.

Mapping the Distribution of Low-Wage Employment

If we are going to consider interventions on the demand side, it makes sense to try to understand what kinds of firms are most likely to be sources of low-wage employment.[3] As before, I define low-wage workers as those who are earning at or below the hourly wage needed to lift a full-time, full-year worker with a family of four (including two children) above the poverty line.

Table 6.1 shows the industry distribution of low-wage and non-low-wage earners in the private sector. Over one-third of private low-wage workers are concentrated in retail, food and drinking, and accommodation. This concentration poses a significant challenge because, as we will see, few employment and training programs are aimed at these sectors.

Adding to the complications that these data pose for program design is the distribution of firm size among low-wage workers. Table 6.2 shows this distribution (in the private sector). It is important to note that the firm size measure includes employees at all locations of the respondent's employer and hence is an overstatement of the size of the actual establishment where the respondent works.

As is apparent, low-wage workers are more likely to be found working for small employers than are better paid employees. This is consis-

Table 6.1 Distribution of Private Sector Low-Wage and Non-Low-Wage Workers (%)

	Low-wage	Non-low-wage
Construction	4.7	8.2
Manufacturing	11.4	18.3
Retail	20.3	10.1
Professional services	9.2	12.3
Food and drinking services	12.5	2.4
Health	9.9	13.0
Agriculture	2.5	0.5
Accommodation	2.6	0.9
Other	26.9	31.4

SOURCE: 2006 Outgoing Rotation Group. Data are limited to the private sector and are weighted by the sample weight and by hours worked. See notes for additional explanation of data preparation.

Table 6.2 Distribution of Low-Wage and Non-Low-Wage Employees by Firm Size (%)

Number of employees	Low-wage	Non-low-wage
<10	23.0	10.3
10–24	14.7	9.7
25–99	17.8	15.4
100–499	13.4	16.7
500–999	4.6	6.8
1,000+	26.3	40.8

SOURCE: March 2006 Current Population Survey. The data are weighted by hours worked in addition to the sample weight.

tent with the long-standing pattern that large firms pay better than do small ones (Hollister 2004).[4] More specifically, 40 percent of low-wage workers are in firms with 24 or fewer employees, and well over half are in firms with fewer than 100 workers. This concentration in small firms has significant programmatic implications that are often overlooked. In general, small firms are difficult for government programs to work with because the managers have little in the way of slack time and resources (and, not incidentally, are often more suspicious of the government than are larger organizations). In addition, many of the more innovative programmatic ideas, such as constructing career ladders, are of limited applicability in smaller organizations. Finally, it is very resource intensive for programs to work with large numbers of small employers, and the payoff, in terms of the number of people affected, is limited.

Taken together, the implication of the industry and employer size distribution of private low-wage workers is that an effective public policy approach to the issue will need to incorporate multiple strategies. Policies aimed at directly working with employers may be less effective in some parts of the labor market, and standard setting efforts may be relatively more important in these sectors.

The Case for Demand-Side Interventions

Public policy aimed at addressing the large low-wage sector has traditionally emphasized education and training, that is, supply side programs aimed at improving people's human capital. Similarly, labor market policy directed at middle-layer job loss has also focused upon retraining and job search. These foci make sense and are certainly appropriate. Consider, for example, the evidence regarding the distribution of basic skills. A 2003 survey of adults in several OECD nations directly measured literacy skills. The survey in the United States was a random representative sample of 3,400 adults and directly tested the respondents on their achievements in three types of literacy: prose skills, document interpretation skills, and numeracy (OECD and Canadian Ministry of Industry 2005). Five levels were identified, with a level one score signifying very low-level skills. In the United States, 20 percent of adults scored at level one in both prose and document skills, and 26 percent scored at level one in numeracy skills. For comparison, in Canada the fractions at these levels were 14 percent, 15 percent, and 19 percent. In Norway they were 7 percent, 8 percent, and 10 percent (p. 50).

Improving human capital is therefore appropriate but it is incomplete. There is also an important case to be made for interventions on the demand side aimed at providing incentives and assistance to firms to improve the quality of their jobs. There is a broad array of evidence that the employment practices of firms, even after controlling for the characteristics of the labor force, make a difference in the employment outcomes of employees. For example, we know that workers do better if they are employed in large firms, in firms that are unionized, in firms that invest in training, and in firms that pay wage premiums above the going rate. As an example of research along these lines, a study of the earnings mobility of low-wage workers that combined longitudinal household data on individuals with data on firms taken from the Unemployment Insurance database found that nearly half of all transitions out of low-wage employment were associated with changes in employers. Because of the longitudinal fixed effect study design, this pattern could be attributed to the characteristics of the firm as opposed to the human capital attributes of the employees (Holzer, Lane, and Vilhuber 2004). Scholars have also asked why some firms pay higher wages than others and have controlled for supply-side variables such as the occupational distribution and human capital endowments of the labor force. In two such studies, Goshen (1991) finds that a firm effect accounts for between 31 and 51 percent of the variation across firms in wages, and Davis and Haltiwanger (1991) find strong plant-level effects in their wage-determination models.

There is some evidence that firms exercise a nontrivial degree of discretion over their employment practices (and hence, by extension, that policy can influence these choices). One kind of evidence is purely anecdotal and is based on comparisons of the policies of different employers operating in the same product market. Many commentators point to the contrasting employment policies of Costco and Wal-Mart, but one might as readily highlight the employment situation of housekeepers in unionized and nonunionized hotels.

Underlying the view that firms can exercise discretion is the idea that human resource policies tend to cluster together in bundles. These bundles characterize distinctive employment strategies. In the popular discussion, this idea is captured by a distinction between "high road" and "low road" policies, but the concept is more subtle than this. The idea of human resource bundles first emerged in research on the automobile industry, where scholars noted that Japanese firms such as Toyota systematically combined job rotation, team production, and high levels of training into a coherent set of policies that improved both productivity and quality. This was contrasted with a quite different bundle of policies which then characterized American automobile producers. This example is instructive in another way: over time, American auto manufacturers studied and learned from Japan and adopted their human resource strategies. This is an important point because it demonstrates that firms, faced with pressures of various kinds and provided with information and support, can in fact respond by implementing new approaches to how they organize their workforces.

Additional data enable us to understand how clusters or bundles of human resource practices are related to low-wage work. This survey, conducted in 2002, is a representative sample of the for-profit private sector workforce (Bond 2003).[5] In these data, 21.5 percent of the workforce is low wage according to the definition used earlier. This figure is very close to the census figure. It is also noteworthy that other employment-related outcomes cluster with the wage pattern. For example, among the low-wage workers, 55.1 percent did not receive health insurance from their employers. In addition, low-wage employers are much less likely to provide training than are other firms: 46.5 percent of low-wage employees reported that their firms offered training compared to 72.3 percent of the rest of the labor force.

This pattern is replicated in other data. Although generalizations are difficult, it is fair to conclude that a central issue is that many companies are not prepared to invest in the skills and careers of their employees, particularly their lower-paid employees, as part of their overall competitive strategy. Indeed, there is extensive evidence that employer investment in training is disproportionately directed toward higher-wage and better-educated workers and away from so-called "frontline" employees. For example, according to the National Household Survey in 1995, among employees in the bottom quintile in earnings, 22 percent received formal training from their employers, whereas among workers in the top income quintile the rate was 40 percent (Ahlstrand, Bassi, and McMurrer 2003, p. 3).

A final question is whether it is in fact reasonable to believe that work can be reorganized so that today's adult low-wage workforce can move into better jobs. Given the pervasive emphasis on the earnings gap between college and high school graduates, an observer might be forgiven for thinking that there is very little room in the job market for people with less than a four-year college degree. This is not correct. It is important to understand that there is a very large layer of jobs that require skills at roughly the level of a two-year associate's degree. According to projections by the Bureau of Labor Statistics, 28 percent of all job openings in the period 2004–2014 will be for jobs that require some college but not a degree. This is a larger figure than the expected openings for jobs that require college degrees (Hecker 2005). Another way of making this point is to note that the occupational category that is projected to generate the largest number of jobs between 2000 and 2014 is "professional and related occupations," and that of those who held these jobs in the 2000–2005 period, 40.5 percent had some college but less than a college degree. Other projections suggest that there will be a number of new jobs available for skilled blue-collar work (machine maintenance, technicians, repair jobs, and the like), and that these too require education in the "some college" or associate's degree range (Goldberger, Lessell, and Biswas 2005).

A FRAMEWORK FOR THINKING ABOUT POLICY

There are a wide variety of tools available for influencing how firms organize their employment systems, and a framework or classification system is helpful. One important distinction is between what might be termed standard setting on the one hand and technical assistance or programmatic interventions on the other. Examples of the former include unionization, minimum and living wage legislation, and community benefit agreements. Examples of the latter are sectoral training programs, labor market intermediaries, and variants of manufacturing extension services.

A second useful distinction is between interventions aimed at improving the quality of existing jobs ("making bad jobs good") and interventions aimed at creating, or retaining, more good jobs. Examples of the first set of policies are efforts to raise wages or to create job ladders in the existing job base, for example, in the retail, health, or hospitality industries. Examples of the second category are economic development programs that utilize labor market tools to attract good jobs or to assist existing firms to compete more effectively and hence to maintain the base of good jobs that already exist.

Table 6.3 organizes possible policy levers in terms of these distinctions. The distinctions in this table are to some extent arbitrary, but they do represent a useful way of thinking about the universe of policy interventions on the demand side. One important question, addressed

Table 6.3 Policy Matrix

	Standard setting	Programmatic
Make bad jobs good	Minimum wage	Career ladders
	Living wages	Intermediaries
	Unionization	Sectoral programs
Create more good jobs	Community benefit agreements	Extension services
	Managed tax incentives	Sectoral programs
		Consortia or partnerships under business or union auspices

below, is whether there is fruitful interaction across the different boxes. For example, when tax incentives are restricted to jobs above a certain quality threshold, it would make sense to provide programmatic assistance to firms to enable them to meet the standards.

Several additional important questions should be kept in mind; one is scale. The employment and training field is full of examples of small boutique programs that seem successful but which either are inherently limited in their impact or have proved very difficult to replicate. It is therefore important to ask to what extent any potential innovation can have an appreciable impact on the problem. The second difficult question is sustainability. Promising programs are often short-lived and prove dependent on unreliable outside funding or a particular confluence of circumstances that led to the program in the first place. Developing mechanisms to build in greater stability is an important challenge.

Standard-Setting Policy

The goal of standard setting is to set a floor on the quality of jobs. The great attraction of this approach is that it is relatively straightforward and has the potential to reach a scale well beyond what is possible with more programmatic interventions.

Standard-setting policy can be thought of as two subgroups: policies put in place by government (such as minimum wages), and others due to private action (such as unions). Turning first to public policy, by far the best known standard aimed at the low-wage labor market is the minimum wage. The federal minimum wage is currently $5.85 an hour. As is well known, there has been a long-term erosion in its real value, and until the recent modest increase it was at its lowest level since 1955. As a fraction of the pay of the average private sector nonsupervisory worker, it was at the lowest level since World War II (Bernstein and Shapiro 2006). In the face of this stagnation, 29 states now have set minimum wages above the federal level. The political power of this issue was demonstrated in the recent midterm elections when six states voted to increase their minimum wage.

Congress recently increased the minimum wage to $7.25 an hour to be achieved in steps by 2009. Exactly how many people would get a wage increase in 2009 depends, of course, on assumptions about inflation and wage growth. It is important to note, however, that the $7.25 an hour standard is still well below the poverty wage for a family of four with one bread-earner working full time and full year.

The contours of the standard debate regarding the minimum wage are familiar. Opponents argue that an increased minimum leads to job loss as firms lay off employees whose productivity falls beneath the standard, whereas advocates argue that the magnitude of the job loss is low and the gains that accrue to people who remain working at the higher wage well exceed any losses. In recent years the balance of opinion has shifted to the latter view, at least for increases in the range under discussion.

Although the discussion of the minimum wage is typically framed in terms of its impact upon the wages and employment of directly affected employees, a broader view suggests that more is at stake. One way to think about this is to ask why one would support a minimum wage instead of relying entirely on a more generous Earned Income Tax Credit (EITC). A simple view would be that the EITC would raise incomes without having the negative employment consequences of the minimum wage. The answer goes to the broader role of the minimum wage in the job market. By establishing a floor, a minimum wage may prevent low-wage employers from competing on the basis of wage costs with firms that are willing to pay above the minimum. Such competition, if permitted, would drive down the overall wage structure. The EITC does not play this role and, in fact, permits firms to maintain low wages and substandard employment terms. This is not a criticism of the EITC—it is an important program with many virtues but it is not a substitute for the kinds of standards embodied by the minimum wage. There is, unfortunately, very little research that addresses this channel of the minimum wage, and it does seem doubtful that the federal minimum at its current low level is important in this regard. However, in principle this is an important part of the case for an effective and binding minimum wage.

Related to this line of argument, in the sense that the minimum wage is about more than just wage levels, is the view that an increased minimum wage would lead firms to adopt a different bundle of human resource practices. On one level this idea has been around for a long time and, in the context of the union literature, has been characterized as the union "shock effect." The argument is that an enforced higher wage prompts a firm to reconsider and redesign its employment and

production system in order to increase efficiency and obtain the productivity that would sustain the higher wage. More recently, economic
theorists studying how firms make decisions about how much training
to provide their workforces have argued that a higher minimum wage
will compress a firm's internal wage structure and lead to higher levels
of training for those at the bottom (Acemoglu and Pischke 1998).

Unionization

In addition to the minimum wage, the other long-standing and obvious strategy for improving employment conditions in the low-wage
labor market is unionization. The potential of unionization is suggested
in Table 6.4 and shows the fraction of various groups that are low-wage
workers according to the definition used earlier.

It is obvious that union status makes a considerable difference in
the probability that an employee will work for low wages. These results
hold in a regression analysis that also controls for industry in addition
to the human capital and demographic variables.[6]

Some recent research suggests that the apparent gains to be had by
unionization is an artifact of various forms of selection bias that cannot
be dealt with by the standard controls. For example, better motivated
workers may join unions, or unions might succeed in organizing firms
which in any case would have paid high wages. Related to this is the
view that the union/nonunion wage gains shown in Table 6.4 reflect the
success of unions in the past but are not reflective of what they can accomplish now (DiNardo and Lee 2004).

These arguments have technical problems and are inconsistent with
other evidence regarding the role unions play in reducing inequality
(see, for example, Card, Lemieux, and Riddell [2003]).[7] But whatever
their merits in the higher reaches of the job market, these arguments are
not credible in the low-wage sector, where the relevant personal characteristics of the workforce do not vary a great deal, and similar national
chains pay quite differently depending on their union status. The common sense pattern in the table is confirmed by accounts of recent union
contracts in low-wage industries. For example, according to HERE, the
Hotel Employees Restaurant Employees union, the average unionized
hotel maid earns $13 an hour, while the national average for the job is
$8.67 (Marshall and Greenhouse 2006).

Table 6.4 Percentage Low Wage By Union Status, Private Sector (%)

	All	Men	Women	High school degree or less	Some college	White	Black	Hispanic
Union	6.9	3.6	13.3	9.7	4.1	6.0	10.1	16.2
Nonunion	19.5	14.8	24.6	32.3	15.7	18.4	29.5	37.5

SOURCE: 2006 Census Outgoing Rotation Group. See notes for description of data preparation.

Unionization in low-wage, particularly immigrant, sectors has been one of the few bright spots for unions in recent years. The success of Justice for Janitors is one notable example, and a similar campaign—Hotel Workers Rising—is under way in the tourist sector. The unions involved in these campaigns—the Service Employees International Union (SEIU), and the Union of Needletrades, Industrial and Textile Employees and HERE, which have merged to form UNITE HERE—are explicitly focusing much of their organizing strategy on the low-wage, often immigrant, labor market. SEIU has been one of the few unions in America to gain membership in recent years. Other unions, such as the American Federation of State, County, and Municipal Employees (AFSCME), have organized low-wage workers in the public sector with some success.

The real concern about the role unions might play in reducing low-wage employment is not whether, when successful, they improve employment conditions but rather the fact that their success rate is poor. The rate of private sector unionization has fallen from 25 percent in 1973 to just over 7 percent today. Although data on success rates in organizing drives are hard to come by, recent research shows that of those organizing drives that lead to an election (and only about half of such drives even get to this stage), only one in five result in a first contract (Ferguson 2006). Later in this chapter I will discuss how this issue might be addressed.

As the union movement has struggled, there has been growth in alternative modes of organizing and representing low-wage workers. Of particular interest is the emergence of strong community organizations and worker centers.[8]

There are several national networks of community organizations that work in low-wage communities and organize around economic issues.[9] These organizations are particularly active in campaigns to raise the state minimum wage, in living-wage campaigns, and in efforts to redirect the targeting of economic development subsidies. In addition, they also organize around job training and other policies directed at low-wage employees. One of the nation's most successful job training programs, Project QUEST, which is described on p. 223, was established by a community organization in San Antonio. The network of affiliated community organizations then replicated it in several other cities in the Southwest.

Worker Centers are organizations that provide legal and social services to low-wage, often immigrant, workers who are employed in the small firms that populate much of the low-wage labor market. These small, scattered employment sites are not attractive targets for traditional union organizing campaigns. The centers started growing in the 1980s, beginning with the first and still best known of these, the Workplace Project in Long Island. Today, there are roughly 35 in the country (Fine 2006, p. 10). In addition to their service function, some centers try to replace street corner hiring with organized hiring halls (for example, near Home Depot stores) that in turn attempt to standardize wages. They also run campaigns aimed at the employment practices of specific employers. Some centers have also pursued a legislative strategy. For example, the Workplace Project succeeded in obtaining passage of the New York Unpaid Wages Prohibition Act, which seeks to stop the practice of employers holding back promised wages from a vulnerable population.

It is clear that in the national context, 35 Worker Centers cannot accomplish a great deal. However, when all of the representational activity outside traditional union channels—community organizations as well as Worker Centers—is added up, it is fair to conclude that there is an important amount of activity. A central and very open question is whether these newer styles of organizing can join together with traditional unions to obtain the power necessary to have a noticeable impact.

New Standard Setting Strategies

As we will see, in recent years much of the creativity in programs has occurred at the state and local levels, and by the same token, it is at these levels of government that innovative ways of setting standards in the labor market have also been implemented. These efforts include living wage campaigns, community benefit agreements, and restrictions on the use of economic development incentives. These efforts combined constitute a sustained national movement to use political power to raise wage levels.

The first living wage ordinance was passed in Baltimore in 1994 as a result of organizing by a community group affiliated with the national Industrial Areas Foundation network. Since then, according to the ACORN Web site that tracks the movement, there are 140 ordinances throughout the country.[10] There is considerable variation in the coverage and structure of the laws, but the majority cover city contractors, city employees, or both. A smaller set of living wage laws are aimed at firms that receive business assistance from public sources.

Living wage campaigns, and the resulting ordinances, have multiple goals. Beyond the direct effect, one important objective is to use the campaigns as an organizing device and to force a public discussion of economic equity. Although difficult to measure, observation of campaigns suggests that living wage campaigns are important in this regard. However, for the purposes of this chapter, we seek to determine the impact of the campaigns upon job quality.

The first point to be made is that the impact, positive or negative, is relatively small given the restricted nature of the ordinances. The estimate for Boston, for example, is that 1,000 employees had wage increases. The largest effort is probably Los Angeles, where estimated impact is on the order of 7,500 workers. However, the Boston experience is more representative. The magnitude of the mandated wage also varies albeit within a limited range. As of 2002 the ordinance in Boston set a wage of $10.25 an hour, while in Los Angeles it was $8.17.

There is an emerging evaluation literature on living wage campaigns. What is striking is that even skeptics concede that the ordinances are successful in raising wages. The debate is over whether there are negative employment effects, but again, even the skeptics accept that if there are negative effects, the wage gains outweigh the costs, and that as a result there is a net benefit to the low-wage group.[11] Studies of the impact on firms do not find major negative effects, and some suggest that turnover is reduced as a result of the higher wages. In short, living wage laws seem to accomplish their mission, but it is important to remember that the mission is very limited in terms of scope.

An extension of the living wage idea is to establish wage (and possibly benefit) standards on an industry basis. For example, a large majority of the Chicago City Council recently passed an ordinance that required large retailers in the city to pay a minimum wage of $9.25 an hour, with scheduled increases to $10.00. In addition, the employers were required to either provide $1.50 an hour (with a scheduled increase to $3.00) in benefits or else supplement the wage by the same amount. This ordinance was vetoed by the mayor, but a campaign is under way to elect enough city councilors to override the veto. A number of advocacy groups are considering or launching similar campaigns in retail and other industries in different parts of the country.[12]

A second initiative aimed at improving job quality through state and local government action manages the use of economic development incentives. These incentives, which are widely used by both states and cities, offer a variety of tax breaks and incentive payments to firms to influence their location and growth decisions. Until recently there was little public discussion or awareness of the terms of these deals. A rough sense of the scope of the problem is that, according to an analysis of Illinois data, 35 percent of jobs subsidized by economic development incentives in 2004 paid less than $27,000 a year. As recently as 1994, only six jurisdictions put any restrictions on the wage levels that could be subsidized by these development incentives. By contrast, the most recent estimate is that 43 states, 41 cities, and 5 counties have wage restrictions in place for at least one of their subsidy programs (cities and states can, of course, have multiple subsidy programs, and there is no estimate what fraction of all such programs have wage standards). In addition, 10 states require that any firm receiving a subsidy provide a public report on the number of jobs that it expects to retain or create as a result of the subsidy and the wage level of the jobs (see Purinton et al. 2003 and McCourt et al. 2006).

Community benefit agreements (CBAs) are in some sense a combination of efforts aimed to control location subsidies and living wage campaigns. The central idea is to identify a large development project that requires city approval. A coalition of community groups then negotiates with the developer regarding first source hiring, wage standards, and other topics such as parking, affordable housing, and recreation. If an agreement can be reached, the coalition becomes an ally of the developer in obtaining the relevant approvals. Among the most active geographies for CBAs has been Los Angeles, where coalitions organized and supported by the Los Angeles Alliance for a New Economy (LAANE) have negotiated agreements in the Los Angeles airport, Staples Center, and Century Blvd. developments. Similar efforts have been initiated in Denver, Milwaukee, Boston, Seattle, and Chicago (for a description of CBAs, see Gross, Leroy, and Janis-Aparicio [2005]). As promising as CBAs are, there are also obvious limitations: they typically only benefit residents in the area of the large-scale development and the labor standards tend to be modest.[13] Nonetheless, they are a creative addition to the toolkit of efforts to use a combination of political and standard setting power to upgrade job quality.

A final important issue regarding standard setting in low-wage labor markets concerns enforcement. There is a perception among advocates that enforcement efforts and effectiveness has declined in recent years. Data on this are hard to come by, but a recent review of patterns in New York City does suggest that there are significant problems, particularly with respect to overtime pay and minimum wages.[14] Improving this situation is the joint responsibility of both the federal government and state Departments of Labor.

PROGRAMS THAT WORK WITH FIRMS

It is slightly unfair but not too far off the mark to characterize the old style approach to service delivery as one in which agencies trained people in occupations for which they thought there was demand and then either simply sent people out to look for work or helped them in the process. In either case, the connection between programs and employers was tenuous at best. While many programs may still have these characteristics, a new model of best practice has emerged in recent years that features much more interaction with employers.

Programs that work with firms to improve the quality of jobs focus on two main strategies. The first is redesigning jobs to create career ladders or to enlarge the content of existing jobs. This strategy implies both working with management to redesign work and providing training and support to employees so that they can meet the additional responsibilities and move up in the workplace. The second, simpler approach is to encourage firms to increase the quantity of training that they make available to lower paid employees in the hope that this will lead to career advancement.

The new program models vary along a number of dimensions: target groups, the auspices under which the programs are managed, and the nature of the services that are provided. What is striking, however, is that they have also coalesced around a common set of what might be termed "best practices" elements. It is these elements that move these innovations beyond the traditional approach of education and training programs and that make these new programs distinctive and important.

The most important of these best practice elements is driven by an understanding that employment and training efforts work best if they connect effectively to both sides of the labor market, that is, to employers as well as clients. In order to accomplish this they work hard to become knowledgeable about the human resource needs of their target group of firms and, in some cases, they also seek to understand how they can contribute to the competitive success of the firms. In short, they seek to appeal to firms as a business proposition, not as a charity, public relations, or welfare effort.

The second feature is that best practice programs make substantial investments in their clients. They reject the quick and dirty training, short-term investments, and simple job search assistance models that characterize much of the traditional education and training system. The investments that the new programs make take a variety of forms: long training periods, more sustained involvement with firms, and higher levels of support to clients in terms of financial assistance and counseling.

There are, however, important differences across the programs. Their auspices vary and include community groups, unions, community colleges, employer organizations, and state governments. The programs also vary in the extent to which they work with incumbent workers versus job seekers.

Much, but not all, of the discussion around these new models tends to focus on two broad program categories: labor market intermediaries and sectoral programs. Labor market intermediaries are organizations that consciously look both ways in the job market, attempting to work with both employers and with individuals. Some intermediaries are passive in that they effectively are just bulletin boards, providing matching services for firms or workers. Others are slightly more ambitious and take job orders from firms and try to find or train employees to fill them. However, the most creative intermediaries provide a range of services to employers, including what might be termed "HR Consulting" aimed at improving job quality. These intermediaries also work with individuals providing training and placement for their client firms. Sectoral programs perform the same functions as do intermediaries, but they have the added characteristic of specializing in a particular industry. They seek to develop deep knowledge of the markets, technology, and labor market circumstances of the industry, and through this knowledge contribute to both the human resource and also the economic growth and development needs of the industry. Both sets of organizations try not only to improve access to jobs but also to help make bad jobs better and to create more good jobs. The relative weight put on these goals varies across different programs. Examples of programs include the following:

Cooperative Home Care Associates (CHCA) works with low-paid home health care aides and seeks to transform the nature of their work by creating a workers' cooperative, providing more training and skill than is typical, and leveraging this to charge a higher than average wage/benefit package and create a larger proportion of full-time work than is the norm. The model has been successful in New York City and is replicated in other locations by the Paraprofessional Health Care Institute.

Boston SkillWorks. Several regions have pulled together funding streams and established intermediaries to work with firms to upgrade low-wage workers. Boston SkillWorks has received funding from public sources and several local and national foundations and is a five-year, $15 million dollar effort. Managed by a local intermediary, Jobs for the Future, it has established career ladder programs in several local hospitals and is working to do the same in the hotel/hospitality industry and in building services. Its goal is to upgrade roughly 2000 incumbent workers and to provide preemployment training to roughly 500 new hires.

Pennsylvania Industry Clusters. A number of states have been very aggressive in pulling together disparate funding streams to create a more unified workforce policy (for a description of some of these efforts see Jobs for the Future [2005]). Many experts in economic development believe that an effective strategy is to identify clusters of firms in the same industry and work with them to address challenges that they have in common. Pennsylvania has applied this idea to its approach toward workforce development. The state identified 9 industry clusters and 17 subclusters. It then established a $20 million annual appropriation to organize and deliver training through cluster-specific "industry partnerships." It also reprogrammed existing federal and state community college funding to target the skill needs of the clusters. Industry partnerships must have an explicit strategy that spells out how the workforce services will improve industry competitiveness and job quality.

Extension Services, such as the Massachusetts Manufacturing Partnership and the Jane Addams Resource Corporation. The Massachusetts program helps firms adopt the Toyota Production system. It works with individual companies and sponsors events at which firms make presentations as well as plant tours. The Massachusetts program is essentially a technology/production assistance program that has a workforce development component. The relative emphases are reversed at the Jane Addams Resource Corporation in Chicago, which works with small manufacturers in a corridor within the city. The activities of Jane Addams show that an extension service can both provide a range of services and serve as a link between the economic development and the workforce components. Jane Addams is part of the Local Industrial Retention Initiative and helps firms obtain various forms of technical assistance and services from city agencies. It runs a large (400 trainees per year) incumbent worker training program, as well as an entry-level machinists training program for unemployed residents. Jane Addams is also active in an effort to develop a small high school devoted to machining skills, and an initiative to benchmark and improve the manufacturing skills training provided by the community colleges within Chicago.

Project QUEST. QUEST is a training program in San Antonio, Texas aimed at the working poor who have high school diplomas. The program works with firms in San Antonio to identify job openings and to identify the skills required. The firms then make a good-faith pledge to hire program graduates and may redesign their jobs to create ladders. The jobs must meet living wage standards. The training is provided by local community colleges and typically lasts one and a half years. The program provides modest financial support and extensive counseling to the clients. It is organized and managed by a nonprofit organization that is closely linked to a community-based organization. Over 2,000 people have participated in QUEST.

What Do These Programs Do?

These programs have various strategies for improving job quality, but the most common are attempts to create career ladders and to enlarge jobs. The most extensive efforts along these lines have been in the health care sector, including hospitals and nursing homes. An example, which comes from programs in Boston, is the creation of a ladder associated with the job title Patient Care Technician. This is a low-level job, essentially the hospital equivalent of the nursing home title Certified Nursing Assistant. An associate's degree or the equivalent is required to move up the ladder from this job in a hospital. Boston SkillWorks worked to create a ladder by encouraging hospitals to establish Patient Care I, II, and III positions with increasing responsibility, and to provide tuition assistance to enable people to study as they moved up the ladder. The new positions on the ladder provided both greater rewards and tangible feedback as people undertook the effort to move up.

There are a large number of efforts around the country to build ladders of this kind in hospitals and nursing homes (Fitzgerald 2006). Many of the largest and best known health care programs have been negotiated by the SEIU union health care locals, although there are also many examples in the nonunion sector, such as the Boston one cited above. The Robert J. Woods Foundation is currently supporting roughly a dozen demonstration programs around the country that focus on how to build more learning opportunities directly into health care workplaces.

There are also small programs to create comparable ladders in other low-wage settings, such as hotels and retail. For example, Work-Source Partners, a firm that helps employers build career ladders, has a small effort under way with the CVS Drugstore chain to create a Retail Management Certificate program to move check-out clerks into pharmacy technician and potentially store manager positions. The effort is supported in part by state (of Massachusetts) training funds and in part by CVS, which finances some coaching and support as well as some paid released time and tuition assistance. It is worth noting that CVS's interest in creating career ladders is long-standing. For example, a case study conducted in 2000 described CVS as exemplary in attempting to upgrade low-skill workers through career paths and training (Ahlstrand, Bassi, and McMurrer 2003, pp. 65–74). Given, however, that the certificate program described above is still characterized as a pilot effort, a reasonable conclusion would be that even in a large organization with a commitment to the issue, change is very slow and incremental.

Some of the efforts, particularly in health care, are quite large. Outside of health care, however, most programs are still small and of the pilot variety. These career ladder programs are typically at least partially funded by public or foundation training resources, although some of the union-linked programs are financed out of funds set aside in collective bargaining agreements. The motivation of employers, beyond social responsibility, is to reduce turnover (with its associated impact on recruiting costs and perhaps customer service) and increase labor supply into occupations for which they are experiencing shortages.

Assessing the Interventions

As promising as career ladder programs are, there are several difficult questions. The vast majority of the efforts are in health care (for reasons discussed below). How far these kinds of programs can extend beyond health care and whether the business case (reduced turnover, better service) is really compelling is unclear. Unfortunately, the most comprehensive review of career ladders suggests that these worries are legitimate. Fitzgerald (2006) reviews career ladder efforts in several other industries than health. For child care she characterizes the current state of play as "embryonic" (p. 63); in education she writes that "neither school officialdom nor the public is entirely convinced that significant skill upgrades are even possible among school paraprofessionals or are worth the money" (p. 92); and in biotechnology she concludes that "it is too early to say much about the results" (p. 118). Only in manufacturing is there very much to show, and here the star example is one program in Wisconsin.

A thoughtful evaluation of the experience of one highly touted program reinforces these worries (FutureWorks 2004). In 2002 Massachusetts launched its BEST (Building Essential Skills through Training) program. The initiative combined Adult Basic Education and flexible job training money and sought to work with firms in health care, financial services, manufacturing, and biotechnology to upgrade workforce skills and to build career ladders. The program was the result of a task force which issued the standard critiques of the employment and training system (narrow and constrained funding streams, and lack of employer involvement), and BEST was a state of the art response with respect to program design and flexible funding. The goal of the program was to create career ladders for low-wage workers in the targeting sectors.

Of the six sectoral programs, two did very poorly on all dimensions because of staffing and implementation issues. The remaining four programs did succeed in training a relatively large number of employees. However, virtually all of the training was short term. Even in the consortia with the greatest employer enthusiasm, it proved very difficult to convince firms to care about anything other than short-term staffing needs. Firms were not willing to invest in career ladders: "Some employers had a hard time visualizing their entry-level workers as higher skilled employees. Others simply lacked the internal capacity required to promote career path development among their entry-level workers" (FutureWorks 2004, p. 21). The report goes on to comment that

> . . . employer support and implementation capacity for career path development is in its infancy. While employers may support the career path notion in theory, few human resource directors, managers, or supervisors . . . have the time or resources required to institutionalize the approach . . . it remains unclear whether limited demand for career path models is due to lack of information (i.e., employers are simply unfamiliar with the concept and need more/ better information about career path models), lack of time and re-

sources (i.e., employers don't have internal resources to develop and implement the approach) or due to employer perceptions regarding entry level workers (i.e., employers have difficulty viewing entry-level workers as future skilled labor). (p. 28)

The evaluation did document a substantial amount of training, particularly in basic skills, but it was unable to attribute any gain in wages or career trajectory to the program.

The BEST program lasted for two years. On one hand, this can be seen as a sustained effort to implement a new model. On the other hand, two years is relatively short in terms of the goal of changing the employment practices of firms. However, what is clear from the experience is that the energy, organizational skills, and resources for such an effort need to come from the program and the intermediary. Few of the employers who were involved were willing to continue the training of entry-level workers after the program ended, much less engage in the organizational changes envisioned by the program (FutureWorks 2004, p. 39).

A more optimistic, but still very mixed, experience in manufacturing was documented in a recent report on a project funded in 2001 three foundations (Mott, Ford, and Annie E. Casey) and managed by the National Association of Manufacturers (NAM) (Whiting 2005). The goal was to assist three local NAM chapters (in Connecticut, Michigan, and Pennsylvania) in their efforts to work with five small and medium-sized manufacturing firms with the dual mission of improving their internal human resource processes and upgrading low-wage employees in their labor forces. Representatives from each association recruited firms to participate and then provided them with technical assistance on their recruitment, training, supervisory, and compensation systems. In addition, the program brokered training services for employees in the firms.

The results of this effort, which ended in 2004, were positive but mixed. The project was slowed initially by the recession and fell one year behind schedule. As a result, the formal evaluation that was planned was scrapped. Recruitment of firms was slow, but in the end 17 firms were involved. The narrative report points to employer reports of improvements in productivity and quality, and a variety of positive comments by employers are cited. These are credible achievements. However, after three years of effort, the best claim in terms of advancement is that a total of 14 promotions and 28 pay increases could be attributed to the program. Furthermore, the employers reported that without a continued subsidy they would be unlikely to continue with the program.

Beyond narrative accounts of specific programs, systematic research on these models is thin. Although these new models have gained substantial attention in policy circles, there are limited data on either their diffusion or effectiveness. A 2002 survey by the National Network of Sector Partners identified 243 organizations that met four criteria: 1) they worked with both employees and employers, 2) they targeted low-wage workers, 3) they provided a mix of services and not simply job placement, and 4) they invested in longer-term career advancement past the placement stage. More than half of these programs were less than 10 years old, and two-thirds of them served 500 or more persons per year. They were housed in a wide range of different kinds of organizations (Marino and Tarr 2004).

The more formal evaluation evidence on these initiatives is promising but incomplete and thin. A pre/post evaluation of Project QUEST found very large gains for participants, and as part of that evaluation, a study of participant files suggested that creaming and self-selection effects could not explain away the gains (Osterman and Lautsch 1996). A qualitative evaluation reached positive conclusions about the ability of sectoral programs to achieve their goals, and a pre/post evaluation of six intermediary and sectoral programs by Public/Private Ventures found, 24 months after program completion, gains from $1–$5 per hour in wages for five of the organizations (Grote and Roder 2005; Pindus et al. 2004).

Alternative Strategies for Working with Firms

The programs described above work with low-wage firms to improve the quality of work by redesigning both jobs and job ladders. The most common alternative (but also complementary) approach is the straightforward one of increasing the training investments that firms make in their low-wage employees so that mobility prospects, within the firm and elsewhere, are improved. Recall the earlier evidence that the pattern of firm training expenditure is biased away from low-wage and frontline workers. Of course, an obvious question is why firms would be willing to train employees if this facilitated their departure to other (albeit better) employers.

There are a range of programs, typically at the state level, that aim to increase employers' investment in training. A number of states provide tax credits to firms for employees who complete certified retraining programs. However, there have been no efforts to assess these programs either in terms of direct impact or whether they expand the scope of training rather than simply subsidize firms for what they would have done in any case (Bosworth 2006, p. 43).[15] There are other ideas for using the tax system and financial aid to increase the training investments of firms, which will be taken up in the next section.

A more direct approach to transforming the employment practices of firms is to provide them with grants to subsidize or incent improved practices. We will see below that a number of states have established state training funds along these lines. There have been virtually no evaluations of these efforts, but one study of a Michigan program in the early 1990s found that firms that received training grants did increase their level of training for the period of the grant (although not beyond) and also achieved productivity gains (in this case, reduced scrap rates) that persisted beyond the grant. The pattern of the training outcomes is good news/bad news. The good news is that the grant did not simply subsidize what the firm would have done anyway. The bad news is that, despite evident performance gains, the HR practices of the firms were not shifted to a "higher road " since the increase in training was not sustained (Holzer et al. 1993).

Other attempts to convince firms to improve their human resource practices rely on publicity and jawboning. For example, the Council for Adult and Experiential Learning (CAEL) in Chicago has organized an effort called Workforce Chicago. This model brings together leading local firms to award and publicize best practice with respect to workforce training. There is considerable local publicity, the political establishment has become involved, and the winning firms hold workshops for other companies on how to implement their practices. There is an active Web site and a quarterly newsletter. In addition, the organization has sought to be a forum for bringing together the business community with the higher education leadership to discuss common issues.

Local political leaders and sponsors find the model compelling enough to try to spread it to other cities. There are comparable efforts now under way in Philadelphia and St. Louis, and CAEL has presented to the National Conference of Mayors. This said, there has been no assessment of how effective this effort is in influencing employment practices (there is a certain "preaching to the choir" element to the effort) or in improving the circumstances of frontline employees in particular.

Some Lessons on Working with Firms

Stepping back from these various efforts, it is useful to ask what are the lessons about the challenges of working with firms to upgrade low-wage workers. A helpful first question is to ask what are the characteristics of the firms that seem willing to work with employment and training programs to upgrade their workforces. In surveying the landscape of programs it is hard to avoid being struck by the disproportionate role that health care firms play in programs. For example, the vast majority of career ladder efforts are in health care. If we ask why this is the case then we can begin to understand what motivates employers.

Health is, as we saw earlier, a sector with large numbers of poorly paid employees and hence is a natural target. In addition, the overall shape of employment in the health sector is conducive to ladders in that there are multiple levels of jobs and a progression path. Other sectors, such as hotels, have more narrow pyramidal employment ladders, offering fewer opportunities for upward movement.

There is, however, more to the story about why health is an attractive target. Health care employers are not footloose; they cannot pull up stakes and move to a location with lower wages. Furthermore, they tend to be dependent on various public policies: licenses, approvals, and the like. Both of these factors lead health care employers to be willing to consider participation in these efforts. Adding to the incentives is that many health care employers experience high turnover and difficulties in maintaining a stable workforce. This increases their costs and also reduces the quality of their services. The programs that we have described promise to address these issues. An additional consideration is that many hospitals are unionized, and the unions, particularly SEIU and ASFCME, have been very interested in building career ladders. A final consideration is that at least a subset of health care employers can be reimbursed via federal and state payment schemes for the expenses of the effort.

When all these factors are taken into account, it is not surprising that efforts to upgrade the quality of work have had the greatest success in health care. But the flip side is that it is also clear why making progress is so difficult in other sectors of the economy where many of the underlying supports and incentives are absent. Accounts of working with firms point to several difficulties (in addition to the absence of the considerations cited above for health). These difficulties can be seen in the BEST initiative, which worked with small employers in a variety of industries and in the NAM project, which focused on small manufacturers. Small and medium-sized firms that employ low-wage workers lack the organizational slack to improve their human resource systems. Their managers are stretched thin, and the human resource specialist (if there is one) also performs multiple functions and lacks the time and resources to radically transform the employment system. A sense of the difficulties can also be gained from the findings of a task force that interviewed small and medium-sized manufacturers in Indiana. The report found that the firms 1) "see no quick payback and little financial incentive since investments in human capital do not receive as favorable tax treatment as investments in physical capital," 2) "fear that they will be unable to secure the benefits of training investments as higher-skilled workers might move to other firms," 3) "are not confident that they can predict changing skill requirements much less design the mix of training and new skill development that will adequately prepare their workers," and 4) "don't know much about the education and training systems" (Ball State University 2003).

Small firms are difficult targets for the reasons cited above and because of the tremendous effort required to reach a substantial number of workers (given that small firms are small). However, there are also significant challenges in working with larger employers. Even in these companies there often is no advocate for transforming the work of low-wage employees. American firms are notorious (in comparison to companies in other countries) for the relative weakness of the human resources function, and hence there is no natural constituency with power pushing for investment in the low-wage workforce (Pfeffer 1994). Furthermore, many managers, in both large and small firms, are skeptical of the gains that could be achieved by upgrading their low-wage workers. It is only when top management "gets religion" that there is an opportunity to work with firms, and the task of propagating that religion and selling it within the organization is slow and difficult.

Summary

In the past decade there has been a good deal of investment and creative experimentation in working with firms to improve job quality. These initiatives have disproved one long-standing misperception: that employment and training policy is ineffective. We know that it is possible to design effective interventions that upgrade the quality of jobs and improve the working experience of low-wage employees. In addition, a clear consensus has emerged around the elements of a best practice model.

Despite these accomplishments, however, it is not clear just how far it is possible to go with interventions of this kind. As the BEST and NAM experiences make clear, making progress is very slow and runs up against the natural difficulties of working with employers who have many other concerns on their minds and who do not have a history of interest in human resource issues. Even some of the more successful models, such as Boston SkillWorks, were many years in the making and impact a relatively small number of employees in a limited range of industries. In addition, there is ample room for knowledge development. We do not know, for example, whether models of this sort are most effective when implemented by community groups, unions, or business associations.

A final issue is that these program models cannot succeed in a policy vacuum. In order for employees to move up a job ladder, or in order for them to simply receive training, traditional training programs need to have an appropriate level of resources. In addition, work supports of various kinds are important to enable the low-wage workers to succeed. The programs are thus challenged on scale along two dimensions: first, whether they can inherently work on a large enough scale to make an impact, and second, whether public resources will be available at an appropriate level to enable whatever degree of success is possible.

MOVING FORWARD

Improving low-wage work is the next frontier of labor market policy. In an era of exploding income inequality and welfare reform that has encouraged many people to join the low-wage labor market, it is essential that the United States systematically asks how to improve the quality of jobs. This challenge is given additional urgency by the evidence that upward mobility out of the low-wage job market is very slow and uneven.

If we look back at the evidence presented in this chapter, several broad conclusions stand out:

- There is a great deal of program activity and creativity on multiple dimensions and using multiple strategies. A wide range of actors, public and private, are involved. There are examples of interventions that work, and other examples of promising interventions should be supported and assessed.

- The program activity, while substantial, is well below any reasonable estimate of what is required based on the universe of need. Perhaps more importantly, it is scattered and in no way constitutes a coherent national strategy or commitment to addressing the challenge of improving job quality.

- Any successful effort to improve the quality of jobs must include both standard setting and programmatic components. The standard setting strategy is important because it is scalable, i.e., it impacts a large number of employers, and because it can influence practices among small firms and firms in sectors such as retail, which are difficult for programmatic efforts to reach. Whenever possible, it is desirable to offer firms programmatic assistance to achieve the standards.

- On the programmatic side, it is important to bring to bear a wide range of institutions, including traditional federal employment and training programs, state customized training, economic development and small firm assistance programs, and new institutions such as intermediaries and sectoral programs.

- This chapter has emphasized efforts to improve the employment practices of firms. It is clear, however, that more traditional human capital training programs are of continuing importance both because of skill gaps in the low-wage labor force and because any effort to work with firms must include strategies for upgrading the workforce.

In short, the matrix presented earlier is a useful guide. We need to make bad jobs better, and we need to create more good jobs. In addition, any effective national strategy should include a combination of carrots and sticks. A strategy that relies entirely on training and economic development programs working directly with individual employers or employer groups could achieve a good deal but is also slow and incomplete in its coverage. A strategy that supports increased unionization and better wage and hour standards would impact a larger number of employees but lacks the tools to help employers meet their responsibilities. Some combination of the two approaches seems optimal.

A Prelude: The Current State of Play

The central Federal Employment and Training program is the Workforce Investment Act (WIA), but in recent years overall funding levels have been flat, and even the diminishing resources that are available have been diverted from training and instead are spent on job-matching functions (the One-Stop Centers).[16] In addition, restrictions on WIA funding mean that very little can be spent on working with firms to upgrade their employment systems. As a result of falling federal investment in the employment and training system, the real action has shifted to the states and to foundations. Foundation funding has been crucially important but is not a sustainable basis for building public policy. State funding for programs working with firms is largely found in the state training funds based on the unemployment insurance system.

These funds were first started by California, with its well-known and largest fund, the Employment and Training Panel (ETP).[17] The California ETP was financed by a small diversion of the unemployment insurance tax into the training fund, which set the pattern for many states. Today there are seven states that finance training funds via some draw on the UI tax system, but there are another 16 states that have comparable funds that simply use an employer tax. These state training funds range quite widely in size, ranging from $100,000 per year in Delaware to over $70 million per year in California. They all support training for incumbent workers, and 14 also support training for new or pre-hire employees. They typically require an application from a firm as well as, often, from a training provider or intermediary. Roughly 10 of the states seem to primarily use their programs as an economic development tool to attract new firms; however, in the remainder of the states the funds are potentially an important resource for improving the prospect of low-wage incumbent employees.

There are relatively few linkages between these funds and other employment and training funding streams. The states vary widely in how they measure impact and potential substitution (firms using the program to support what they would do anyway), and overall there is little that can be said with confidence in terms of assessment. The great advantage of these funds (in addition to simply the existence of the resources) is that they tend to be much more flexible than federal money with respect to targeting and allowable activities. However, as noted, many of these funds do not address issues in the low-wage labor market, and only half of the states have any such funds in the first place.

The other key player is the community college system. These institutions are by far the largest occupational training organizations, and many of their students are low-income adults. In 2000, among all college students, 29.6 percent were in community college occupational training programs, and another 28.7 percent were in other community college tracks. Of the students enrolled in occupational training, 64 percent were in associate's degree programs, with the remainder in certificate programs (Bailey et al. 2004). The profile of the students suggests that community colleges touch the working poor population to a nontrivial extent. Fifty-five percent of students in occupational programs are 24 or older, 39 percent are minority, and two-thirds attend part-time. Eighty percent of community college students work full or part time while in school (Brock and LeBlanc 2005, p. 2). Another indication is that among first-time community college students between the ages of 25 and 64 in 1995–1996, 71 percent were in the lower two income quintiles compared to 50 percent of younger students (Prince and Jenkins 2005, p. 2). Most of what community colleges do is straightforward education and training—not the kind of activity that has been the focus of this chapter. However, many community colleges have implemented customized training programs that work directly with firms in their regions.

The Road Ahead

Today there is no national framework or set of institutions for supporting efforts to upgrade low-quality jobs. The lack of these institutions in the labor market field has been contrasted with the creation of LISC, the Enterprise Foundation, and the Low Income Tax Credit as an integrated national effort to address housing quality.[18] Several national foundations (notably Ford, Casey, and Mott) have sought to build equivalent institutions for the low-wage labor market. The foundations have succeed impressively in funding demonstration efforts and also in supporting nonprofits that provide technical assistance. However, in the long run a model based on foundation support is not sustainable nor can it operate on the appropriate scale.

As already noted, there are promising strategies for working with firms, many of which have been implemented by an impressive range of actors, including business associations, non-profits, labor market intermediaries, and unions. One central problem, however, is that these efforts are underresourced. It is, of course, not surprising to hear a claim that more money is needed, but the problem goes beyond simply the level of funding. In general, the existing federal funding structure does not support what some have termed the "core intermediary functions" of organizing firms, working with their human resource staff, designing career ladders, and supporting employees. Rather than seeing these functions as central, federal programs view them as overhead or "administration" and sharply limit the amount of resources available.

Taking into account both the federal and state funding streams and the substantive issues raised by these streams, two important federal policy initiatives are attractive. The first aims to create a federal program and framework to support innovative intermediaries and other programmatic initiatives. The second tries to change the incentive structure confronting firms as they decide how much to invest in their employees.

The Department of Labor should establish a "Low Wage Challenge Fund" for supporting programs that work with firms to upgrade the jobs of their low-wage workers. In addition to directly funding programs, matching resources should be available to incentivize states to establish or increase their customized training fund programs and to orient these programs toward the low-wage/low-skill workforce.

The Low Wage Challenge Fund would systematically fund policy entrepreneurship. As already noted, the past decade has seen an impressive flowering of new program designs. At the same time it is also true that there is a series of unanswered questions about these efforts that need to be studied and evaluated, not the least of which is the standard question about impact. In addition, these programs vary considerably in their auspices (who sponsors and runs them), in the role played by support services, and in whether they aim at particular industries or sectors or whether they provide broad occupational training.

The fund would be structured to play the same role, but on a larger scale, that the foundation world is currently playing. That is, the fund would support innovative program models and also seek to leverage the resources of other systems, notably the state training funds and the community college system.

The goals would be to provide incentives for states that currently do not have such funds to establish them (about half the states) and to move the funds away from their smokestack-chasing character and toward well-designed training for low-wage employees. There are already best practice states in this regard. For example, New Jersey has a "Supplementary Workforce Fund For Basic Skills," which provides resources for literacy and Adult Basic Education training in firms, and Florida gives extra points in its application process to proposals that focus on low-wage workers.

The goal of working with community colleges is to take advantage of the resources of this very large system that already educates large numbers of low-wage workers. Including the manufacturing extension services in this effort is also desirable because it speaks to the need to maintain the base of good jobs that we already have.

It is worthwhile to use federal resources to match and stimulate state training funds and community college programs because it levers additional resources. In return for federal matching, the state training funds should establish procedures to assure that any support they provide to firms represents a net addition to the firms' training efforts directed to low-wage workers (and does not simply substitute for what the firm would otherwise have done), and that the programs are subject to credible evaluation.

The second broad goal is to reorient public policy to alter the incentive structure facing firms and to encourage them to improve the quality of the jobs that they offer. A key issue here is training expenditures. As we have seen, employer training is biased against low-wage workers. A few states attempt to address this problem by offering tax credits to firms that increase their investment in training their less well-paid employees; however, these programs are scattered and little is known about them. A federal tax credit for incremental (additional) training that was directed to low-wage employees would be an important step forward. It would be important to design the credit so that it targets the group of employees who need the extra boost and so that it is not a windfall that rewards firms for what they would do regardless. There are also good reasons to insist that the training lead to a general credential that provides mobility to the employee, although this needs to be weighed against likely reluctance of firms to invest in training that encourages their employees to leave. (A proposal along these lines can be found in Bosworth [2006]).

Strengthening Standards in the Low-Wage Labor Market

An increase in the federal minimum wage is long overdue. In addition, it is important to find ways to level the playing field for union organizing. The real concern about the role unions might play in reducing low-wage employment is not whether, when in place, they improve employment conditions but rather the fact that their success rate is poor. These negative trends in membership and campaign success rates continue even though numerous surveys suggest that a substantial fraction of unorganized employees would like to be represented by unions (see Freeman 2007). This pattern suggests that something is broken in the system established by the National Labor Relations Act.

A good deal of effort is being devoted internally in the union movement to raise the rate of union success. These efforts include putting more resources into organizing, being more strategic in designing organizing campaigns, and considering new models of representation, such as membership organizations without collective bargaining rights. On the national agenda are attempts to reform labor law to speed up elections and to reduce the incentives of employers to delay and to engage in unfair labor practices. One currently popular (in union circles) proposal calls for card-check campaigns. Such procedures are of growing importance (see Brudney 2005). There is not uniform agreement, even among those sympathetic to unions, that the card-check strategy is the best approach. However, it is clear that finding ways to level the playing field for unions in the low-wage labor market is an important component of any strategy.

The third arrow in the standard setting quiver is to strengthen the use of economic development incentives to create good jobs. Here it is important to continue the trend of assuring that tax abatements and economic development subsidies are only available if they lead to good jobs. Much of the responsibility for this rests in state governments, and the role of the federal government would be to advocate and diffuse best practice. However, federal programs should also walk the talk with respect to the wage standards embodied in the Workforce Investment Act, TANF training programs, and other federal efforts.

CONCLUSION

America is a wealthy country, and in recent years productivity has resumed its upward climb. Yet despite this success, low-wage work is not only far more prevalent than seems appropriate, but the share of employment that is below acceptable standards is increasing. The difficulty that low-wage workers have in escaping the bottom of the labor market makes these patterns even more troubling.

The first step to addressing this is a real national commitment to the problem. There have been periods—for example, the New Deal or the War on Poverty—when labor market issues have been a central concern of public policy. Unfortunately, in recent years this has not been the case, and advocates have not been able to articulate a convincing narrative that makes the case for serious policy steps to address the bottom of the job market. Nor has the political will been present. The success of recent state-level minimum wage campaigns and local living wage campaigns suggests that the political situation may be shifting. However, years of skepticism about what government can accomplish have undermined confidence that the problem can be resolved. As a result, the challenge remains of making a convincing case that effective policy is possible.

This chapter has described a multilevel strategy for improving job quality at the bottom of the labor market. A combination of standard setting and assistance to employers in upgrading their human resource policies holds promise. In my view both prongs of strategy are essential. A pure programmatic job training or sectoral strategy will run into significant difficulties of scale and will also have problems reaching the smaller firms, which are significant employers of low-wage workers. Standard setting plays a key role of giving firms incentives to participate in the programmatic efforts because those initiatives enable them to more productively achieve the standards. In addition, standard setting will reach smaller firms while programmatic approaches may not.

For these efforts to succeed, adequate resources need to be available for job training, for work support, and to support the intermediary organizations that work with firms. Much of the real work needs to be done at the local and state levels, but the federal government has a central role to play both with respect to resources and standards. This chapter has tried to be realistic about what is possible and to recognize the limitations of any set of programs. At the same time, there is reason to be optimistic, and an ambitious commitment to upgrading low-wage work can have an impact. We have learned a great deal about what works, and the next step is to implement what we have learned on a large enough scale to make a real difference.

Notes

1. This is based on an analysis of the census Outgoing Rotation Group (ORG) data. The wage standard is based on the poverty level for a family of four and assumes 2,080 hours of work a year. In 2006, this implied an average wage of $9.83 or less. The wage levels for the previous years are adjusted using the CPI to 2006 levels. The sample is limited to adults 25–64 years old who worked in the private sector, and only data in the fourth month rotation are analyzed here. There is an extensive literature regarding the use of ORG data that includes complications regarding the use (or nonuse) of allocated wages, the treatment of topcoding, and the elimination of outliers (among other concerns). In my analysis I have followed the data preparation steps described in Lemieux (2006), which represent the standard steps in the literature. Specifically, I use only nonallocated wages, eliminate outliers according to Lemieux's rules, and adjust for topcoding using the conventions of Lemieux.

2. In the private sector, if we weight each observation by the number of weekly hours worked, then 16.5 percent of hours overall are low wage.

3. For this purpose, the March Current Population Survey is more useful than the Outgoing Rotation Group data used above because, although its hourly wage data are less precise, it contains data on firm size. The wage data are less precise because they have to be estimated using usual hours worked per week and usual weekly earnings. The processing of the data follows Lemieux (2006). The data are weighted by hours worked. The industry and size variables refer to the longest job held during the year while the wage variable is an average over the whole year. I have eliminated anyone who was self-employed at the time of the interview as well as people who report that more than 10 percent of their total annual earnings was due to self-employment.

4. Hollister argues that in recent years the traditional firm size effect on wages has weakened.

5. The data are nationally representative of people ages 25–64 in the for-profit sector who speak either English or Spanish.

6. Both an OLS and a logit regression were run in which the dependent variable was the probability of being low wage and the independent variables included controls for sex, race, education, and a series of industry dummy variables. In the OLS regression the coefficient was 0.109 and highly significant. In the logit the coefficient on union was 1.36 and also highly significant.

7. The research is based on examining what happens to wages in situations where unions win or lose an election by a very small margin. The argument is that in such cases the various forms of selection bias are eliminated. However, it is possible that an effective union can win an election by a large margin due to its power rather than to selection bias explanations, and in such a case the wage gains should be attributed to the union effect. In addition, in a growing number of cases agreements are achieved via card-check and not by elections.

8. The discussion of community organizations draws from Osterman (2003). The discussion of Worker Centers draws from Fine (2006) and from Gordon (2005).

9. These networks include the Industrial Area Foundation, Direct Action Research Training (DART), PICO National Network, Gamamiel, and the Association of Community Organizations for Reform Now (ACORN). The first four organize heavily through congregations and hence are often termed "faith-based" organizations. One recent estimate is that there are 133 of these faith-based organizations throughout the country.

10. See www.livingwagecompaign.org.

11. The skeptical view is summarized and reviewed in Neumark and Adams (2004). The more positive view is summarized in Thompson and Chapman (2006).

12. A resource for data on these campaigns is the Brennan Center for Justice at the New York University Law School.

13. In the case of the Staples agreement the wage standards for 70 percent of the jobs in the project were set at between $7.72 and $8.97 an hour and $100,000 was set aside to support training.

14. According to the research, several surveys show that 67 percent of domestic workers receive no overtime pay even though they are entitled to it, 59 percent of

restaurant employees have the same problem, and small retail stores in Brooklyn routinely violate wage and hour laws. See Brennan Center for Justice (2006).

15. Bosworth reports that these tax credits are available in Rhode Island, Georgia, Arizona, Colorado, Connecticut, Kentucky, Louisiana, and Mississippi.

16. WIA Adult Formula funding declined from $945 million in fiscal year 2002 to $865 million in fiscal year 2006, and of these funds only about 40 percent are actually spent on training, a substantially lower share than under JTPA. See The Workforce Alliance, 2006, pp. 12–13.

17. The material in this paragraph draws from King and Smith (2006).

18. I owe this analogy to John Colborn of the Ford Foundation.

References

Acemoglu, Daron. 1999. "Changes In Unemployment and Wage Inequality: An Alternative Theory and Some Evidence." *American Economic Review* 89(5): 1259–1278.

Acemoglu, Daron, and Jorn-Steffen Pischke. 1998. "Why Do Firms Train? Theory and Evidence." *Quarterly Journal of Economics* 113(1): 79–119.

Acs, Greg, and Pamela Loprest. 2004. *Leaving Welfare: Employment and Well-Being of Families that Left Welfare in the Post-Entitlement Era*. Kalamazoo, MI: W.E. Upjohn Institute for Employment Research.

Ahlstrand, Amanda, Lauri J. Bassi, and Daniel P. McMurrer. 2003. *Workplace Education for Low Wage Workers*. Kalamazoo, MI: W.E. Upjohn Institute for Employment Research.

Autor, David, Lawrence Katz, and Melissa Kearney. 2006. "The Polarization of the U.S. Labor Market." NBER Working Paper no. 11986. Cambridge, MA: National Bureau of Economic Research.

Bailey, Thomas, Timothy Leinbach, Marc Scott, Mariana Alfonso, Gregory Kienzl, and Benjamin Kennedy. 2004. "The Characteristics of Occupational Students In Post-Secondary Education." CCRC Brief no. 21. New York: Community College Research Center, Teachers College.

Ball State University. 2003. "Indiana Manufacturing Education and Training Initiative: Final Report." Muncie, IN: Center for Organizational Resources, Ball State University.

Bernstein, Jared, and Maury Gittleman. 2003. "Exploring Low-Wage Labor with the National Compensation Survey." *Monthly Labor Review* 126(11-12): 3–12.

Bernstein, Jared, and Isaac Shapiro. 2006. "Nine Years of Neglect: Federal Minimum Wage Remains Unchanged for Ninth Straight Year, Falls to Lowest Level in More than Half a Century." Economic Policy Institute Issue

Brief no. 227. Washington, DC: Economic Policy Institute and Center on Budget and Policy Priorities.

Bond, James. 2003. *Highlights of the National Study of the Changing Workforce*. New York: Families and Work Institute.

Bosworth, Brian. 2006. "Strengthening Employer Support for the Postsecondary Education of Working Adults." Somerville, MA: Futureworks.

Brennan Center for Justice at NYU School of Law. 2006. *Protecting New York's Workers: How the State Department of Labor Can Improve Wage-and-Hour Enforcement*. New York: Brennan Center for Justice. http://brennancenter. org/dynamic/subpages/download_file_47027.pdf (accessed October 17, 2006).

Brock, Thomas, and Allen LeBlanc with Casey McGregor. 2005. "Promoting Student Success in Community College and Beyond: The Opening Doors Demonstration." New York: MDRC.

Brudney, James. 2005. "Neutrality Agreements and Card Check Recognition: Prospects for Changing Paradigms." *Iowa Law Review* 90: 819–886.

Card, David, Thomas Lemieux, and W. Craig Riddell. 2003. "Unionization and Wage Inequality: A Comparative Study of the U.S., the U.K., and Canada." NBER Working Paper no. 9473. Cambridge, MA: National Bureau of Economic Research.

Davis, Steve, and John Haltiwanger. 1991. "Wage Dispersion between and within U.S. Manufacturing Plants, 1963–86." *Brookings Papers on Economic Activity: Microeconomics* 1991: 115–200.

DiNardo, John, and David Lee. 2004. "The Economic Impacts of Unionization on Private Sector Employees." NBER Working Paper no. 10598. Cambridge, MA: National Bureau of Economic Research.

Ferguson, John-Paul. 2006. "The Eye of the Needle: Surviving Union Organizing Drives." Mimeo. Cambridge, MA: Sloan School of Management, Massachusetts Institute of Technology.

Fine, Janice. 2006. *Worker Centers: Organizing Communities at the Edge of the Dream*. Ithaca, NY: Cornell University Press.

Fitzgerald, Joan. 2006. *Moving Up in the New Economy: Career Ladders for U.S. Workers*. Ithaca, NY: Cornell University Press.

Freeman, Richard. 2007. "Do Workers Still Want Unions? More than Ever." EPI Briefing Paper no. 182. Washington, DC: Economic Policy Institute.

FutureWorks. 2004. "Building Essential Skills Through Training (BEST), Final Evaluation Report." Boston: Commonwealth Corporation, and Arlington, MA: FutureWorks.

Goldberger, Sue, Newell Lessell, and Radha Roy Biswas. 2005. *The Right Jobs: Identifying Career Advancement Opportunities for Low-Skilled Workers*. Boston: Jobs for the Future.

Gordon, Jennifer. 2005. *Suburban Sweatshops: The Fight for Immigrant Rights*. Cambridge, MA: Harvard University Press.

Goshen, Erica. 1991. "Sources of Intra-Industry Wage Dispersion: How Much Do Employers Matter?" *Quarterly Journal of Economics* 106(3): 869–884.

Gross, Julian, with Greg LeRoy and Madeline Janis-Aparicio. 2005. *Community Benefit Agreements: Making Development Projects Accountable*. Washington, DC: Good Jobs First, and Oakland, CA: California Partnership for Working Families.

Grote, Mae Watson, and Anne Roder. 2005. *Setting the Bar High: Findings from the National Sectoral Employment Initiative*. New York: Public/Private Ventures.

Hecker, Daniel. 2005. "Occupational Employment Projections to 2014." *Monthly Labor Review* 128(11): 70–101.

Hollister, Matissa. 2004. "Does Firm Size Matter Anymore? The New Economy and Firm Size Effects." *American Sociological Review* 69(5): 659–676.

Holzer, Harry. 2004. "Encouraging Job Advancement Among Low-Wage Workers: A New Approach." Brookings Institute Policy Brief no. 30. Washington, DC: Brookings Institution.

Holzer, Harry, Richard Block, Marcus Cheatham, and Jack Knott. 1993. "Are Training Subsidies for Firms Effective? The Michigan Experience." *Industrial and Labor Relations Review* 46(2): 625–636.

Holzer, Harry, Julia Lane, and Lars Vilhuber. 2004. "Escaping Low Earnings: The Role of Employer Characteristics and Changes." *Industrial and Labor Relations Review* 57(4): 560–578.

Jobs for the Future. 2005. *Building Skills, Increasing Economic Vitality: A Handbook of Innovative State Policies*. Boston: Jobs for the Future.

King, Christopher, and Tara Smith. 2006. "Financing Workforce Intermediaries." Working paper, December. Boston: Jobs for the Future.

Lemieux, Thomas. 2006. "Increasing Residual Wage Inequality: Compositional Effects, Noisy Data, or Rising Demand For Skill?" *American Economic Review* 96(3): 461–498.

Marino, Cindy, and Kim Tarr. 2004. "The Workforce Intermediary: Profiling the Field of Practice and Its Challenges." In *Workforce Intermediaries for the Twenty-first Century*, Robert Giloth, ed. Philadelphia: Temple University Press, pp. 93–123.

Marshall, Carolyn, and Steven Greenhouse. 2006. "Eye on Presidency and Ear on Hotel Workers' Grievances." *New York Times*, October 16, A:20.

McCort, Jeff, with Anna Purinton, Philip Mattera, and Greg LeRoy. 2006. *Subsidizing Low-Wage Jobs: An Analysis of the First Development Deals Disclosed Under Illinois' New Accountability Law*. Washington, DC: Good Jobs First.

Neumark, David, and Scott Adams. 2004. "The Economic Effects of Living Wage Laws: A Provisional Review." *Urban Affairs Review* 40(2): 210–245.

OECD and Canadian Ministry of Industry. 2005. *Learning A Living, First Results of the Adult Literacy and Life Skills Survey.* Paris: Organisation for Economic Co-operation and Development.

Osterman, Paul. 2003. *Gathering Power: The Future of Progressive Politics in America.* Boston: Beacon Press.

Osterman, Paul and Brenda Lautsch. 1996. "Project QUEST: A Report to the Ford Foundation." Cambridge, MA: Massachusetts Institute of Technology.

Pfeffer, Jeffrey. 1994. *Competitive Advantage through People: Unleashing the Power of the Work Force.* Boston: Harvard Business School Press.

Pindus, Nancy, Carolyn O'Brien, Maureen Conway, Conaway Haskins, and Ida Rademacher. 2004. "Evaluation of the Sectoral Employment Demonstration Program." Washington, DC: Urban Institute.

Prince, David, and David Jenkins. 2005. "Building Pathways to Success for Low Income Adults Students: Lessons for Community College Policy and Practice from a Statewide Longitudinal Tracking Study." New York: Community College Research Center, Teachers College.

Purinton, Anna, with Nasreen Jilani, Kristen Arant, and Kate Davis. 2003. *The Policy Shift to Good Jobs.* Washington, DC: Good Jobs First.

Theodos, Brett, and Robert Bednarzik. 2006. "Earnings Mobility and Low-Wage Workers in the United States." *Monthly Labor Review* 129(6): 34–47.

Thompson, Jeff, and Jeff Chapman. 2006. "The Economic Impact of Local Wage Laws." EPI Briefing Paper no. 170. Washington, DC: Economic Policy Institute.

Uchitelle, Louis. 2006. "Two Tiers, Slipping into One." *New York Times*, February 26, 3:1.

Whiting, Basil. 2005. "The Retention and Advancement Demonstration Project: A Case Study." Washington, DC: Center For Workforce Success, National Association of Manufacturers.

Workforce Alliance. 2006. "Training Policy in Brief, An Overview of Federal Workforce Development Policies." Washington, DC: Workforce Alliance.

7

Boosting the Earnings and Employment of Low-Skilled Workers in the United States

Making Work Pay and Removing Barriers to Employment and Social Mobility

Steven Raphael
University of California, Berkeley

The last few decades of the twentieth century witnessed fairly dramatic changes in the labor market outcomes and socioeconomic status of American workers at the bottom of the earnings distribution. Earnings of the least skilled adults either stagnated or fell. Moreover, labor force participation and employment have declined considerably, suggesting a reduction in demand for the labor of the least skilled and an accompanying withdrawal from the labor force on the part of many low-skilled workers unwilling to accept diminished wages.

Certain economy-wide developments have affected the employment prospects of all low-skilled workers regardless of race or gender. For example, the well-documented changes in the earnings distribution beginning in the late 1970s have increased the relative returns to postsecondary schooling as well as the returns to experience (Katz and Autor 1999).[1] Nonetheless, certain social and institutional developments are likely to have had disproportionate impacts on the labor market prospects of certain subgroups within the population of low-skilled adults. For example, the prison incarceration rate between the late 1970s and the present more than quadrupled. That has had a disproportionate impact on less-educated black men and has left in its wake large groups of less-educated men who are hampered by their criminal histories in their search for employment.[2] As a further example, the expansion of the Earned Income Tax Credit (EITC), welfare reform, the Medicaid expansions, and the introduction of the State Children's Health Insurance program (SCHIP) greatly increased the relative returns to work over welfare for poor women with children.

This chapter documents the relative economic performance of low-skilled disadvantaged workers in the United States and identifies key factors that have either enhanced their economic security or that are becoming increasingly important barriers to steady employment and self-sufficiency. As the introduction suggests, there are important differences by gender. Low-skilled men are currently participating in the labor force at rates that are extremely low by historical comparison, which suggests that procuring and maintaining steady employment has become a serious problem for this particular group. The analysis below demonstrates that the unprecedented decline in employment and participation among men is only partially explained by the decline in earnings potential. Thus, boosting the employment rates of low-skilled men will require both supply-side incentives that make work pay and demand-side efforts aimed at increasing employer willingness to hire from this particular labor pool.

Low-skilled women have fared better in recent decades, experiencing more modest declines in earnings and changes in employment ranging from modest decreases to substantial increases. The greatest gains in employment are found for those women most likely to have been affected by the institutional changes to the nation's safety net during the 1990s, in particular poor and near-poor women with children.

I analyze and offer several policy proposals designed to boost the employment and earnings of the least-skilled workers. First, I discuss several recent proposals to substantially expand the Earned Income Tax Credit (EITC) for childless adults. I analyze the likely costs of these proposals, the degree to which the expansions would actually benefit workers at the bottom of the income distribution, the potential effect of such expansions on the incentive to marry, and the likely impact on take-home earnings and employment. My preferred proposal is a hybrid of two proposals, one by Edelman, Holzer, and Offner (2006) and the other by Berlin (2007). It combines an expanded credit for childless adults with a targeted liberalization of the benefits calculation for the poorest married couples. While the employment effects of such an expansion are likely to be modest, the impact on annual income and material poverty is substantial and would go part of the way toward reducing the real decline in earnings experienced by low-skilled workers over the past three decades. Moreover, modest changes to the current system could eliminate the marriage penalty inherent in the EITC for the poorest couples at relatively little public expense.

Second, I offer several policy proposals intended to remove some of the educational and employment barriers that hinder the reentry of former prison inmates into mainstream society. Specifically, I propose that

- Summary disqualification of former inmates and those with felony convictions from participating in federal public assistance programs and from receiving financial aid for education should be reversed.

- Employment bans based on former convictions and occupational licensing restrictions should be based on the content of one's criminal record and not applied in a blanket manner. Moreover, when used, employment bans should be based on conviction rather than arrest records. Any bans on the employment of felons mandated by law should be based on the content of one's previous behavior as well as the time that has elapsed.

- We should increase investment in labor market intermediaries that specialize in building relationships with employers willing to hire ex-offenders and in placing former inmates into sustainable employment.

- States should incentivize desistance from criminal activity by expunging certain criminal records after a fixed time period has elapsed.

While the challenges faced by former inmates in the legitimate labor market are many, these modest proposals would eliminate key barriers to employment that affect increasing proportions of low-skilled men, at little cost in terms of public safety.

WHO ARE THE LOW-EARNERS IN THE UNITED STATES AND HOW HAVE THEY FARED?

Here I use data from the 1980, 1990, and 2000 Public Use Microdata Samples (PUMS) from the U.S. Census of Housing and Population to characterize the low-wage population and to document recent trends in earnings, employment, and institutionalization rates. I restrict the analysis to adults 18 to 55 years of age that are out of school, that are not in the military, and that do not report self-employment income. I measure each person's hourly earnings by dividing total annual wage and salary earnings by total annual hours worked (measured by weeks worked last year multiplied by usual hours worked). For those individuals who did not work in the previous year or who are institutionalized at the time of interview, I compute hourly earnings by assigning the median hourly wage for workers in the same year, gender, race or ethnicity, education, and labor market experience group.[3] Thus, average wages for all workers in the sample measure the actual wages for some and the potential earnings of those who do not participate in the labor force, based on the earnings of comparable individuals employed at some point during the year.

An important strength of the PUMS data concerns the fact that the data covers the institutionalized population (including inmates in jails and prisons and inpatients in mental hospitals) as well as the noninstitutionalized. As I discuss below, the institutionalized population now makes up a sizable proportion of many demographic subgroups among the low-skilled adult population. Thus, the ability to characterize institutionalization trends is central to fully comprehending the current state of the low-skilled adult population in the United States.

Who Are the Low-Earning Adults in the United States?

Tables 7.1 and 7.2 describe how the distributions of the male (Table 7.1) and female (Table 7.2) populations have changed between 1980 and 2000 for all adults in my sample and for adults in the bottom quarter of the earnings potential distribution. Each table presents the proportion of the population accounted for by four mutually exclusive racial or ethnic groups (non-Hispanic white, non-Hispanic black, non-Hispanic

Table 7.1 Comparison of All Out-of-School Men 18 to 55 with Similar Men in the Bottom Quarter of the Earnings Potential Distribution

	1980		2000	
	All men	Low-wage men	All men	Low-wage men
White	0.800	0.627	0.684	0.506
Less than high school	0.173	0.273	0.063	0.126
High school graduate	0.324	0.220	0.239	0.214
Some college	0.171	0.074	0.199	0.111
College graduate	0.208	0.061	0.188	0.059
Black	0.114	0.254	0.126	0.269
Less than high school	0.047	0.140	0.025	0.095
High school graduate	0.042	0.084	0.056	0.126
Some college	0.016	0.027	0.032	0.044
College graduate	0.008	0.008	0.014	0.009
Asian	0.015	0.016	0.038	0.032
Less than high school	0.003	0.006	0.004	0.008
High school graduate	0.004	0.005	0.008	0.010
Some college	0.003	0.002	0.008	0.006
College graduate	0.006	0.003	0.017	0.008
Hispanic	0.071	0.103	0.145	0.184
Less than high school	0.038	0.069	0.064	0.099
High school graduate	0.020	0.024	0.048	0.063
Some college	0.008	0.008	0.024	0.019
College graduate	0.005	0.003	0.011	0.006
Immigrant	0.071	0.082	0.159	0.152
Institutionalized	0.018	0.150	0.038	0.247
Disabled	0.084	0.350	0.139	0.248

SOURCE: Author's tabulations from the 1980 and 2000 Public Use Microdata Samples (PUMS) of the U.S. Census of Housing and Population.

Asian, and Hispanic), the distribution of a given group's share by level of educational attainment, and the proportion who are immigrant, institutionalized, or who report a work-limiting disability.

The prime-age adult male population has become less white, more Hispanic, and more Asian. The fraction of all men that are black has increased slightly. Within racial groups, the distribution of educational attainment has shifted decisively towards higher levels for whites and

Table 7.2 Comparison of All Out-of-School Women 18 to 55 with Similar Women in the Bottom Quarter of the Earnings Potential Distribution

	1980		2000	
	All women	Low-wage women	All women	Low-wage women
White	0.798	0.772	0.695	0.617
Less than high school	0.161	0.226	0.051	0.095
High school graduate	0.387	0.367	0.230	0.240
Some college	0.136	0.108	0.225	0.168
College graduate	0.114	0.072	0.193	0.118
Black	0.118	0.126	0.131	0.136
Less than high school	0.043	0.065	0.019	0.039
High school graduate	0.048	0.047	0.053	0.064
Some college	0.017	0.011	0.041	0.027
College graduate	0.010	0.004	0.019	0.007
Asian	0.017	0.017	0.043	0.052
Less than high school	0.004	0.005	0.006	0.010
High school graduate	0.005	0.006	0.010	0.014
Some college	0.003	0.003	0.009	0.010
College graduate	0.005	0.004	0.018	0.018
Hispanic	0.066	0.084	0.125	0.187
Less than high school	0.035	0.054	0.048	0.100
High school graduate	0.021	0.022	0.041	0.058
Some college	0.007	0.005	0.025	0.022
College graduate	0.003	0.002	0.012	0.009
Immigrant	0.075	0.088	0.148	0.219
Institutionalized	0.004	0.010	0.005	0.018
Disabled	0.069	0.131	0.112	0.143

SOURCE: Author's tabulations from the 1980 and 2000 Public Use Microdata Samples (PUMS) of the U.S. Census of Housing and Population.

blacks. Across groups, Hispanics constitute an increasing proportion of those with the lowest level of educational attainment. In addition to these changes, the proportion of immigrants among the male population has more than doubled, the proportion with a work-limiting disability has increased by over 60 percent, and the proportion in institutions has increased by over 200 percent. The change in the proportion that is institutionalized reflects the net effect of two offsetting trends: the proportion of the male population in mental hospitals has declined continuously since 1980, while the proportion in local jails and state and federal prisons has greatly increased (Raphael and Stoll 2007).

For men in the bottom quarter of the earnings distribution there are some notable facts. In both 1980 and 2000, racial and ethnic minorities are considerably overrepresented among low earners while white males are underrepresented. Changes between 1980 and 2000 have reinforced this pattern: there has been a decline in the proportion that is white of 0.12, an increase in the proportion that is black of 0.015, an increase in the proportion that is Asian of 0.016, and an increase in the proportion that is Hispanic of 0.081. Low earners are considerably more educated on average in 2000 than they were in 1980. Roughly 49 percent of low-earning males in 1980 had less than a complete high school education, compared to 33 percent in 2000. Conversely, the proportion with a high school diploma increased from 33 to 41 percent. In contrast to the overall trend, the proportion of low-earning workers with a work-limiting disability declined from 0.35 to 0.25.

One of the most dramatic differences between the trends for low-income men and the trends for all men concerns the large absolute increase in institutionalization rates. In 2000, nearly one quarter of men whose earnings potential fell in the bottom quarter of the earnings distribution were institutionalized, and most of these men were in state or federal prisons or jail. This represents a nearly 10-percentage-point increase since 1980.

For women, Table 7.2 reveals that the overall distributions of the adult female population across racial or ethnic groups and levels of educational attainment are comparable to those of men (as shown in Table 7.1) in both years. For low-wage women, however, white women account for much larger proportions of the low-wage population in both years as compared to men. The proportion of immigrants and the proportion of disabled increase for women overall. Among low-wage women, the proportion that is immigrant more than doubles while the proportion with work-limiting disabilities increases slightly. The most notable difference relative to men concerns institutionalization trends. There is a very slight increase from a very low level in 1980 in the overall proportion of women in institutions (from 0.004 to 0.005). Among low-earnings women, the increase is larger (from 0.010 to 0.018), yet much smaller than that observed for men.

Trends in Wages, Employment, and Institutionalization for Disaggregated Subgroups

Table 7.3 presents the average log wages for men and women for 1980, 1990, and 2000 by race or ethnicity and by level of educational attainment; it also shows the change for each decade. Note that since wages are expressed in logs, the change between any two years is approximately equal to the proportional change in hourly earnings. For the entire period, potential wages decline for all men who do not have a college degree or more, and the largest declines occur for men with less than a complete high school education. Among the least educated white men, wages decline by roughly 22 percent between 1980 and 2000, with most of the decline occurring during the 1980s. For black and Hispanic high school dropouts, hourly wages decline overall by 17 percent, again with most of the wage loss occurring in the earlier decade. There are also sizable declines in the hourly wages of male high school graduates. These patterns clearly reveal the growing returns to education among men and are consistent with the findings of previous research.[4]

Wage trends for women are quite different from those for men. Perhaps the most notable differences pertain to wage levels for a given group and at a given point in time. There are large intergender disparities favoring males in each year within each race or ethnicity education group. However, these within-group disparities decline between 1980 and 2000.

The declines in hourly wages for women with the least skills are considerably more modest than the comparable declines experienced by men. For example, the hourly wages of white women with less than a high school diploma declined by 10 percent between 1980 and 1990 and then increased by 3 percent over the subsequent decade. The comparable changes for similarly educated white men are declines of 18 percent between 1980 and 1990 and 4 percent thereafter. Similarly, the hourly wages of white female high school graduates increased by roughly 2 percent between 1980 and 2000 while the wages of corresponding white men declined by 14 percent.

Prior research on the labor supply responses of men and women suggests that declines in hourly wages should result in a decline in employment among those experiencing the wage change. A decrease in wages reduces the rate at which an individual can convert his nonmarket time into money by supplying his time to the formal labor market.

To the extent that people value their time, a decline in the wages that one's labor will command is likely to induce one to either supply less time or withdraw from the labor force entirely.[5] Thus, in conjunction with the patterns in Table 7.3, this simple theory predicts that employment rates should have declined considerably for low-skilled men and less so for low-skilled women.

Indeed, employment does tend to decline for those demographic groups experiencing the largest declines in earnings. Table 7.4 presents the proportion of each group employed at the time of the census interview for the same race/ethnicity-education-gender groups displayed in Table 7.3. There are sizable declines in the employment rates of the least skilled male workers. Between 1980 and 2000, the employment rate for white high school dropouts declined by 14 percentage points, while employment for white high school graduates fell roughly 7 percentage points. For black men, there are large declines in employment for all groups with the exception of college-educated black men, and there is an especially large decline (27 percentage points) for black high school dropouts. By 2000, only one-third of prime-age, black male high school dropouts were employed on a given day, compared to nearly two-thirds in 1980.

For the least skilled men the declines in employment rates during the 1990s are of equal magnitude to, or larger than, the declines observed during the 1980s. By contrast, nearly all of the wage losses for these groups occur during the 1980s, suggesting that factors beyond declining wages are also driving the poor employment outcomes of less-skilled men.

Low-earning women experienced smaller wage losses than men from comparable demographic groups and with similar levels of educational attainment, and thus one would expect *a priori* that declines in employment would be more modest for women. In fact, with the exception of black and Asian women having less than a high school degree, the employment rates of all groups increased during the 1980s. Juhn and Potter (2006) demonstrate that this increase in labor force participation represents the tail end of a long trend towards greater participation among women of all skill levels. Between 1990 and 2000, this trend appears to have slowed, with modest to moderate declines in employment among women from all racial or ethnic groups and all levels of educational attainment.

Table 7.3 Average Log Wages for Men and Women 18 to 55 Years of Age by Race/Ethnicity, Educational Attainment, and Year

	1980	1990	2000	1980–1990	1990–2000
		Panel A: Men			
White					
Less than high school	2.57	2.39	2.35	-0.18	-0.04
High school graduate	2.71	2.58	2.57	-0.13	-0.01
Some college	2.82	2.77	2.77	-0.05	0.00
College graduate	3.07	3.12	3.17	0.05	0.05
Black					
Less than high school	2.33	2.19	2.16	-0.14	-0.03
High school graduate	2.47	2.35	2.36	-0.12	0.01
Some college	2.62	2.58	2.60	-0.04	0.02
College graduate	2.88	2.92	2.96	0.04	0.04
Asian					
Less than high school	2.37	2.24	2.26	-0.13	0.02
High school graduate	2.59	2.44	2.41	-0.15	-0.03
Some college	2.69	2.68	2.68	-0.01	0.00
College graduate	3.03	3.08	3.15	0.05	0.07
Hispanic					
Less than high school	2.35	2.19	2.18	-0.16	-0.01
High school graduate	2.53	2.39	2.33	-0.14	-0.06
Some college	2.68	2.62	2.60	-0.06	-0.02
College graduate	2.92	2.93	2.92	0.01	-0.01

Panel B: Women

	1980	1990	2000	1980–1990	1990–2000
White					
Less than high school	2.09	1.99	2.02	-0.10	0.03
High school graduate	2.24	2.21	2.26	-0.03	0.05
Some college	2.38	2.41	2.47	0.03	0.06
College graduate	2.68	2.79	2.87	0.11	0.08
Black					
Less than high school	2.04	1.96	2.00	-0.08	0.04
High school graduate	2.21	2.15	2.19	-0.06	0.04
Some college	2.35	2.37	2.44	0.02	0.07
College graduate	2.75	2.82	2.86	0.07	0.04
Asian					
Less than high school	2.13	2.07	2.10	-0.06	0.03
High school graduate	2.29	2.25	2.26	-0.04	0.01
Some college	2.41	2.49	2.53	0.08	0.04
College graduate	2.69	2.79	2.91	0.10	0.12
Hispanic					
Less than high school	2.04	1.95	1.96	-0.09	0.01
High school graduate	2.21	2.16	2.16	-0.05	0.00
Some college	2.33	2.37	2.40	0.04	0.03
College graduate	2.61	2.74	2.76	0.13	0.02

SOURCE: Author's tabulations from the 1980, 1990, and 2000 Public Use Microdata Samples (PUMS) of the U.S. Census of Housing and Population.

Table 7.4 Proportion Employed for Men and Women 18 to 55 Years of Age by Race/Ethnicity, Educational Attainment, and Year

Panel A: Men

	1980	1990	2000	1980–1990	1990–2000
White men					
Less than high school	0.75	0.68	0.61	−0.07	−0.07
High school graduate	0.87	0.86	0.80	−0.01	−0.06
Some college	0.91	0.91	0.88	0.00	−0.03
College graduate	0.95	0.95	0.94	0.00	−0.01
Black					
Less than high school	0.60	0.46	0.33	−0.14	−0.13
High school graduate	0.73	0.66	0.57	−0.07	−0.09
Some college	0.79	0.76	0.71	−0.03	−0.05
College graduate	0.89	0.89	0.86	0.00	−0.03
Asian					
Less than high school	0.75	0.69	0.63	−0.06	−0.06
High school graduate	0.84	0.83	0.73	−0.01	−0.10
Some college	0.91	0.90	0.80	−0.01	−0.10
College graduate	0.94	0.93	0.89	−0.01	−0.04
Hispanic					
Less than high school	0.77	0.73	0.64	−0.04	−0.09
High school graduate	0.83	0.79	0.69	−0.04	−0.10
Some college	0.88	0.86	0.79	−0.02	−0.07
College graduate	0.92	0.92	0.86	0.00	−0.06

Panel B: Women

	1980	1990	2000	1980–1990	1990–2000
White					
Less than high school	0.43	0.45	0.44	0.02	−0.01
High school graduate	0.60	0.67	0.67	0.07	0.00
Some college	0.66	0.76	0.76	0.10	0.00
College graduate	0.73	0.82	0.81	0.09	−0.01
Black					
Less than high school	0.43	0.39	0.37	−0.04	−0.02
High school graduate	0.62	0.62	0.58	0.00	−0.04
Some college	0.73	0.76	0.74	0.03	−0.02
College graduate	0.86	0.90	0.86	0.04	−0.04
Asian					
Less than high school	0.49	0.47	0.48	−0.02	0.01
High school graduate	0.60	0.62	0.57	0.02	−0.05
Some college	0.68	0.73	0.66	0.05	−0.07
College graduate	0.72	0.75	0.70	0.03	−0.05
Hispanic					
Less than high school	0.39	0.41	0.37	0.02	−0.04
High school graduate	0.58	0.60	0.53	0.02	−0.07
Some college	0.67	0.73	0.68	0.06	−0.05
College graduate	0.74	0.80	0.75	0.06	−0.05

SOURCE: Author's tabulations from the 1980, 1990, and 2000 Public Use Microdata Samples (PUMS) of the U.S. Census of Housing and Population.

One interesting pattern evident in Table 7.4 concerns the within-group gender disparities in employment rates. In 1980 and 1990, men are more likely to be employed than comparable women in every group displayed in the table, with the sole exception of black college graduates in 1990. While this gender disparity varies considerably across groups, differentials on the order of 10 to 15 percentage points are typical. In the year 2000, comparable gender differences are observed among whites, Asians, and Hispanics. For blacks, however, the employment rates of males have deteriorated far enough to render the male-female employment rate differentials negative for most educational groups.

Finally, Table 7.5 presents the proportion institutionalized at the time of the census survey. The proportion institutionalized is composed disproportionately of inmates of local jails and state and federal prisons. The table reveals stark intergender, interracial, and cross-educational group disparities in the incidence of incarceration and the change in this incidence over this two-decade period. The largest increases are observed for black males with less than a high school degree. Between 1980 and 2000, the proportion institutionalized increased from roughly 8 percent to 27 percent of this population, a number similar in magnitude to the 33 percent of this group that is employed. The incarceration rate for men without a high school diploma more than doubled for whites and Asians, and nearly doubled for Hispanics, although the levels are considerably lower than those observed for blacks. The incarceration rates for women are quite low, although the rate for black women tripled—from 0.01 to 0.03—between 1980 and 2000.

The proportion of men who have ever served time in prison is certainly larger than the proportion incarcerated at any given point in time. The U.S. prison population is characterized by a high rate of turnover: nearly one-half of the population is released each year, and slightly over half is admitted (Raphael and Stoll 2007). The Bureau of Justice Statistics estimates that a black male born in 2001 has a 33 percent chance of serving prison time at some point in his life. The BJS also estimates that roughly 20 percent of all adult black males and 3 to 4 percent of white males have served time at some point in their lives (Bonczar 2003). In previous research on the California state prison system, I estimated the proportion of adults males by race, age, and education who had served time in the state prison system. Roughly one-third of prime-age (25 to 44) white men with less than a high school education had been through the state prison system. For black men with less than a high school education, a prior prison spell was nearly certain (Raphael 2006).

These trends indicate that to a greater extent than ever before, low-skilled men who are not institutionalized are likely to have felony convictions and prison experience in their past. Combined with relatively easy access to criminal records and employers actively screening for this factor, this trend indicates that this particular development has become an increasingly important handicap for low-skilled men in the legitimate labor market.

TO WHAT EXTENT DO CHANGES IN WAGES EXPLAIN RECENT EMPLOYMENT AND INCARCERATION TRENDS?

Thus, relatively less-educated men and women have both experienced declines in earnings since 1980, but men have experienced the most severe declines. These wage patterns correspond to uniform decreases in the employment rates of the least educated men, including particularly large declines for black men, and mixed patterns with regard to the changes in employment for the least educated women. Concurrently, the proportion of males incarcerated and not working has increased—by a great amount for certain subgroups (black men in particular), and by a more moderate yet significant amount for less-skilled men more generally.

Certainly, these changes in earnings, employment, and institutionalization rates are related, and the causality runs in multiple directions. Declining wages are likely to induce some to withdraw from the labor force. Moreover, decreases in the returns to legitimate work increase the relative returns to criminal activity, a factor that will increase the proportion of the population at risk of becoming incarcerated and, ultimately, the incarceration rate. Finally, men fail to accumulate human capital while incarcerated (Raphael 2006), may be stigmatized by the label of ex-offender when seeking legitimate employment (Holzer, Raphael, and Stoll 2006, 2007; Pager 2003), and may experience an erosion of their legitimate work skills and an augmentation of their propensity to engage in crime while incarcerated. These factors are all likely to negatively influence employment and earnings.

Table 7.5 Proportion Institutionalized for Men and Women 18 to 55 Years of Age by Race/Ethnicity, Educational Attainment, and Year

Panel A: Men

	1980	1990	2000	1980–1990	1990–2000
White					
Less than high school	0.03	0.05	0.07	0.02	0.02
High school graduate	0.01	0.02	0.03	0.01	0.01
Some college	0.01	0.01	0.02	0.00	0.01
College graduate	0.00	0.00	0.00	0.00	0.00
Black					
Less than high school	0.08	0.15	0.27	0.07	0.12
High school graduate	0.04	0.08	0.12	0.04	0.04
Some college	0.04	0.08	0.08	0.04	0.00
College graduate	0.02	0.02	0.02	0.00	0.00
Asian					
Less than high school	0.01	0.02	0.03	0.01	0.01
High school graduate	0.01	0.01	0.02	0.00	0.01
Some college	0.00	0.01	0.01	0.01	0.00
College graduate	0.00	0.00	0.00	0.00	0.00
Hispanic					
Less than high school	0.03	0.05	0.05	0.02	0.00
High school graduate	0.02	0.04	0.05	0.02	0.01
Some college	0.01	0.03	0.03	0.02	0.00
College graduate	0.01	0.01	0.01	0.00	0.00

Panel B: Women

	1980	1990	2000	1980–1990	1990–2000
White					
Less than high school	0.01	0.01	0.02	0.00	0.01
High school graduate	0.00	0.00	0.00	0.00	0.00
Some college	0.00	0.00	0.00	0.00	0.00
College graduate	0.00	0.00	0.00	0.00	0.00
Black					
Less than high school	0.01	0.02	0.03	0.01	0.01
High school graduate	0.00	0.01	0.01	0.01	0.00
Some college	0.00	0.01	0.01	0.01	0.00
College graduate	0.00	0.00	0.00	0.00	0.00
Asian					
Less than high school	0.00	0.00	0.00	0.00	0.00
High school graduate	0.00	0.00	0.00	0.00	0.00
Some college	0.00	0.00	0.00	0.00	0.00
College graduate	0.00	0.00	0.00	0.00	0.00
Hispanic					
Less than high school	0.00	0.01	0.00	0.01	−0.01
High school graduate	0.00	0.00	0.00	0.00	0.00
Some college	0.00	0.00	0.00	0.00	0.00
College graduate	0.00	0.00	0.00	0.00	0.00

SOURCE: Author's tabulations from the 1980, 1990, and 2000 Public Use Microdata Samples (PUMS) of the U.S. Census of Housing and Population.

The first two factors suggest that diminished wages are likely to be partially responsible for the low employment rates of low-skilled men and perhaps for their newly high incarceration rates. Put simply, if people at the bottom of the earnings distribution are not working because working pays less than it used to, and are engaging in more criminal activity as a side product, then addressing this problem requires making legitimate work pay. Tables 7.3, 7.4, and 7.5 do indeed suggest that those groups suffering the largest wage losses also exhibit the largest employment declines and the largest increases in incarceration, although the patterns across groups and the timing aren't perfect. Hence, to the extent that society could alter existing taxes and subsidies to improve the take-home pay of low-earning workers, policymakers may be able to turn the tide on some of these more adverse developments.

In this section, I address two related questions that will provide the analytical research findings to more thoroughly investigate this policy idea. Specifically, to what extent are recent employment trends driven by falling wages? Concurrently, how much of the increase in institutionalization rates can be attributed to poorer labor market opportunities?

Declining Wages and the Employment Rates of Low-Skilled Men and Women

To assess the extent to which declining wages drive declining employment rates, one needs to assess the degree to which labor supply behavior is responsive to changes in potential earnings. The theoretical concept used by economists to describe this behavioral response is the labor supply elasticity. The supply elasticity is defined as the percentage change in employment among a given group caused by a 1-percentage-point change in wages.

In Appendix 7A, I describe the details of a procedure that I use to estimate the labor supply responsiveness of men and women to changes in wages. While I do not discuss the details here, I will note that the estimation method accounts for the institutionalized and the possibility that the labor supply decision may ultimately affect the probability of an incarceration spell. The elasticity estimates from this analysis are presented in Figures 7.1 and 7.2. The estimates from a model that uses all men indicates a moderate degree of responsiveness of employment to wages, with a high-end labor supply elasticity estimate of roughly 0.2

Figure 7.1 Labor Supply Elasticity Estimates For Men, Based on Census Microdata by Race or Ethnicity

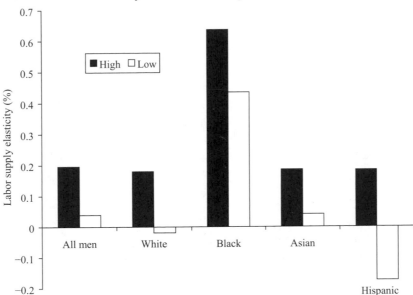

SOURCE: Author's calculations based on the regression model estimates from the 1980, 1990, and 2000 Public Use Microdata Samples (PUMS) of the U.S. Census of Housing and Population.

(indicating that a 10 percent decrease in wages would cause a 2 percent decrease in employment). Race-specific estimates suggest that black men are most responsive to changes in wages.

In general, women's supply behavior is more responsive to wage changes than that of men. The low-end overall elasticity estimate for women is nearly double the high-end estimate for men (0.4 vs. 0.2). In addition, the elasticity estimates for black and Hispanic women are particularly large. This range of elasticity estimates for both men and women is in line with the results discussed in Devereux (2003), Juhn (1992), Juhn and Potter (2006), and Pencavel (1997, 2002).

Using these elasticity estimates and the wage changes documented in Table 7.3, it is possible to calculate the degree to which declining wages explain recent employment patterns.[6] I present the results from these calculations in Table 7.6. The first column presents actual changes

Figure 7.2 Labor Supply Elasticity Estimates For Women, Based on Census Microdata by Race or Ethnicity

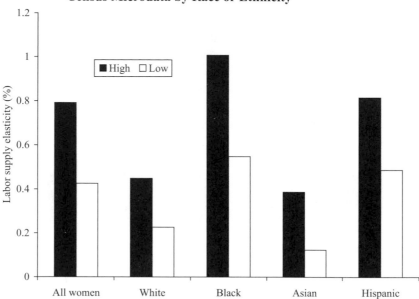

SOURCE: Author's calculations based on regression model estimates from the 1980, 1990, and 2000 Public Use Microdata Samples (PUMS) of the U.S. Census of Housing and Population.

in employment rates between 1980 and 2000 for the race and education groups depicted in Tables 7.3 through 7.5. The second column presents the change in employment predicted by the actual change in wages for this group using the high race-specific elasticity estimate from the values presented in Figures 7.1 and 7.2. The final column presents a similar calculation using the low elasticity estimate for the given race and gender group.

For the least educated men, declining earnings explains relatively small, but not unsubstantial, portions of the decline in employment rates. For white men without a high school degree, the predicted changes in employment attributable to declining wages range from no change to a decline of 3 percentage points. For black men without a high school degree, 4 to 6 percentage points of the 27-percentage-point decline can be attributed to a negative supply response to falling wages, constituting 16 to 22 percent of the decline. Similarly, for black men with high school diplomas (the modal category for this group of men), declining wages explain 3 to 5 percentage points of the 16-percentage-point decline between 1980 and 2000 (roughly 18 to 30 percent of the decline). Thus, reversing wage trends for low-skilled men would likely lead to increases in employment rates, but the increases would fall far short of undoing the employment declines witnessed in recent decades.

Among women, only black and Hispanic women experienced substantial declines in employment between 1980 and 2000, and even for these groups, the declines are modest in comparison to those for men. For black women with less than a high school degree, roughly 16 percent of the decline in employment is attributable to declining wages. For comparable Hispanic women, however, half to all of declining employment can be attributed to lower wages in 2000.

To be sure, the relative returns to work for the less skilled have been influenced by various policy developments over this time period that are not reflected in their hourly wages. For poor women with children, welfare reform, the expansion of the EITC, Medicaid expansions, and the introduction of the State Children's Health Insurance Program (SCHIP) have greatly increased the returns to work. In fact, with the EITC affecting take-home pay by as much as 40 percent for some workers, the hourly wage provides a rather imprecise measure of the marginal return to an additional hour of work for the least skilled women.

The wages of childless men as well as those of men who are noncustodial fathers have not been influenced by these developments. In fact, for many of these men, the marginal return to working has likely been eroded by child support policies that garnish the wages of men with arrearages and impose large marginal taxes on legitimate labor market earnings, while (in cases where their former partners and children are receiving public assistance) passing little to none of the collected revenues on to their dependents (Edelman, Holzer, and Offner 2006; Primus 2006). Thus, for low-skilled men as well, observable hourly wages provide a noisy and perhaps biased gauge of the after-tax rewards from work.

Nonetheless, these tabulations do indicate that the phenomenon of falling wages provides a partial explanation for the eroding employment rates of the least skilled, especially for less-educated African Americans.

Table 7.6 Comparison of Actual Changes in Employment Rates to Changes Predicted by Labor Supply Elasticity Estimates

| | Panel A: Men | | |
	Actual change in employment rates, 1980–2000	Predicted change, largest elasticity estimates	Predicted change, smallest elasticity estimates
White			
Less than high school	−0.14	−0.03	0.00
High school graduate	−0.07	−0.02	0.00
Some college	−0.03	−0.01	0.00
College graduate	−0.01	0.02	0.00
Black			
Less than high school	−0.27	−0.06	−0.04
High school graduate	−0.16	−0.05	−0.03
Some college	−0.08	−0.01	−0.01
College graduate	−0.03	0.05	0.03
Asian			
Less than high school	−0.12	−0.02	0.00
High school graduate	−0.11	−0.03	−0.01
Some college	−0.11	0.00	0.00
College graduate	−0.05	0.02	0.00
Hispanic			
Less than high school	−0.13	−0.02	0.02
High school graduate	−0.14	−0.03	0.03
Some college	−0.09	−0.01	0.01
College graduate	−0.06	0.00	0.00

Panel B: Women

	Actual change in employment rates, 1980–2000	Predicted change, largest elasticity estimates	Predicted change, smallest elasticity estimates
White			
Less than high school	0.01	-0.01	-0.01
High school graduate	0.07	0.01	0.00
Some college	0.10	0.03	0.01
College graduate	0.08	0.06	0.03
Black			
Less than high school	-0.06	-0.02	-0.01
High school graduate	-0.04	-0.01	-0.01
Some college	0.01	0.07	0.04
College graduate	0.00	0.10	0.05
Asian			
Less than high school	-0.01	-0.01	0.00
High school graduate	-0.03	-0.01	0.00
Some college	-0.02	0.03	0.01
College graduate	-0.02	0.06	-0.01
Hispanic			
Less than high school	-0.02	-0.03	-0.02
High school graduate	-0.05	-0.02	-0.01
Some college	0.01	0.04	0.02
College graduate	0.01	0.09	0.05

SOURCE: Author's analysis of data from the 1980, 1990, and 2000 Public Use Microdata Samples (PUMS) of the U.S. Census of Population and Housing.

Declining Wages and the Increased Incarceration Rates of Men

There is now considerable evidence that economically motivated crime increases with unemployment and decreases as average wages rise, especially the average wages of low-skilled workers (Fagan and Freeman 1999; Freeman 1987; Gould, Weinberg, and Mustard 2002; Grogger 1998; and Raphael and Winter-Ebmer 2001). A higher average propensity to commit crimes will result in a larger prison population (Raphael and Stoll 2007). These two effects jointly describe the pathway between the eroding labor market position of low-skilled adults and the increase in incarceration. Simply stated, when work pays less, more people shun work and turn to crime. The more people that commit crimes, the higher the proportion at risk for incarceration and the greater the incarceration rate.

In Appendix 7B, I outline a strategy for estimating the effect of the decline in wages described in Table 7.3 on the increase in incarceration rates discussed above. The method requires drawing on existing estimates of the responsiveness of criminal activity to changes in wages, estimating the risk of incarceration conditional on engaging in crime, and estimating the time one is likely to serve conditional on being caught and incarcerated. The results of this exercise are presented in Table 7.7. The table presents estimates for men only, since the changes in institutionalization rates are quite modest for women. The first column of figures presents the actual change in the proportion institutionalized, the next column presents the change predicted by wage changes between 1980 and 2000, and the final column presents the ratio of the predicted to the actual change. For relatively less-educated white men, declining wages predict an increase in the institutionalization rate equal to approximately 15 percent of the actual increase. By comparison, the proportion of the actual increase for low-educated black men predicted by their change in wages is quite small (on the order of 2 to 3 percent). This is driven largely by the much larger increases in institutionalization rates for black men. The figures for Asian and Hispanic men are more in line with those for whites. For Hispanic high school dropouts, declining wages predict roughly 18 percent of the increase in incarceration rates.

These results suggest that declining earnings explain a small portion of the overall increase in incarceration. In previous research with

Table 7.7 Comparison of Actual Changes in Institutionalization Rates for Men and Predicted Changes Based on Changes in Hourly Wages

	Actual change in institutionalization rates, 1980–2000	Predicted change in institutionalization rates given wage changes	Ratio, predicted/actual
White			
Less than high school	0.037	0.005	0.134
High school graduate	0.019	0.003	0.166
Some college	0.008	0.001	0.141
College graduate	0.001	−0.002	−2.250
Black			
Less than high school	0.190	0.004	0.020
High school graduate	0.077	0.002	0.032
Some college	0.042	0.000	−0.011
College graduate	0.006	−0.002	−0.300
Asian			
Less than high school	0.021	0.002	0.118
High school graduate	0.012	0.004	0.338
Some college	0.007	0.000	0.032
College graduate	0.000	−0.003	—
Hispanic			
Less than high school	0.021	0.004	0.182
High school graduate	0.033	0.005	0.136
Some college	0.016	0.002	0.113
College graduate	0.004	0.000	0.000

NOTE: See text for discussion of predicted changes in institutionalization rates. The predictions make use of the absolute changes in log hourly wages between 1980 and 2000, presented in Table 7.3.
SOURCE: Author's tabulations based on data from the 1980, 1990, and 2000 Public Use Microdata Samples (PUMS) of the U.S. Census of Population and Housing.

Michael Stoll (Raphael and Stoll 2007), I have estimated that declining wages for low-skilled men are responsible for no more than 13 percent of the increase in incarceration rates between 1980 and 2000. Nonetheless, small decreases in incarceration caused by, for example, a wage subsidy may generate substantial social savings. Correction expenditures per prison year are on the order of $35,000 a year (Donohue 2007). In 2005, there were approximately 1.5 million prison inmates. If a targeted wage subsidy were to reduce the prison population by a modest 5 percent, 75,000 fewer inmates would be incarcerated on any given day, generating savings in corrections expenditures of roughly $2.6 billion. Moreover, this figure would increase considerably if we were to account for some of the harder-to-price social costs of incarceration (including the impact on families and public health) as well as the value in stolen goods or losses from the crimes averted. Thus, even small effects such as those in Table 7.7 deserve serious consideration.

CRIMINAL RECORDS AND THE EMPLOYMENT PROSPECTS OF LOW-EARNING MALES

To be sure, the relatively poor labor market outcomes for very low-skilled men and women are driven largely by skill deficits and a general lack of job readiness. This is true of low earners in years past as well as the present and of workers at the bottom of the earnings distribution in other market economies as well as ours. Nonetheless, the recent U.S. experience is one where earnings and employment have eroded while the formal level of educational attainment among the least skilled has actually increased. These incongruous trends suggest that factors beyond skills have operated to chip away at the relative and absolute economic position of these adults.

In this section, I discuss the likely impacts of the large increases in the proportion of low-skilled men with criminal records on their employment and earnings prospects. We have already seen that male incarceration rates have increased considerably, as has the proportion of men with prison time in their past. Here, I explore the mechanisms through which a prior incarceration experience is likely to affect earnings and employment not only in the immediate future but throughout one's lifetime.

Incarceration and the Accumulation of Work Experience

Serving time interrupts one's work career. The extent of this interruption depends on both the expected amount of time served on a typical term as well as the likelihood of serving subsequent prison terms. The average prisoner admitted during the late 1990s on a new commitment faced a maximum sentence of three years and a minimum of one year—with many serving time closer to the minimum (Raphael and Stoll 2004). If this were the only time served for most, then the time interruption of prison would not be that substantial.[7]

However, many people serve multiple terms in prison, either because of the commission of new felonies or because of violation of parole conditions after their release. A large body of criminological research consistently finds that nearly two-thirds of ex-inmates are re-arrested within a few years of release from prison (Petersilia 2003). Moreover, a sizable majority of the re-arrested will serve subsequent prison terms. Thus, for many offenders, the typical experience between the ages of 18 and 30 is characterized by multiple short prison spells with intermittent, and relatively brief, spells outside of prison.

In previous longitudinal research on young offenders entering the California state prison system, I documented the degree to which prison interrupts the early potential work careers of young men. I followed a cohort of young men entering the state prison system in 1990 and gauged the amount of time served over the subsequent decade (Raphael 2006). This analysis is summarized in Table 7.8. Panel A presents estimates of the distribution of the total amount of time served, comprising multiple prison terms. The median inmate serves 2.79 years during the 1990s, with the median white inmate (3.09 years) and median black inmate (3.53 years) serving more time and the median Hispanic inmate (2.23 years) serving less time.[8] Roughly 25 percent of inmates served at least five years during the 1990s while another 25 percent served less than 1.5 years.

However, as a gauge of the extent of the temporal interruption, these figures are misleading. Cumulative time served does not account for the short periods of time between prison spells where inmates may find employment yet are not able to solidify the employment match with any measurable amount of job tenure. A more appropriate measure of the degree to which incarceration impedes experience accumulation would be the time between the date of admission to prison for the first term served and the date of release from the last term.

Panel B of Table 7.8 presents the quartile values from the distribution of this variable. For the median inmate, five years elapses between the first date of admission and the last date of release. For median white, black, and Hispanic inmates, the comparable figures are 6.2, 6.4, and

Table 7.8 Quartile Values of the Total Time Served during the 1990s and the Time between the Date of First Admission and Date of Last Release for the 1990 Prison Cohort Between 18 and 25 Years of Age

Panel A: Distribution of Total Time Served

	25th percentile	50th percentile	75th percentile
All Inmates	1.44	2.79	4.81
White	1.43	3.09	5.12
Black	1.93	3.53	5.45
Hispanic	1.29	2.23	3.97

Panel B: Distribution of Time between the Date of First Admission and the Date of Last Release

	25th percentile	50th percentile	75th percentile
All Inmates	1.86	4.99	8.71
White	2.01	6.17	9.11
Black	2.88	6.42	9.16
Hispanic	1.44	3.65	7.62

NOTE: Tabulations are based on all individuals between the ages of 18 and 25 that entered the California state prison system during 1990 serving the first term of a commitment. Tabulation of the percentiles of the two time distributions are based on all terms served over the subsequent 10 years.

SOURCE: Author's tabulations of administrative records provided by the California Department of Corrections.

3.7 years, respectively. For approximately one-quarter of inmates, nearly nine years pass between their initial commission to prison and their last release. In other words, one-quarter of these inmates spent almost the entire decade cycling in and out of prison.

Spending five years of one's early life (6.4 years for the median black offender) cycling in and out of institutions must impact one's earnings prospects. Clearly, being behind bars and having only short spans of time outside of prison prohibit the accumulation of job experiences during a period of one's life when the returns to experience are the greatest.

Does Having Been in Prison Stigmatize Ex-Offenders?

The potential impact of serving time on future labor market prospects extends beyond the failure to accumulate work experience. Employers are averse to hiring former prison inmates and often use formal and informal screening tools to weed ex-offenders out of the applicant pool. Given the high proportion of low-skilled men with prison time on their criminal records, such employer sentiments and screening practices represent an increasingly important employment barrier, especially for low-skilled African American men.

Employers consider criminal records when screening job applicants for a number of reasons. For starters, certain occupations are closed to felons under local, state, and in some instances federal law (Hahn 1991). In many states employers can be held liable for the criminal actions of their employees. Under the theory of negligent hiring, employers can be required to pay punitive damages as well as damages for loss, pain, and suffering for acts committed by an employee on the job (Craig 1987). Finally, employers looking to fill jobs where employee monitoring is imperfect may place a premium on trustworthiness and screen accordingly.

In all known employer surveys where employers are asked about their willingness to hire ex-offenders, employer responses reveal a strong aversion to hiring applicants with criminal records (Holzer, Raphael, and Stoll 2006, 2007; Pager 2003). For example, over 60 percent of employers surveyed in the Multi-City Study of Urban Inequality (MCSUI) indicated that they would "probably not" or "definitely not" hire applicants with criminal histories, with "probably not" being the modal response. By way of contrast, only 8 percent responded similarly when queried about their willingness to hire current and former welfare recipients.

The ability of employers to act on an aversion to ex-offenders, and the nature of the action they take in terms of hiring and screening behavior, will depend on their access to applicants' criminal histories. If an employer can and does access criminal records, the employer may simply screen out applicants based on their actual arrest and conviction records. In the absence of a formal background check, an employer may act on an aversion to hiring ex-offenders using perceived correlates of previous incarceration, such as age, race, and level of educational attainment, to attempt to screen out those with criminal histories. In other words, employers may statistically profile applicants and avoid hiring those from demographic groups with high rates of involvement in the criminal justice system (Holzer, Raphael, and Stoll 2006).

The audit study by Pager (2003) offers perhaps the clearest evidence of employer aversion to hiring ex-offenders and the stigma associated with having served time in prison. The study uses male auditors matched on observable characteristics—including age, education, general appearance, demeanor, and race—to assess the effects of prior prison experience on the likelihood that each auditor is called back for an interview. The author finds consistently sizable negative effects of prior prison experience on the likelihood of being called back by the employer, with callback rates for the auditor with prior prison time one-half that of the matched coauditor.

Summary

Incarceration is likely to negatively affect the earnings and employment prospects of former inmates. On the supply side, incarcerated felons fail to accumulate work experience during a period of life when earnings tend to increase the fastest. The time out of the labor force while incarcerated, as well as the longer time of tenuous attachment to the labor force while cycling in and out of prison, permanently alters the lifetime earnings path of former inmates for the worse. On the demand side, employers consistently express a strong reluctance to hire workers with criminal records. This reluctance is driven in part by liability fears and by a premium placed on trustworthiness, but also by public policy that legally prohibits employers from hiring convicted felons in certain job categories. In sum, the greater incidence of involvement with the criminal justice system that has occurred over the past three decades has most certainly negatively affected the prospects of the least-skilled U.S. adults.

IMPROVING THE PROSPECTS OF LOW-SKILLED ADULTS: EXPANDING THE EITC AND REMOVING EMPLOYMENT BARRIERS FOR FORMER INMATES

I have documented a severe erosion of the earnings and employment of less-skilled men in the United States and less detrimental developments for less-skilled women. While the sources of these trends are certainly complex, there are direct policy levers under the control of federal and state government that could be effectively employed to reverse them. From among these, raising the minimum wage would most directly increase the earnings of the lowest-paid workers. While economists debate the likely employment effects of raising the minimum wage, there is solid research suggesting that modest increases have very little effect on employment while increasing the total amount of income earned by the least skilled (Card and Krueger 1994).[9] Moreover, the earnings of the least skilled are low primarily because of their low skills. Improving our primary, secondary, and postsecondary educational systems as well as augmenting the resources devoted to workforce development would clearly benefit our lowest earners (the topic of discussion in the chapter in this volume by Lerman).

In this section, I offer and analyze two proposals for improving the take-home earnings of the least skilled workers and for boosting the employment rates of those who should be working yet are participating in the formal labor force at historically low levels. First, I discuss several current proposals for expanding the Earned Income Tax Credit to single childless workers and offer a hybrid proposal that combines what I see as the best elements of each. Second, I discuss several steps that federal, state, and local policymakers could take to improve the chances of former inmates and convicted felons and aid the reentry of recently released inmates into conventional society.

Expanding the EITC

First introduced in the 1970s, the EITC has become one of the most important antipoverty policies in the United States. At a current cost of approximately $40 billion, the EITC distributes income to low-earning workers primarily in families with children, although there is a modest benefit for childless workers between 25 and 65 years of age. EITC benefits are calculated as a fraction of annual earnings up to a maximum and are phased out at a gradual rate for income earned beyond a further threshold. For example, for a married couple with two children in 2007, the EITC provides an additional $0.40 for each dollar earned up to $11,790, totaling a maximum annual benefit of $4,716. The benefit level is held constant until family earnings reach $17,390 and then is reduced by $0.21 for each dollar earned above this threshold until the benefit is completely phased out (which occurs at $39,783). Since benefits are conditional on having positive earnings, the EITC provides a strong incentive to participate in the labor force, although the program does provide an incentive for many workers who are already working to work fewer hours a year.[10]

The expansions of the EITC during the 1990s had very large impacts on the employment and after-tax incomes of those adults most affected (Meyer and Holtz-Eakin 2001; Meyer and Rosenbaum 2001). However, these expansions had little impact on the earnings of single noncustodial parents or childless single adults with very low earnings, as nearly all of the extra resources devoted to the program went to households with children. In light of this fact, there are several recent proposals to expand the EITC for childless adults and noncustodial parents (Berlin 2007; Center for American Progress 2007; Danziger and Gottschalk 2005; Edelman, Holzer, and Offner 2006).

The attractiveness of such proposals lies both in their simplicity and in their direct effect on the earnings of the least skilled. Rising earnings inequality and declining wages, driven by a host of factors, have adversely affected the material well-being and employment rates of the least skilled workers. Thus, making work pay through a wage subsidy will directly counter these trends regardless of their source, and improve the material well-being of the poor, while providing them with a strong incentive to engage in the legitimate labor market and perhaps a disincentive to engage in criminal activity. To be sure, the existing proposals vary in three ways: 1) cost, 2) the degree to which the benefits are targeted towards the lowest earners, and 3) the degree to which these expansions affect incentives in other respects, such as marriage. Moreover, along these three dimensions no one proposal dominates.

Here, I analyze several variants of two recent proposals to expand the EITC, and I fashion a simple hybrid of the two proposals that addresses the marriage penalty while maintaining the well-targeted nature of the current EITC. The two existing plans that I analyze are as follows:

The Edelman, Holzer, and Offner (EHO) Proposal. In their book, *Reconnecting Disadvantaged Young Men*, Peter Edelman, Harry Holzer, and Paul Offner (2006) offer a plan for a targeted expansion of the EITC toward single childless workers and noncustodial parents.

The plan calls for a 20 percent wage subsidy for the first $7,500 in earnings, yielding a maximum subsidy of $1,500. Beyond earnings of $10,000, the subsidy is taxed away at the rate of $0.15 per dollar until it is completely phased out at $20,000 in annual earnings. The proposal also calls for disregarding one-half of the earnings of the lower-earning spouse in two-earner families for the purposes of calculating EITC benefits. In the analysis below, I assume that all workers aged 18 to 65 who meet the income criteria are eligible for the childless credit. Note that this proposal is quite similar to that recently offered by the Center for American Progress Task Force on Poverty.[11]

The Berlin Proposal. In a recent working paper, the president of MDRC, Gordon Berlin (2007), proposes a targeted expansion of the EITC singles benefit along with a change in the manner in which family income is tabulated for the purposes of the credit. Regarding the childless credit, Berlin proposes an expansion for all adults 21 to 54 years of age who work full time, at a rate of 25 cents per dollar earned through $7,800 of earnings, with a phaseout beginning for earnings beyond $14,400 at a rate of $0.16 per additional dollar earned (with a total phaseout income level of $26,587). Berlin also proposes that EITC benefits be calculated based on individual income rather than family income. Thus, in a two-earner household with two children, the higher-earning worker would claim the children for the purposes of the EITC, and the benefit attributable to this worker's earnings would be calculated accordingly. The lower-earning worker would qualify for the childless credit.

To highlight the relative characteristics of these two proposals, I simulate the costs, impacts on the income distribution, and impacts on average earnings of these two plans (and, by extension, the likely impacts on employment). For the sake of simplicity, I modify the existing proposals somewhat to highlight the tradeoffs in the two approaches. Specifically, I apply the EHO childless credit phase-in and phaseout rates as well as the income thresholds to the Berlin plan. In addition, I assume that all workers between the ages of 21 and 54 are eligible for benefits under the Berlin plan irrespective of whether they have full-time or part-time status. I also consider an enhanced EHO plan that extends the 20 percent earnings subsidy through $10,000 in annual earnings, effectively giving a 20 percent raise to a full-time minimum-wage worker. Finally, I consider a hybrid plan that combines elements of the EHO and Berlin proposals. Specifically, I combine the EHO childless credit for all workers aged 18 to 65 with the Berlin income calculation rules applied selectively to families with earnings equal to or less than $30,000 a year. For qualified households with earnings above $30,000, I apply the income determination rules in the EHO proposal.[12]

I use the March 2006 Current Population Survey (CPS) to simulate how each of these proposals would have affected individuals' outcomes in tax year 2005.[13] Table 7.9 displays cost estimates of total EITC disbursements using the parameters of each of these proposals to calculate EITC benefits for eligible families and individuals. Before proceeding, we should note a number of qualifications. First, these simulations predict a total cost for the current system of roughly $30 billion for tax year 2005, which is approximately $5 to $6 billion below actual costs. In isolation, this fact suggests that the costs simulated in the table may be biased downward. Biasing the estimates in the other direction, I am assuming a 100 percent take-up rate for all available benefits. In practice, take-up of the EITC is not universal, especially for the childless credit, and thus this assumption is likely to bias costs upwards. Finally, the cost estimates in Table 7.9 do not account for any behavioral labor supply response among potential recipients—i.e., the cost estimates simply apply the alternative benefit formulations to those who work, without considering the likely impact of expanded employment. However, as I will discuss shortly, the employment effects of each of these proposals are likely to be quite modest, thus minimizing the importance of this particular behavioral effect on costs.

With these caveats in mind, the simulation suggests that the EHO plan would increase total EITC costs by roughly $18 billion, the enhanced EHO plan would increase them by $35 billion, the Berlin proposal by $26 billion, and the hybrid proposal by $20 billion. For the Berlin proposal, my cost estimate is close to that cited by the author in the original working paper (approximately $29 billion). For the EHO proposal, my cost estimate is nearly double that cited by the authors ($9.8 billion), although this discrepancy is nearly completely accounted for by the difference in the assumed take-up rate.[14] Nonetheless, the costs estimates reveal a clear ordering, with the EHO proposal the least costly, the enhanced EHO proposal the most expensive, and the Berlin and hybrid proposals at intermediate cost points. As the enhanced EHO

Table 7.9 Simulated Costs of Various Proposals to Expand the Earned Income Tax Credit to Single Childless Adults and to Mitigate the Inherent Marriage Penalty

Simulated costs using the 2006 distribution of wage and salary earnings (millions of 2006 dollars)

Beneficiary category	Existing system	EHO proposal	Enhanced EHO proposal	Berlin proposal	Hybrid EHO-Berlin proposal
Single and childless	1,269	20,062	33,878	13,840	20,062
Married, no children	516	3,166	3,737	7,172	3,788
Married with children	13,383	15,203	15,202	25,251	16,571
Single parents	14,315	14,615	14,615	14,615	14,615
Total	29,783	53,046	67,433	60,879	55,037
Difference relative to existing		18,165	35,551	25,997	20,156

NOTE: Blank = not applicable. Costs are simulated using data from the March 2006 Current Population Survey. See text for exact description. The EHO-proposed expansion includes a 20 percent credit for single childless adults up to $7,500 in earnings that is phased out after $10,000 in earnings at a rate of 0.15. The EHO proposal also includes disregarding half of the earnings of the lower-paid spouse in calculating the EITC benefit for married couples. The enhanced EHO proposal is similar with the exception that the 20 percent credit for a single childless adult applies to the first $10,000 in earnings and is phased out after reaching $12,000. The Berlin proposal applies the single childless benefit. The Berlin proposal uses the EHO single childless benefit formula applied only to single adults between 21 and 55. The proposal also uses individual income rather than combined income in calculating the EITC credit for married couples. For married couples with children, the higher earner's income is used to calculate the credit with children, while the lower earner receives the childless EHO credit. The Hybrid EHO-Berlin proposal is the EHO proposal with one modification: the EITC benefit for married couples with total wage and salary income of less than $30,000 is computed using the individual calculations in the Berlin proposal. The benefit for married couples with higher incomes is computed using the EHO disregard.
SOURCE: Author's tabulations from the March 2006 Current Population Survey.

proposal would have the largest impact on the take-home pay of low-income workers, and thus the largest likely effect on employment, the cost estimates reveal the fairly obvious tradeoff between impact size and cost.

Table 7.10 investigates where in the earnings distribution the additional dollars expended under each proposal land. To construct this table, I first simulated tax-paying units by assuming that all single childless adults as well as single parents file individual returns and that all married adults file joint returns. I then stratified the distribution of wage and salary earnings across these tax filing units into 10-percent slices, or deciles, ordering them from lowest to highest. The figures in Table 7.10 give the percentage of the additional dollars spent under each proposal (i.e., the last row of figures in Table 7.9) that would accrue to each income decile.

The table reveals quite large disparities in how well-targeted these proposals are towards the bottom of the earnings distribution. The additional dollars spent under the EHO and the enhanced EHO proposals are heavily concentrated in the bottom three deciles of the earnings distribution, with 91 percent of the former and 89 percent of the latter accruing to tax-filing units that have less than $20,000 in annual income. Some of the additional benefits do hit higher up in the income distribution, since married couples with incomes as high as $51,000 a year would qualify for benefits under the EHO proposal.[15] However, in proportional terms, the amount accruing to units with earnings above $40,000 is trivial. For the Berlin proposal, only 49 percent of the additional dollars hit the bottom 30 percent of the income distribution, with a much higher proportion (38 percent) escaping above the median income. These figures suggest that there are many households where a relatively high-earning spouse is married to a relatively low-earning spouse whose income would qualify for the childless benefit. The hybrid proposal, on the other hand, reveals that a targeted application of the income eligibility calculations under the Berlin proposal (restricted to households with incomes below $30,000) preserves the targeting of the EHO proposal with relatively few additional benefits accruing to high-income households and a relatively modest increase in total costs above the base EHO proposal.

While the EHO proposal and its variants are well targeted, the Berlin proposal wins out in terms of the implicit marriage penalty. Table

Table 7.10 Distribution of Additional Dollars Spent Above the Existing Credit by the Deciles of the Wage and Salary Earnings of Simulated Tax-Filing Units

Deciles of the earnings distribution	% additional dollars going to each earnings decile under the following proposals			
	EHO proposal	Enhanced EHO proposal	Berlin proposal	Hybrid EHO-Berlin proposal
D1: <6,000	21	13	9	19
D2: 6,001–13,000	49	41	26	45
D3: 13,001–20,000	21	35	14	20
D4: 20,001–25,743	1	6	4	4
D5: 25,744–34,000	3	2	9	7
D6: 34,001–42,500	3	2	11	3
D7: 42,501–55,000	1	0	13	1
D8: 55,001–73,500	0	0	7	0
D9: 73,501–102,000	0	0	4	0
D10: 102,001 and up	0	0	3	0

NOTE: The figures in the table give the percentage of the additional dollars spent above the current system that would accrue to tax filing units of the given income class. The nature of the proposals is discussed in the notes to Table 7.9 and in the text.
SOURCE: Author's tabulations from March 2006 Current Population Survey.

7.11 calculates the credit for a two-earner family in which each working adult earns $10,000 per year (roughly the earnings of a full-time minimum wage worker). Hypothetical credits are tabulated for married, for unmarried, and by the number of dependent children. While the actual financial effect of marriage will differ in magnitude and, sometimes, in sign from those presented in Table 7.11 for households with different income mixes, two full-time low-paid workers provide a good baseline for policy intended to reduce poverty and aid the lowest paid workers in the country. In general, the marriage disincentives will be higher for higher-income couples in most of the proposals analyzed here.

As can be seen, the current EITC, when considered in isolation, creates modest disincentives to marry. The largest penalty occurs for couples with one child ($683). The EHO proposal as well as the enhanced EHO proposal tend to exacerbate this problem. For a couple with no children, marriage reduces total credit income by roughly $1,950. The effect is somewhat smaller for couples with one child (−$1,500) and two or more children (−$964). These penalties are considerably larger for the enhanced EHO proposal.

In contrast, there is no marriage penalty under the Berlin proposal. Since benefits are calculated according to individual rather than joint income, the proposal has a neutral impact on household formation. This is clearly an attractive design feature. However, it comes at the expense of poorer targeting of the benefit dollars, as was illustrated in Table 7.10. The hybrid proposal also eliminates the marriage penalty for this low-income couple. However, the penalty is shifted further up the income distribution, specifically towards couples with combined incomes of $30,000 or higher. Aggregate benefits for such higher-income couples are smaller than for lower-income couples and account for a smaller percentage of annual income. Thus one might argue that in such instances the marriage penalty associated with the EITC is likely to have less of an influence on behavior than when the credit is larger, both absolutely and proportionally.

In our discussion of employment and earnings trends, the role of declining wages in explaining the declining employment of low-skilled men and women was heavily emphasized. One might ask whether the proposed expansions analyzed here would appreciably alter employment by greatly increasing the returns to formal work. Among the lowest earners without children, such as those earning minimum wage, the

Table 7.11 Calculation of the EITC Benefits for a Couple (Each of Whom Earns $10,000 per Year) When Married and When Unmarried, Under the Existing System and Under Each Proposed Expansion

	Number of children		
	None	One	More than one
Existing system			
Married	0	2,237	3,864
Unmarried	325	2,910	4,197
Penalty	−325	−673	−333
EHO proposal			
Married	1,050	2,747	4,536
Unmarried	3,000	4,247	5,500
Penalty	−1,950	−1,500	−964
Enhanced EHO			
Married	1,550	2,747	4,536
Unmarried	4,000	4,747	6,000
Penalty	−2,450	−2000	−1,464
Berlin proposal			
Married	3,000	4,247	5,500
Unmarried	3,000	4,247	5,500
Penalty	0	0	0
Hybrid EHO-Berlin			
Married	3,000	4,247	5,500
Unmarried	3,000	4,247	5,500
Penalty	0	0	0

NOTE: Figures in the table represent the EITC benefit, under the existing system and under each proposal, that a two-earner couple, in which each spouse earns $10,000 per year, would receive when married and when unmarried. The nature of the proposals is discussed in the note to Table 7.9 and in the text.

SOURCE: Author's tabulations based on the Earned Income Tax Credit (EITC) program parameters for the 2005 tax year.

proposed expansions would substantially raise earnings (by as much as 20 percent), effectively countering the ground lost between 1980 and the present. However, even among the least skilled, the proportion earning the minimum wage is low, and thus for many the proposed expansions will only subsidize part of annual earnings, with some low-skilled workers likely to be operating within the phaseout income range.

To assess the overall effects of these expansions on take-home pay and their potential to draw certain groups into the labor market, I have tabulated average annual earnings for certain subgroups of the population with extremely low employment rates and characterized the benefits under each of these proposals as a proportion of annual earnings. The proportional increase, when combined with estimates of the supply responsiveness of these groups, provides ballpark estimates of the boost to employment rates one might expect from the expansions discussed here.[16]

Table 7.12 presents the proportional increases in annual income that would be generated by the proposed expansions for selective groups of low-skilled males with very low employment rates. All tabulations pertain to single, childless men with the additional characteristics indicated in the table. The first column demonstrates that the existing system has virtually no effect on earnings (less than half of a percent) and thus likely has no effect on individual decisions to work among these men. The EHO/Hybrid proposal[17] provides a notable increase in annual income, ranging from 2 to 6 percent, for all groups depicted; the largest increase (6 percent) occurs for black high school dropouts between 18 and 25 years of age. The enhanced EHO proposal has the largest proportional effects on income; it shows increases among young high school dropouts of 8 percent for all groups with the exception of Asian men, who would see a 5 percent increase. The Berlin proposal has the smallest effect on earnings among the new proposals; its effects range from 1 to 4 percent, and most men characterized in the table experience increases on the order of 2 percent.

How much of an increase in employment might we expect from these expansions? When combined with the labor supply elasticity estimates discussed above, the earnings increases in Table 7.12 are likely to have very modest effects on employment. For example, the EHO proposal is predicted to alter the employment rate of all black male dropouts by roughly 1 percentage point, while the larger enhanced EHO proposal might increase the employment rate of young black dropouts by as much as 2 percent. Given the lower responsiveness of less skilled men in the other racial or ethnic groups, the employment effects are likely to be even smaller.

As an overall assessment of the proposals, it is clear that no one proposal dominates, and that each has relative advantages and disad-

Table 7.12 EITC Credit as a Proportion of Annual Earnings for Select Groups of Single Childless Less-Educated Men, Under the Existing System and Under the Various Proposed Expansions

	Existing system	EHO and hybrid proposal[a]	Enhanced EHO proposal	Berlin proposal
White, less than high school				
18–55	0.00	0.03	0.05	0.02
18–25	0.00	0.05	0.08	0.02
26–35	0.00	0.02	0.04	0.02
Black, less than high school				
18–55	0.00	0.04	0.05	0.03
18–25	0.00	0.06	0.08	0.03
26–35	0.01	0.04	0.06	0.04
Asian, less than high school				
18–55	0.00	0.02	0.03	0.01
18–25	0.00	0.04	0.05	0.02
26–35	0.00	0.02	0.04	0.02
Hispanic, less than high school				
18–55	0.00	0.03	0.05	0.02
18–25	0.00	0.04	0.08	0.03
26–35	0.00	0.03	0.05	0.03

NOTE: Figures provide the average credit under each system, divided by the average annual wage and salary earnings for workers in the given demographic group. All calculations apply to single, childless men. The nature of each proposal is described in the notes to Table 7.9 and in the text.
[a] For single childless men, the EHO and hybrid proposals are identical.
SOURCE: Author's tabulations based on data from the 1980, 1990, and 2000 Public Use Microdata Samples (PUMS) of the U.S. Census of Population and Housing.

vantages. The EHO proposal costs less and delivers more income to the lowest-earning workers.[18] However, the expanded childless credit exacerbates the marriage penalty inherent in the current system. The Berlin proposal eliminates this penalty, but at a higher cost and for a less well-targeted program. The hybrid model, I believe, combines the strengths of both proposals, yielding a well-targeted expansion that reduces, or for some eliminates, the disincentive to marry. While the marriage disincentives are pushed further up the earnings distribution, one can reasonably argue that the behavioral impact of the penalty is likely to be smaller for higher-income couples.

The small projected employment effects of these expansions are disappointing and suggest that substantially increasing employment through supply-side incentives would require a much bigger and costlier expansion than the proposals analyzed here. Nonetheless, the proposals represent considerable increases in the incomes of the workers at the very bottom of the distribution, increases that will greatly improve their material well-being and provide strong incentives for a small slice of the nation's poorest adults to engage in legitimate work.

Policies to Remove Barriers to Employment for Ex-Offenders

Spending time in prison or having a prior felony conviction in one's history is becoming an increasingly common characteristic of low-skilled workers, especially for low-skilled minority men. While the causes of this increased interaction with the criminal justice system are varied, the lion's share of this development is attributable to changes in sentencing policy that have both increased the average time that an offender spends behind bars and enlarged the scope of behavior punished by a spell of incarceration (Raphael and Stoll 2007). My analysis of employment trends found that only a small part of the decline in employment rates among the least-skilled men can be explained by declining wages, suggesting the limits of policies designed to boost take-home earnings. Fully addressing the employment crises for these men requires directly addressing the barriers to employment created by one's official criminal past.

Facilitating the successful reentry of former inmates and felons into noninstitutionalized society is an extremely complex problem that will most likely require substantial investments in training, social services, employment services, and postrelease monitoring (see the discussions in Petersilia [2003] and Travis [2005]). The sheer size of this population—roughly 600,000 inmates are released each year and nearly 5 percent of the adult male population has served time—is indicative of the enormity of this challenge. Nonetheless, there are simple steps that the state and federal government could take that would not compromise public safety yet would eliminate some of the challenges that former inmates and felons face in procuring employment and avoiding extreme poverty after their release.

To begin with, the summary disqualification of former inmates and those with felony convictions from participating in federal public assistance programs and from receiving financial aid for education should be reversed. Currently, those with prior drug felony convictions are prohibited from receiving federal financial education assistance. Moreover, the 1996 Personal Responsibility and Work Opportunity Reconciliation Act made drug felons ineligible for food stamps and cash assistance for life. States could adopt the federal ban on food stamps and cash assistance as is, or pass legislation to modify or eliminate the ban. States are not authorized to eliminate the ban on financial aid (Legal Action Center 2004).

The only possible rationale for such collateral punishment of drug offenders is that by enhancing punishment fewer people will engage in drug crimes. However, the deterrence effects of incarceration itself are hotly debated among those who study the determinants of crime (Lee and McCrary 2005; Levitt 1998), with much research suggesting that the likely effects are quite small. With this in mind, the deterrent effects of much more removed, and perhaps less salient, punishments such as a lifetime ban on food stamps receipt or becoming ineligible for Pell grants must certainly generate very little in the way of crime reduction. Such bans, however, do make it more difficult for released offenders to avoid extreme poverty and to turn their lives around. Financial aid through the Pell grant program is one of the main sources of assistance for those attending community college, an important source of training and secondary education for less-skilled adults. Food stamps very effectively provide basic assistance to meet the most fundamental needs of the poor. Banning former felons from participating in these programs is frankly counterproductive. Those states that maintain complete or partial bans on participation in public assistance should drop them, and the federal governments should reverse the ban on drug offenders receiving educational assistance.

Employment bans based on former convictions and occupational licensing restrictions should be based on the content of one's criminal record and not applied in a blanket manner. Moreover, when used, employment bans should be based on conviction rather than arrest records. Any bans on the employment of felons mandated by law should be based on the nature of one's previous behavior as well as the time that has elapsed since the felony was committed. In their analysis of the consideration that states give to criminal records, the Legal Action Center (2004) found that in nearly all states there is no standard or statute governing the consideration that employers and occupational licensing agencies are required to give to an employee who has a criminal history. In many states, employers can fire anyone who is found to have a criminal history regardless of the gravity of the offense, the time since conviction, or the relevance of the past behavior to one's current job responsibility. In addition, employers are generally free to consider and discriminate based upon one's criminal history in hiring, with most states allowing employers to consider arrests not leading to conviction.

Holzer, Raphael, and Stoll (2006) demonstrate that most employers of low-skilled labor check criminal records in some manner (either by directly asking the applicant, by paying a private firm, or by performing a query of the state criminal history repository), and that the proportion of employers that check has increased considerably over the decade of the 1990s. The high propensity to check, the complete discretion in considering past criminal records, and the high proportion of men with prior convictions all indicate a need for some governing standard that addresses the interests of employers but also recognizes the employment needs of former inmates and those with prior convictions. With this in mind, states should prohibit firms from considering prior arrests that did not result in a conviction when making decisions about the hiring or firing of an employee. Moreover, publicly mandated employment bans of former felons for specific jobs as well as licensing bans should be based on the content of specific offenses or offender characteristics. In general, a more considerate and rational process for determining the suitability of former prisoners for employment in certain occupations is needed.

We should invest more in labor market intermediaries that specialize in the reentry employment needs of recently released inmates. When asked, many employers express an extreme reluctance to hire former inmates. However, a sizable minority indicate that they are indeed willing to hire offenders and actually do so, as measured by recent hiring outcomes. Governmental as well as nonprofit entities devoted to workforce development often serve an important informational role in matching clients to employers, which greatly minimizes the search costs for both parties. For a specific group of clients who face a stigma in searching for work, such job search assistance is likely to be particularly important.

Moreover, over time such intermediaries establish long-term relationships and credibility with employers and are thus more effective in placing their clients in employment. Because over the past decade many more people have been incarcerated for relatively less serious offenses, intermediaries should easily be able to identify the most job-ready candidates and offer up a steady supply of reentering former inmates who are prescreened and likely to be solid employees, or at least of comparable quality to an employer's average hire.

Given the scale of the flow of inmates out of prison each year (on the order of 600,000), there is a large potential role for agencies and nonprofits devoted to minimizing employment search costs, prescreening workers for employers, and aiding those who are reentering in becoming ready for conventional employment.

States should incentivize desistance from criminal activity by expunging certain criminal records after a fixed time period has elapsed. In a recent analysis, Kurlycheck, Brame, and Bushway (2006) raise the important question of whether unfettered employer access to criminal records can be justified by the legitimate concerns of employers and the public. They assess whether the rate at which young offenders desist from offending as time passes since the last offense merits limiting employer access to arrest and conviction information for sufficiently distant past offenses. The authors demonstrate that for a cohort of young men in Philadelphia the likelihood of a repeat offense declines precipitously as time accrues since the last offense. This pattern is consistent with both a causal effect of staying clean and a remaining population of former offenders that becomes increasingly selected with time since the last offense (to be specific, selection occurs towards a low propensity to offend). For policy purposes, however, the exact source of this pattern is irrelevant. Based on this pattern, the authors argue that limiting employer access to criminal records beyond a certain time period may effectively limit the collateral consequences of prison while not necessarily exposing employers and the public to sufficiently higher risk to warrant keeping access to the records open.

This simple proposal carries many advantages. Clearly, being able to procure and retain gainful employment is practically a necessary condition for the successful reintegration of former inmates into noninstitutionalized society. The expunging of one's past offenses following a determined period of desistance will certainly improve the labor market prospects as well as the life prospects of former offenders. Moreover, the prospect of having one's record wiped clean after a given period of desistance provides an incentive for former inmates to change their behavior.

Nonetheless, this proposal may have unintended negative consequences if employers care about prior criminal activity and engage in indirect and imperfect screening practices. In other words, limiting an employer's ability to access criminal records or to ask about criminal convictions may not preclude employers from using potential signals of earlier run-ins with the law in making hiring and promotion decisions. At a minimum, employers may be able to effectively identify ex-offenders through such signals as education, where one comes from, or through unaccounted-for gaps in one's employment history. At worst, employers may systematically discriminate against workers who come from groups that they *perceive* to have a high propensity to offend, such as young black men (Holzer, Raphael, and Stoll 2006). This important issue of how employers may respond to limits on access is key to designing a policy that not only allows employers to take into account aspects of an individual's history that are legitimately related to assessing potential job performance, but also protects those who, through the passage of time, have demonstrated the irrelevance of their past infractions to their future performance.

There are several key choice variables that should be considered in designing an information policy that balances the ability of employers to have access to relevant information about applicants and employees with the interests of former offenders who have managed to stay out of trouble. First and foremost among these choice variables is the length of the time limit placed on criminal history inquiries. If the limit that is set is too short, employers will not have confidence in formal checks and thus will employ informal screens as a supplement, undoing much of the potential benefit to ex-offenders from suppressing such information in the first place. To the extent that the limit is too long, few offenders will benefit and there will be little added incentive to stay clean because of the prospect of an expunged record. Kurlycheck, Brame, and Bushway (2006) focus on the seven-year limit set in the federal statute pertaining to the trucking industry. Clearly, more research on employer hiring practices with a focus on this specific question would greatly inform this choice.

A second choice variable concerns the starting point for the time period framing the criminal record. The authors advocate for a start date corresponding to the date of the most recent conviction, arguing that since few employers have access to incarceration information, time since incarceration is irrelevant. However, one can imagine that, with the knowledge that records are purged after seven years, employers may still downgrade applications from young men whom they suspect have served some time. Knowing that a clean criminal record check is consistent with either 1) never having offended, or 2) having offended and potentially served time but having had no contact with the criminal justice system for the past seven years, provides considerably more information than the alternative of ignoring incarceration.

A third important choice variable concerns whether there are some offenses that should never be purged. One might make the argument that someone who has served time for a felony sex offense should never work with children, or that workers with prior serious violent offenses should not be placed in jobs that involve providing security. Again, a better understanding of how employers consider such mitigating factors would provide useful information for forming a viable policy prescription.

Regardless, the growing numbers of noninstitutionalized felons raise important policy questions regarding reintegration and the manner in which society can ease and facilitate the transition of former offenders into productive and stable lives. Stable employment is clearly key. To the extent that we can improve the prospects of former offenders without substantially harming the interests of employers, and while providing a positive incentive to desist from criminal offending, we should do so.

CONCLUSION

The past three decades have not been kind to low-skilled workers in the United States. In addition to low-skilled adults experiencing substantial real declines in hourly earnings, their employment rates, especially those for low-skilled minority men, have dropped to historic lows. Concurrently, the incarceration rates of these same adults have increased tremendously, to the point where for certain subgroups of the adult male population the likelihood of being institutionalized at any given point in time is nearly equal to the likelihood of being employed or the likelihood of being noninstitutionalized yet idle.

These developments are clearly related. I have demonstrated the effects of declining wages on employment and incarceration rates. There is also a growing body of research suggesting a reverse causal link from prior incarceration to employment outcomes. This line of research, combined with the disturbing incarceration trends that I have documented, indicates that the problems faced by ex-offenders represent an increasingly important and daunting challenge to antipoverty policy in the United States.

I have offered and analyzed two sets of policy responses by state and federal policymakers to these developments: 1) expanding the EITC for childless adults and noncustodial parents, and 2) taking steps to eliminate some of the official barriers to employment and impediments to reentry for former prison inmates and convicted felons. These clearly address only a small set of the problems faced by low-income adults. Yet action on these fronts would most certainly be helpful.

Appendix 7A

Estimating Labor Supply
Elasticities by Race and Gender

I use data from the 1980, 1990, and 2000 census PUMS files to estimate the labor supply elasticities for men and women overall and for men and women by race and ethnicity. I then use these estimates to assess the degree to which changes in employment between 1980 and 2000 can be attributable to changes in wages. The supply elasticity estimates come from estimating the equation

$$(7A.1) \quad E_{exry} = \alpha_y + \beta_e + \kappa_x + \gamma Ln W_{exry} + \varepsilon_{exry},$$

where E_{exry} is the employment rate for adults in our sample in education group e (less than high school, high school graduate, some college, college plus), in labor market experience group x (5 years or less, 6 to 10 years, 11 to 15 years, 16 to 20 years, 21 to 25 years, 26 to 30 years, 31 to 35 years, and 36-plus years), in racial group r (white, black, Asian, or Hispanic), and in year y (1980, 1990, and 2000), $Ln W_{exry}$ is the corresponding average of log wages for members of this group, ε_{exry} is a mean-zero error term, α_y represents a year-specific fixed effect, and β_e represents a fixed effect for all adults in the education group e, and κ_x represents a fixed effect for experience groups. The coefficient γ gives the responsiveness of employment for members of the group to a change in average log wages. The labor supply elasticity is defined by the equation

$$\eta = \frac{W}{E} \frac{\partial E}{\partial W} = \frac{1}{E} \frac{\partial E}{\partial \ln W}.$$

Since γ provides an estimate of ∂E, calculating the elasticity requires dividing through by the employment rate. Since I'm dividing through by the average employment rate, the elasticity should be interpreted as the responsiveness of the group at the mean. The inclusion of year-fixed effects as well as education- and experience-fixed effects means that the elasticity estimates are identified using variation in the changes in employment and earnings occurring within education and experience groups across racial or ethnic groups.

I estimate Equation (7A.1) separately for men and women to derive overall estimates of the responsiveness of male and female labor supply. I also estimate the following modified specification

(7A.2) $E_{exry} = \alpha_y + \beta_e + \kappa_x + \delta \times Black_{exry} + \lambda \times White_{exry} + \eta \times Asian_{exry}$

$+ \gamma_0 LnW_{exry} + \gamma_1 LnW_{exrt} \times Black_{exry} + \gamma_2 LnW_{exry} \times White_{exry}$

$+ \gamma_3 LnW_{exry} \times Asian_{exry} + \varepsilon_{exry}$,

where $Black_{exry}$ is a dummy variable equal to one if the group is black and zero otherwise, and $White_{exry}$ and $Asian_{exry}$ are similar dummy variables indicating white and Asian demographic subgroups. This specification allows the supply responsiveness to changes in wages to vary by race and ethnicity. The base coefficient γ_0 indicates the responsiveness of Hispanic labor supply (the group omitted by the dummy variables) to changes in wages. The coefficient on the interaction term between the black dummy and log wages, γ_1, indicates the degree to which black labor supply responsiveness differs from Hispanic labor supply responsiveness. The overall responsiveness of black labor supply requires adding the based coefficient, γ_0, and the coefficient on the interaction term, γ_1. Similar derivations would yield the labor supply responsiveness for whites and Asians. Note that the addition of race-specific dummy variables indicates that supply responsiveness is being estimated using variation in the changes in employment and earnings occurring within education and experience groups and within racial or ethnic groups. Again, converting the responsiveness parameter into an elasticity estimate requires dividing by the race-specific mean employment rate.

Equations (7A.1) and (7A.2) are estimated using employment rates and earnings potential for all men and women, institutionalized as well as noninstitutionalized. Thus, any impact of wage changes on institutionalization operating through withdrawal from the formal labor force will be reflected in the elasticity estimates.

Table 7A.1 presents the results of this analysis. For both men and women, I present estimation results for all adults in the sample and for adults with a high school degree or less. Parameter estimates for the coefficient on log wages and the interaction terms with log wages are presented in the top half of the table, while the implied elasticity estimates (the calculations represented graphically in Figures 7.1 and 7.2) are presented in the bottom half. The high elasticity estimates in Figures 7.1 and 7.2 use the largest race-specific estimates from the table, while the lowest are based on the smallest.

Table 7A.1 Estimated Effects of Log Wages on the Likelihood of Being Employed at the Time of Interview for Men, and the Corresponding Implied Labor Supply Elasticities

	Men				Women			
	All men		Men with a high school diploma or less		All women		Women with a high school diploma or less	
	(1)	(2)	(3)	(4)	(5)	(6)	(7)	(8)
Log wage	0.159	0.136	0.029	-0.120	0.279	0.258	0.449	0.378
	(0.039)	(0.039)	(0.079)	(0.093)	(0.049)	(0.050)	(0.083)	(0.093)
Log wage × white	—	0.019	—	0.105	—	-0.104	—	-0.110
		(0.018)		(0.035)		(0.024)		(0.049)
Log wage × black	—	0.265	—	0.364	—	0.086	—	0.157
		(0.023)		(0.039)		(0.028)		(0.059)
Log wage × Asian	—	0.019	—	0.150	—	-0.179	—	-0.165
		(0.032)		(0.107)		(0.040)		(0.045)
Implied labor supply elasticities								
Overall	0.196	—	0.039	—	0.426	—	0.792	—
White	—	0.180	—	-0.019	—	0.227	—	0.449
Black	—	0.637	—	0.435	—	0.548	—	1.008
Asian	—	0.186	—	0.041	—	0.124	—	0.388
Hispanic	—	0.184	—	-0.170	—	0.488	—	0.816
R^2	0.892	0.930	0.885	0.918	0.902	0.924	0.884	0.903
N	449	449	239	239	447	447	239	239

(continued)

Table 7A.1 (continued)

NOTE: Standard errors are in parentheses. Dashes indicate that the variable in question was not included in the regression specification, therefore the data are not available. All models are based on regressions of the proportion of employment on average log wages based on demographic cells defined by year, level of educational attainment, labor market experience, and race/ethnicity. See text for the number of categories within each dimension and the specific definitions. All regressions include dummies for year-fixed effects, education group–fixed effects, experience group–fixed effects, and race-fixed effects and are based on data from the 1980, 1990, and 2000 censuses. All models are weighted by the sum of the sample weights within the defined cells. Supply elasticities are calculated by dividing the point estimate for the effect of log wages on employment by the average employment rate for the group in question.

SOURCE: Author's tabulations based on data from the 1980, 1990, and 2000 Public Use Microdata Samples (PUMS) of the U.S. Census of Population and Housing.

Appendix 7B

Assessing the Contribution of Declining Wages to Increases in Incarceration Rates

Let c be the likelihood that an individual chosen at random commits a crime, and p be the likelihood of being caught and convicted, conditional on committing a crime. Let θ be the rate at which inmates are released from prison. Assume that c is a function of legitimate wages—i.e., $c = c(w)$—where $c'(w) < 0$. Raphael and Stoll (2007) demonstrate that under these assumptions the long-run equilibrium incarceration rate will be equal to

(7B.1) $\quad Inc = \dfrac{c(w)p}{c(w)p + \theta}$.

In Equation (7B.1), incarceration increases in the transition probability from nonincarceration to incarceration ($c(w)p$) and decreases in the transition probability out of prison (θ). Differentiating Equation (7B.1) with respect to wages yields the expression

(7B.2) $\quad \dfrac{\partial Inc}{\partial w} = \dfrac{\partial Inc}{\partial c} \times \dfrac{\partial c}{\partial w} = \dfrac{\theta}{(cp + \theta)^2} \times p \times \dfrac{\partial c}{\partial w}$,

where the dependence of c on w is suppressed for simplicity. In practice, cp is a very small number (generally below 0.003) while θ is relatively large (around 0.5). If we set $cp = 0$, Equation (7B.2) is reduced to

(7B.3) $\quad \dfrac{\partial Inc}{\partial w} = \dfrac{\partial Inc}{\partial c} \times \dfrac{\partial c}{\partial w} = \dfrac{1}{\theta} \times p \times \dfrac{\partial c}{\partial w}$.

If we assume that the time-served distribution is exponential, then the first term provides the expected value of time served. Thus Equation (7B.3) becomes

(7B.4) $\quad \dfrac{\Delta Incarceration}{\Delta \ln W} = E(T) \times p \times \dfrac{\Delta Crime}{\Delta LnW}$.

Equation (7B.4) illustrates that the increase in incarceration caused by a decrease in wages will operate through the product of three factors. Moving from right to left on the right hand side of Equation (7B.4), a decline in wages will increase criminal activity (that is to say, $\dfrac{\Delta Crime}{\Delta \ln W}$ will be negative). This in turn will increase incarceration in proportion to the probability of being apprehended and sentenced, conditional on having committed a crime (the parameter, p). Finally, the ultimate effect on the overall incarceration rate will be larger the longer the expected amount of time the sentenced prisoner will serve (given by $E(T)$ in Equation [7B.4]). Thus with estimates for each of these factors, and with the wage trends presented in Table 7.3, one could estimate the proportion of the increase in institutionalization rates depicted in Table 7.5 that can be attributable to declining wages.

I draw estimates for each of these factors from various sources. Grogger (1998) estimates that the effect of a change in the natural log of hourly earnings on the likelihood of engaging in income-generating activity is approximately −0.25. I use this number for the change in crime caused by a change in log wages. Based on an analysis of criminal offending and incarceration among respondents of the NLSY79 data set, and the increased risk of incarceration over the past 20 years, I estimate that the likelihood of being caught and incarcerated among those who are actively engaged in income-generating criminal activity is 0.06 (see Raphael and Stoll [2007] for details). With regard to expected time served, the median inmate in the United States serves a term of slightly more than two years on a given prison spell. However, those offenders coaxed into criminal activity by declining wages are likely to commit fewer and less serious crimes relative to those already incarcerated. Thus, here I assume that such marginal offenders that wind up in prison or jail serve no more than 1.5 years on average. Multiplying these three parameters suggests that the value of the derivative in Equation (7B.1) is equal to −0.0225. Multiplying this estimate by the actual change in wages for any given subgroup provides an estimate of the predicted increase in incarceration caused by the change in the group's wages.

Notes

I thank Timothy Bartik, Adam Carasso, Sheldon Danziger, Harry Holzer, Susan Houseman, Robert Reich, and Eugene Smolensky for their much-valued input.

1. Among the many explanations for the increase in earnings inequality over the past three decades, some of the most common include skill-biased technological change that has increased demand for high-skilled workers and reduced demand for low-skilled workers (Autor and Katz 1999), the erosion of the real value of the minimum wage (DiNardo, Fortin, and Lemieux 1996), increased international trade with less-developed nations (Borjas, Freeman, and Katz 1997), and increased labor market competition from low-skilled immigrants (Borjas 2003; Freeman, Katz, and Borjas 1997).

2. Between 1975 and 2005, the number of state and federal prisoners per 100,000 U.S. residents increased from 111 to 491, constituting a 342 percent increase over this time period and a ratio of 4.42 inmates in 2005 to 1 inmate 30 years earlier. Between 1980 and 2005, the number of inmates in local and county jails increased from 81 per 100,000 to 252 per 100,000, a 211 percent increase and a ratio of 3.11 inmates in 2005 to 1 inmate a quarter-century earlier. For details, see Raphael and Stoll (2007) and the Bureau of Justice Statistics (2007).

3. The computation is based on four mutually exclusive race categories (non-Hispanic white, non-Hispanic black, non-Hispanic Asian, and Hispanic), nine educational attainment groups (no schooling, fourth grade or less, fifth through eighth grade, ninth, tenth, eleventh, and twelfth grades, one to three years of college, and college-plus), year (1980, 1990, or 2000), gender, and eight potential labor market experience groups (5 years or less, 6 to 10 years, 11 to 15 years, 16 to 20 years, 21 to 25 years, 26 to 30 years, 31 to 35 years, and 36-plus years). I measure labor market experience by assuming an entry age of 16 for workers with less than a high school education, 18 for high school graduates, 20 for those with some college, and 22 for college graduates. For workers who are institutionalized, I assume that they have not worked in the previous year since for many of these workers the long form of the PUMS is completed using administrative records that are likely to vary in quality across institutions (Butcher and Piehl 2006).

4. See Autor and Katz (1999) for a general discussion of wage trends in the United States. Juhn (2003) also computes wages for nonparticipants using the average wage of workers in matching demographic groups who work fewer than 13 weeks for the computation. Here I match to median wages for workers in one's demographic group without placing a restriction on weeks worked, because preliminary analysis revealed workers with unusually high wages among those working few weeks. This latter pattern most likely reflects measurement error in the "weeks worked" variable in the IPUMS-CPS database.

5. That is to say, the substitution effect associated with a decline in wages militates towards supplying less time to the labor market. The income effect of lower wages, however, will in isolation induce one to supply more time to the labor market

and consume less free time. While these two effects are offsetting and thus imply that a decrease in wages may correspond to an increase in time supplied, much of the recent empirical research on the labor supply effects of diminished low-skilled wages suggests that the net effect on labor supply has been negative (Devereux 2003; Juhn 1992, 2003; Pencavel 1997, 2002).

6. I calculate the predicted change in employment attributable to declining wages by multiplying the supply elasticity by the actual proportional decline in wages and by the base employment rate for each group in 1980.

7. Of course, I am not saying that a year in prison is not costly. However, a year's absence from the labor market during the beginning of one's career would have only a small effect on accumulated experience.

8. The California inmate population is roughly evenly distributed between whites, Hispanics, and blacks and is overwhelmingly male.

9. Research on the employment effects of raising the minimum wage suggests that small increases result in negligible levels of job destruction, though large increases do indeed reduce employment. The impact on total earnings accruing to minimum-wage workers depends on how sensitive the demand for labor is to changes in wages. Most research suggests that demand for low-skilled workers is relatively inelastic, and thus an increase in the minimum wage leads to a total increase in the aggregate wage bill accruing to low-wage workers.

10. In particular, for households with incomes in the region of the benefits schedule between the maximum benefit threshold and the phaseout threshold, the EITC increases income without altering the marginal return to an additional hour of work. Simple economic theory predicts that such an increase in income would induce most people to work fewer hours. Workers whose income places them in the phaseout region of the benefits schedule have particularly strong incentives to work fewer hours, as the phaseout rate reduces the hourly wage by 21 percent while the benefit provides a positive increase in income. Existing research suggests that the negative incentive effects are particularly strong for secondary earnings in two-parent families (Eissa and Hoynes 2004).

11. In the report, *From Poverty to Prosperity: A National Strategy to Cut Poverty in Half*, The Center for American Progress (2007) proposes an expansion of the EITC nearly identical to that in Edelman, Holzer, and Offner (2006), with the addition that the childless tax credit be made available to all adults over age 24 and to adults between 18 and 24 who are not enrolled in school. The report also calls for an expansion of the phase-in rate for families with three or more children to 45 percent. Currently, a phase-in rate of 40 percent applies to all families with two or more children. Thus, the proposal would not affect the phase-in rate for two-child families while increasing the rate for larger families.

12. An alternative form of this hybrid would be to calculate benefits based on individual income for some phase-in period (say the first three years of marriage as proposed in Edelman, Holzer, and Offner [2006]).

13. I use the March 2006 CPS to first classify all adults by marital status and by whether they have dependents under 18. The four possibilities are then used to simulate tax filing units, where presumably single childless workers file inde-

pendent returns, single parents file returns as a head of household, and married couples file joint returns.

14. Edelman, Holzer, and Offner (2006) assume a take-up rate of the childless benefit of 0.67 and limit the credit to workers aged 21 to 64. Imposing these two restrictions lowers my cost estimates for this plan to $8.6 billion, quite close to the $9.8 billion estimate offered by the authors.

15. Under the EHO proposal, the highest possible phaseout income would be for a married couple with two or more children. Using the 2006 EITC phaseout total, total earnings must satisfy the equation $Income_h + 0.5 \times Income_l \leq 38,348$, where the first term is the income of the higher-earning spouse and the second term is the income of the lower-earning spouse. The highest possible total income that is still eligible for a benefit is approximately $51,000. However, the benefit accruing to such a household would be miniscule.

16. This method basically ignores how the EITC affects the returns to the marginal hour. To be sure, for many workers who receive the EITC credit, the credit increases take-home pay while providing an incentive to reduce hours worked. With this caveat in mind, the calculated employment effects are offered as baseline estimates for the purposes of bounding the employment effect from above. Nonetheless, the fact that most recipients receive the EITC as a once-per-year lump-sum payment may indicate that the connection between the benefits calculation parameters and the returns to additional work on the margin may be blurred for most. If this is the case, these simple calculations would provide reasonable first approximations.

17. For "single with no dependents under 18," the EHO proposal and the hybrid proposal are identical.

18. The analysis above looks at the proportion of income accruing to the deciles of the simulated tax-filing units. Analysis of the absolute dollars accruing to these deciles also reveals larger absolute benefits for households in the bottom three deciles.

References

Berlin, Gordon L. 2007. "Rewarding the Work of Individuals: A Counterintuitive Approach to Reducing Poverty and Strengthening Families." MDRC working paper. New York: MDRC. http://www.mdrc.org/publications/443/workpaper.pdf (accessed July 11, 2007).

Bonczar, Thomas P. 2003. *Prevalence of Imprisonment in the U.S. Population, 1974–2001.* Bureau of Justice Statistics Special Report, NCJ 197976. Washington, DC: U.S. Department of Justice, Office of Justice Programs. http://www.ojp.usdoj.gov/bjs/pub/pdf/piuspol.pdf (accessed July 11, 2007).

Borjas, George J. 2003. "The Labor Demand Curve *Is* Downward Sloping: Reexamining the Impact of Immigration on the Labor Market." *Quarterly Journal of Economics* 118(4): 1335–1374.

Borjas, George J., Richard B. Freeman, and Lawrence F. Katz. 1997. "How Much Do Immigration and Trade Affect Labor Market Outcomes?" *Brookings Papers on Economic Activity* 1(1997): 1–67.

Bureau of Justice Statistics. 2007. *Key Crime and Justice Facts at a Glance.* Washington, DC: U.S. Department of Justice, Office of Justice Programs, Bureau of Justice Statistics. http://www.ojp.usdoj.gov/bjs/glance .htm#Corrections (accessed July 20, 2007).

Butcher, Kristin F., and Anne Morrison Piehl. 2006. "Why Are Immigrants' Incarceration Rates So Low? Evidence on Selective Immigration, Deterrence, and Deportation." Working Paper 13229. Cambridge, MA: National Bureau of Economic Research. http://www.nber.org/papers/w13229 (accessed July 11, 2007).

Card, David, and Alan B. Krueger. 1994. "Minimum Wages and Employment: A Case Study of the Fast-Food Industry in New Jersey and Pennsylvania." *American Economic Review* 84(4): 772–793.

Center for American Progress. 2007. *From Poverty to Prosperity: A National Strategy to Cut Poverty in Half.* Report and Recommendations of the Center for American Progress Task Force on Poverty. Washington, DC: Center For American Progress.

Craig, Scott R. 1987. "Negligent Hiring: Guilt By Association." *Personnel Administrator* 32(October): 32–34.

Danziger, Sheldon H., and Peter Gottschalk. 2005. "Diverging Fortunes: Trends in Poverty and Inequality." In *The American People: Census 2000*, Reynolds Farley and John Haaga, eds. New York: Russell Sage Foundation, pp. 49–75.

Devereux, Paul J. 2003. "Changes in Male Labor Supply and Wages." *Industrial and Labor Relations Review* 56(3): 409–428.

DiNardo, John, Nicole M. Fortin, and Thomas Lemieux. 1996. "Labor Market Institutions and the Distribution of Wages, 1973–1992: A Semiparametric Approach." *Econometrica* 64(5): 1001–1044.

Donohue, John J. 2007. "Assessing the Relative Benefits of Incarceration: The Overall Change of the Previous Decades and the Benefits on the Margin." Working paper. New Haven, CT: Yale University.

Edelman, Peter, Harry J. Holzer, and Paul Offner. 2006. *Reconnecting Disadvantaged Young Men.* Washington, DC: Urban Institute.

Eissa, Nada, and Hilary Williamson Hoynes. 2004. "Taxes and the Labor Market Participation of Married Couples: The Earned Income Tax Credit." *Journal of Public Economics* 88(9–10): 1931–1958.

Fagan, Jeffrey, and Richard B. Freeman. 1999. "Crime and Work." *Crime and Justice: A Review of Research* 25(1999): 225–290.

Freeman, Richard B. 1987. "The Relation of Criminal Activity to Black Youth

Employment." *Review of Black Political Economy* 16 (1–2): 99–107.

Gould, Eric D., Bruce A. Weinberg, and David B. Mustard. 2002. "Crime Rates and Local Labor Market Opportunities in the United States: 1979–1997." *Review of Economics and Statistics* 84(1): 45–61.

Grogger, Jeff. 1998. "Market Wages and Youth Crime." *Journal of Labor Economics* 16(4): 756–791.

Hahn, Jeffrey M. 1991. "Pre-Employment Information Services: Employers Beware." *Employee Relations Law Journal* 17(1): 45–69.

Holzer, Harry J., Steven Raphael, and Michael A. Stoll. 2006. "Perceived Criminality, Criminal Background Checks and the Racial Hiring Practices of Employers." *Journal of Law and Economics* 49(2): 451–480.

———. 2007. "The Effect of an Applicant's Criminal History on Employer Hiring Decisions and Screening Practices: Evidence from Los Angeles." In *Barriers to Reentry? The Labor Market for Released Prisoners in Post-Industrial America*, Shawn D. Bushway, Michael A. Stoll, and David Weiman, eds. New York: Russell Sage Foundation.

Juhn, Chinhui. 1992. "The Decline in Male Labor Force Participation: The Role of Declining Market Opportunities." *Quarterly Journal of Economics* 107(1): 79–121.

———. 2003. "Labor Market Dropouts and Trends in the Wages of Black and White Men." *Industrial and Labor Relations Review* 56(4): 643–662.

Juhn, Chinhui, and Simon Potter. 2006. "Changes in Labor Force Participation in the United States." *Journal of Economic Perspectives* 20(3): 27–46.

Katz, Lawrence F., and David H. Autor. 1999. "Changes in the Wage Structure and Earnings Inequality." In *Handbook of Labor Economics,* Vol. 3A, Orley C. Ashenfelter and David Card, eds. Amsterdam: Elsevier/North-Holland, pp. 1463–1555.

Kurlycheck, Megan C., Robert Brame, and Shawn D. Bushway. 2006. "Scarlet Letters and Recidivism: Does An Old Criminal Record Predict Future Offending?" *Criminology and Public Policy* 5(3): 483–504.

Lee, David S., and Justin McCrary. 2005. "Crime, Punishment, and Myopia." NBER Working Paper 11491. Cambridge, MA: National Bureau of Economic Research.

Legal Action Center. 2004. *After Prison: Roadblocks to Reentry, A Report on State Legal Barriers Facing People with Criminal Records*. New York: Legal Action Center.

Levitt, Steven D. 1998. "Juvenile Crime and Punishment." *Journal of Political Economy* 106(6): 1156–1185.

Meyer, Bruce D., and Douglas Holtz-Eakin, eds. 2001. *Making Work Pay: The Earned Income Tax Credit and Its Impact on America's Families*. New York: Russell Sage Foundation.

Meyer, Bruce D., and Dan T. Rosenbaum. 2001. "Welfare, the Earned Income Tax Credit, and the Labor Supply of Single Mothers." *Quarterly Journal of Economics* 116(3): 1063–1114.

Pager, Devah. 2003. "The Mark of a Criminal Record." *American Journal of Sociology* 108(5): 937–975.

Pencavel, John. 1997. "Changes in Male Work Behavior and Wages." Working Paper 97-046. Stanford, CA: Stanford University.

———. 2002. "A Cohort Analysis of the Association between Work Hours and Wages among Men." *Journal of Human Resources* 37(2): 251–274.

Petersilia, Joan. 2003. *When Prisoners Come Home: Parole and Prisoner Reentry*. Oxford: Oxford University Press.

Primus, Wendell. 2006. "Improving Public Policies to Increase the Income and Employment of Low-Income Nonresident Fathers." In *Black Males Left Behind*, Ronald B. Mincy, ed. Washington, DC: Urban Institute, pp. 211–248.

Raphael, Steven. 2006. "The Socioeconomic Status of Black Males: The Increasing Importance of Incarceration." In *Public Policy and the Income Distribution*, Alan J. Auerbach, David Card, and John M. Quigley, eds. New York: Russell Sage Foundation, pp. 319–358.

Raphael, Steven, and Michael A. Stoll. 2004. "The Effect of Prison Releases on Regional Crime Rates." In *Brookings-Wharton Papers on Urban Affairs*, William G. Gale and Janet Rothenberg Pack, eds. Washington, DC: Brookings Institution, pp. 207–255.

———. 2007. "Why Are So Many Americans in Prison?" National Poverty Center Working Paper #07-10. Ann Arbor, MI: National Poverty Center, University of Michigan.

Raphael, Steven, and Rudolf Winter-Ebmer. 2001. "Identifying the Effect of Unemployment on Crime." *Journal of Law and Economics* 44(1): 259–284.

Travis, Jeremy. 2005. *But They All Come Back: Facing the Challenges of Prisoner Reentry*. Washington DC: Urban Institute Press.

The Authors

Katharine G. Abraham is a professor of survey methodology at the University of Maryland and former commissioner of the U.S. Bureau of Labor Statistics. Her recent research activities have focused primarily on issues related to the measurement of labor market activity, though she also has maintained an active interest in labor market policy topics.

Timothy J. Bartik is a senior economist at the W.E. Upjohn Institute for Employment Research. His research includes the benefits and costs of state and local economic development policies, local labor market policies to reduce urban poverty, and the economic development effects of early childhood programs.

Susan N. Houseman is a senior economist at the W.E. Upjohn Institute for Employment Research. Her research areas of interest include temporary help employment, outsourcing, and nonstandard work arrangements; older workers and retirement; and comparative labor market policies in Japan and Europe.

Lori G. Kletzer is a professor of economics at the University of California, Santa Cruz, and a senior fellow at the Peterson Institute for International Economics. Her current research focuses on the domestic labor market effects of globalization—specifically, on developing measures of the scope and consequences of services trade and offshoring.

Robert I. Lerman is a professor of economics at American University, a senior fellow at the Urban Institute, and a research fellow of the Institute for the Study of Labor (IZA) in Bonn, Germany. His research focuses on how education, employment, and family structure work together to affect economic well-being.

Paul Osterman is deputy dean and Nanyang Professor of Human Resources and Management at the Massachusetts Institute of Technology's Sloan School of Management and is also a professor in the Department of Urban and Regional Planning at MIT. His research has to do with changes in work organization within companies, career patterns and processes within firms, economic development, urban poverty, and public policy surrounding skills training and employment programs.

Steven Raphael is a professor of public policy at the University of California, Berkeley. He studies low-wage labor markets, poverty, and the economics of crime and incarceration, and has written on various aspects of racial inequality in the United States, the economics of immigration, and the social benefits and costs of recent developments in U.S. corrections policy.

Katherine Swartz is a professor of health policy and economics at the Harvard School of Public Health. Her current research interests focus on the population without health insurance and efforts to increase access to health care coverage, reasons for and ways to control episodes of care that involve extremely high expenditures, and how we might pay for expanded health insurance coverage.

Index

The italic letters *f, n,* and *t* following a page number indicate that the subject information of the heading is within a figure, note, or table, respectively, on that page.

Middle-income workers, 7, 151
  job growth for, 1, 204
  problems facing, 2–6, 13, 205
  retirement savings and, 171–172
Minimum wage, 299*n*1
  EITC and, 282–283
  federal and/or state settings for, 212–
    214, 216
  improving job quality with, 11, 237
  as mitigating institution, 7, 14–15*n*11,
    211*t,* 300*n*9
Mining sector, 85, 129*f*
Mississippi, tax credits in, 241*n*15
Missouri, St. Louis, and CAEL-like
    efforts, 228–229
Moderately-skilled workers, focus
    shifted from, 119
Mott Foundation, low-wage labor market
    efforts of, 235

NAAL. *See* National Assessment of
    Adult Literacy
NAEP. *See* National Assessment of
    Educational Progress
NAFTA-TAA, creation of, 145
NAM. *See* National Association of
    Manufacturers
National Assessment of Adult Literacy
    (NAAL), literacy and math test
    scores, 33–36, 40
National Assessment of Educational
    Progress (NAEP), cognitive skill
    test scores of, 33, 51
National Association of Manufacturers
    (NAM), career ladder
    development and, 226–227, 230
National Employer Survey, 25–26
National Governors Association, as
    policy academy sponsor, 189
National health care, 111, 113*n*1
National Household Education Survey, 39
National Labor Relations Act, reforms,
    237
National Network of Sector Partners, 227
National Skill Standards Board (NSSB),
    38, 63

National Vocational Qualifications
    (NVQs), as U.K. skill certification,
    37, 72*n*10
NCLB. *See* No Child Left Behind Act
NCSAW. *See* New Commission on the
    Skills of the American Workforce
Netherlands, The, health coverage in, 10,
    98–99, 111, 114*n*12
"New Basics" curriculum, 17*n*15, 44–45,
    52
New Commission on the Skills of the
    American Workforce (NCSAW),
    findings, 19, 28
New Jersey, 49, 236
New York (state), 216
  Brooklyn, and overtime pay, 241*n*14
  New York City, projects, 219, 221
No Child Left Behind (NCLB) Act,
    literacy intent of, 44
Noncognitive skills, 9, 21, 45
  demand for, 20, 26–27
  personal responsibility among, 20, 25
  SCANS, 25, 36, 45
Nonelderly workers, 234
  changing demographics of, 95, 124,
    161
  childless, and EITC, 246–247, 275,
    276, 277–278, 279*t,* 285*t,* 300*n*11
  employment by education, gender and
    race, 253, 256–257*t,* 258
  health coverage for, 4, 81, 108–109
  literacy skills of, 28, 33–35, 208
  low-wage, in U.S., 248–252, 254–255*t*
  WIA program for, 184, 186*t,* 187*t,*
    188, 191, 195*n*9, 241*n*16
Nonfarm business sector, productivity of,
    2, 13*n*3
Nonimmigrant visas, labor supply and,
    134–138, 155*n*13, 155*nn*15–17
Nonprofit organizations, job training by,
    48
Norway, 88, 208
NSSB. *See* National Skill Standards
    Board
NVQs. *See* National Vocational
    Qualifications

About the Institute

The W.E. Upjohn Institute for Employment Research is a nonprofit research organization devoted to finding and promoting solutions to employment-related problems at the national, state, and local levels. It is an activity of the W.E. Upjohn Unemployment Trustee Corporation, which was established in 1932 to administer a fund set aside by Dr. W.E. Upjohn, founder of The Upjohn Company, to seek ways to counteract the loss of employment income during economic downturns.

The Institute is funded largely by income from the W.E. Upjohn Unemployment Trust, supplemented by outside grants, contracts, and sales of publications. Activities of the Institute comprise the following elements: 1) a research program conducted by a resident staff of professional social scientists; 2) a competitive grant program, which expands and complements the internal research program by providing financial support to researchers outside the Institute; 3) a publications program, which provides the major vehicle for disseminating the research of staff and grantees, as well as other selected works in the field; and 4) an Employment Management Services division, which manages most of the publicly funded employment and training programs in the local area.

The broad objectives of the Institute's research, grant, and publication programs are to 1) promote scholarship and experimentation on issues of public and private employment and unemployment policy, and 2) make knowledge and scholarship relevant and useful to policymakers in their pursuit of solutions to employment and unemployment problems.

Current areas of concentration for these programs include causes, consequences, and measures to alleviate unemployment; social insurance and income maintenance programs; compensation; workforce quality; work arrangements; family labor issues; labor-management relations; and regional economic development and local labor markets.